Vito Acconci//William Anast[illegible]er// Paul Auster//Jacquelynn Bae[illegible]ri// Georges Bataille//Walead Beshty/[illegible]baum// Claire Bishop//George Brecht//Guy Brett//Benjamin H.D. Buchloh//Sophie Calle//Stanley Cavell//John Cage//Lynne Cooke//Tacita Dean//Gilles Deleuze// Anna Dezeuze//Brian Eno//Cerith Wyn Evans//Fei Dawei//Russell Ferguson//Fischli & Weiss//David Frankel//Branden W. Joseph//Allan Kaprow//Klara Kemp-Welch//Siegfried Kracauer//Jacques Lacan// Sarat Maharaj//Cildo Meireles//John Miller//Robert Morris//Alexandra Munroe//Bruce Nauman//Gabriel Orozco//Cornelia Parker//Gabriel Pérez Barreiro// Robert Rauschenberg//Jasia Reichardt//Gerhard Richter//Julia Robinson//Luc Sante//Brad Spence// Ann Temkin//Marcia Tucker//Keith Tyson//Sarah Valdez//Katharina Vossenkuhl//La Monte Young

Chance

Whitechapel Gallery
London
The MIT Press
Cambridge, Massachusetts

Edited by Margaret Iversen

CHA NCE

Documents of Contemporary Art

Co-published by Whitechapel Gallery
and The MIT Press

First published 2010

Whitechapel Gallery is the imprint of Whitechapel Gallery Ventures Limited

ISBN 978-0-85488-177-2 (Whitechapel Gallery)
ISBN 978-0-262-51392-0 (The MIT Press)

A catalogue record for this book is available from the British Library

Library of Congress Cataloging-in-Publication Data

Chance / edited by Margaret Iversen.
p. cm. – (Whitechapel, documents of contemporary art)
Includes bibliographical references and index.
ISBN 978-0-262-51392-0 (pbk. : alk. paper)
1. Chance in art. 2. Arts, Modern–20th century.
3. Arts, Modern–21st century. I. Iversen, Margaret.
NX456.5.C46C48 2010
701'.8–dc22
2009047477

10 9 8 7 6 5 4 3 2 1

Series Editor: Iwona Blazwick
Executive Director: Tom Wilcox
Commissioning Editor: Ian Farr
Project Editor: Hannah Vaughan
Design by SMITH: Namkwan Cho, Victoria Forrest
Printed and bound in China

Cover, Bas Jan Ader, *Fall II*, 1970, 16mm film, 19 seconds, black and white, silent. Colour production still. © Estate of Bas Jan Ader. Courtesy of Patrick Painter Inc., Los Angeles

Whitechapel Gallery Ventures Limited
77-82 Whitechapel High Street
London E1 7QX
www.whitechapelgallery.org
To order (UK and Europe) call +44 (0)207 522 7888
or email MailOrder@whitechapelgallery.org
Distributed to the book trade (UK and Europe only)
by Central Books
www.centralbooks.com

The MIT Press
55 Hayward Street
Cambridge, MA 02142
MIT Press books may be purchased at special quantity discounts for business or sales promotional use. For information, please email special_sales@mitpress.mit.edu or write to Special Sales Department, The MIT Press, 55 Hayward Street, Cambridge, MA 02142

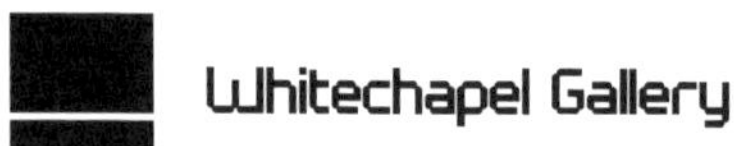

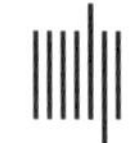

Documents of Contemporary Art

In recent decades artists have progressively expanded the boundaries of art as they have sought to engage with an increasingly pluralistic environment. Teaching, curating and understanding of art and visual culture are likewise no longer grounded in traditional aesthetics but centred on significant ideas, topics and themes ranging from the everyday to the uncanny, the psychoanalytical to the political.

The Documents of Contemporary Art series emerges from this context. Each volume focuses on a specific subject or body of writing that has been of key influence in contemporary art internationally. Edited and introduced by a scholar, artist, critic or curator, each of these source books provides access to a plurality of voices and perspectives defining a significant theme or tendency.

For over a century the Whitechapel Gallery has offered a public platform for art and ideas. In the same spirit, each guest editor represents a distinct yet diverse approach – rather than one institutional position or school of thought – and has conceived each volume to address not only a professional audience but all interested readers.

La Monte Young, *Composition 1960 #10*, 1960

PERFORMANCE, PROCESS, POSSIBILITY

What triggered this piece were the mice. We had a big influx of field mice that summer, in the house and in the studio. They were so plentiful that even the cat was getting bored with them. I was sitting around the studio being frustrated because I didn't have any new ideas, and I decided that you just have to work with what you've got. What I had was this cat and the mice, and I happened to have a video camera in the studio that had infra-red capability. So I set it up and turned it on at night and let it run when I wasn't there, just to see what I'd get.

Bruce Nauman, On *Mapping the Studio I (Fat Chance John Cage)*, 2001

Margaret Iversen
Introduction//The Aesthetics of Chance

Chantal Akerman's *News from Home* (1976) is a film about a newcomer to New York – Akerman herself – which conveys brilliantly her slightly estranged visual excitement in the city. The film consists of carefully set up long takes with a fixed camera. For one sequence, she placed a camera in a subway car opposite the sliding doors. The train arrives at a station where the doors part to reveal a chance composition of pillars and people on the platform. The doors slide shut and the process is repeated several times. The filmmaker obviously hopes that at each stop the doors will frame a striking composition, but she has no way of controlling the outcome. It is this gap between intention and outcome that seems crucial to the meaning of chance in art. The question then becomes: Why should artists deliberately set up such a gap in their practice? And why should the viewer find it so engaging? This book aims to answer these questions and to outline a history of chance procedures since around 1900.

'Chance' has been used to characterize a very broad spectrum of practices including the readymade, collage, expressionist painting, performance, participation and more. While I will touch on some of these, I intend to restrict my focus mainly to those chance procedures that involve setting up some quite formal procedure or mechanical apparatus for capturing chance occurrences. Akerman's use of the sliding doors as a large, slow camera shutter is a good example of this. Once the apparatus or instruction is determined the artist then adopts a posture of waiting to see what will happen. It is rather different, then, from strategies involving high-risk spontaneity where outcomes are just as unpredictable, but where the posture is one of making something happen rather than waiting to see what will happen.

Duchamp, Cage and Fluxus

In 1913–14, Marcel Duchamp made an important work called *3 Standard Stoppages* generated by a rather elaborate and exacting instruction recorded in his box of notes for the year 1913: 'if a straight horizontal thread one metre long falls from a height of one metre onto a horizontal plane distorting itself as it pleases and creates a new shape of the measure of length – Three patterns obtained in more or less similar conditions ...' The instruction dictates the initial conditions of this mock experiment, but it does not determine the outcome; on the contrary, the instruction is a device for evading authorial or artistic agency and so generating chance events and unexpected results. Once the threads were affixed to a dark ground, wooden templates or rulers were formed in accordance with these new wavy units of length. The piece offers an ironic alternative to the standard metre. Duchamp put the fixed threads and rulers in a disused croquet case where they became what he called 'canned chance'. This work stands as an early and exemplary case of the systematic use of chance in art. It consists of an instruction for a controlled experiment which in turn opens the work to the unpredictable effects of forces, objects, experiences – in this case gravity – while at the same time limiting authorial control.

Duchamp's wooden templates were used to generate the network of lines that connect the bachelors to the sieves in the lower section of his *The Bride Stripped Bare by her Bachelors, Even*, known as the *Large Glass* (1915–23). It is now widely acknowledged that the *Glass* is one of the most important works of art of the twentieth century. If that is so, then it must also be the case that chance procedures are just as important for subsequent art practice as the readymade, for Duchamp's great work is a panorama of chance procedures, just as his *Tu m'* is said to be a 'panorama of the index'.[1] The *Glass* is so familiar that one does not need to elaborate this point in detail. It is enough to note what other features of the work are generated by chance. The draft pistons at the top owe their shape to another experiment repeated three times: a square piece of net was hung above a radiator so that hot air currents distorted the shape of the net, which was recorded photographically. The shots are distributed in a pattern obtained by launching paint-tipped match sticks with a toy cannon – an intentional act, but designed to defeat that intention to some degree. The delicate colour of the sieves was made by fixing with varnish dust accumulated over several months when the glass lay horizontal in the studio. In addition, in 1926, the glass was shattered in transit. Duchamp glued the pieces together and declared himself pleased with this accidental (un)finishing touch – an unplanned chance occurrence – that accorded so well with the spirit of the work. One consequence of this last dramatic chance event is that shattered glass has been a repeated motif in subsequent art – from Ed Ruscha's *Nine Swimming Pools and a Broken Glass* and his more recent *Busted Glass* series of paintings, to Walead Beshty's ongoing 'FedEx' sculptures – glass boxes that since 2005 have been undergoing continual damage as they are sent long distances to be exhibited.

Duchamp's engagement with chance procedures resulted in objects that were eventually displayed in the museum. Many artists who followed his example, however, were more inclined to document the experiment itself and to disseminate the work in the form of photography, film or video. A classic example of this practice is a book made by Ed Ruscha that documents an instructional collaborative project: *Royal Road Test* (1967). Its mock experimental character is signalled in the title. It is the record of a performance involving Ruscha and two friends who threw a typewriter out of the window of a speeding car. Ruscha says that Mason Williams spontaneously threw the typewriter and only later did they decide to go back and record the wreckage. In the book, however, the crime is presented as premeditated, since the first photograph in it shows a Royal typewriter sitting innocently on a desk top. In an email, Ruscha explained this as follows: 'The photo of the intact typewriter was added after the original one was thrown from the car. The act of throwing the typewriter was spontaneous and then we re-created the 'before' photo by finding a duplicate typewriter.'[2] The remainder of the photographs show the perpetrators turned detectives, recording the scene of a crime or accident – the wreckage strewn across the Arizona desert. In a very similar way, the photographs in *Thirty-four Parking Lots in Los Angeles* (1967), are the result of a combination of instruction, performance and chance. Ruscha gave an aerial photographer instructions to photograph empty parking lots around LA, thereby revealing hitherto unnoticed herringbone patterns and variegated oil stains. The instructional aspect of Ruscha's books connects them with similar strategies in some strands of conceptual art in the late sixties and seventies.[3] In my view, the brilliance of Lawrence Weiner's *Statements* of 1968, such as *A 36" x 36" REMOVAL TO THE LATHING OR SUPPORT WALL OF PLASTER OR WALL BOARD FROM A WALL*, is the unanticipated pattern of pipes and wires that are exposed when the minimal instruction is *performed* – although, admittedly, this rather goes against the grain of his own *STATEMENT OF INTENT* (1969): 'The piece need not be built ...'

The marked performative aspect of Duchamp's and Ruscha's pieces suggests other examples of the use of chance in work more closely aligned with performance art. Contemporary with Ruscha were a group of artists who in 1962 were to become part of the Fluxus group. They developed ideas promulgated by the experimental composer, John Cage. Cage is a key figure in this narrative as he taught a number of artists in the 1950s at Black Mountain College (including Robert Rauschenberg) and at the New School in New York (including Allan Kaprow). Although Cage was building on avant-garde musical traditions, he was quick to see the relevance of Duchamp to his work and visual artists were equally quick to acknowledge Cage as an inspiration. He took the principle of allowing chance to generate composition to its logical conclusion, first with a complex system using *I Ching* coins and later by leaving performers a great deal of scope in their interpretation of a score. This latter strategy, 'indeterminacy,' lent itself to the idea of creating a dense field of resonating sound rather than a melodic, linear musical experience. The multi-layered, sometimes three-ringed events orchestrated by Cage foreshadowed the rise of Happenings. Cage was thus a leader in the avant-garde project of diminishing the distance between art and life. However, he always insisted on the importance of the instructional frame: 'Life without structure is unseen. Pure life expresses itself within and through a structure.'[4]

A key factor in Cage's aesthetic sensibility was his keen interest in Zen Buddhism. This aspect of his work is perhaps best illustrated by his famous piece *4' 33"* (1952), in which the performer is instructed to sit at the piano, open the lid, and play nothing for fixed periods. The purpose of this is to allow the ambient sounds in the room to be heard. It is the frame. It also indicates an important shift from expressing to listening. Cage's synthesis of Duchampian chance procedures and Zen meant that he put chance to work in a particular way, that is, to open the mind to more intense awareness of the world and nature. For Cage, using chance procedures meant imitating nature in her underlying principles rather than simply copying appearances. This idea of Nature as essentially chance-driven is strange to us, but after the theories of quantum mechanics and Heisenberg's uncertainty principle, it's not such an implausible view. Albert Einstein, exasperated by theories of the unpredictability of sub-atomic particles, wrote in a letter, 'God does not play dice.' But nature definitely does: for example, although much emphasis is placed on Darwin's deterministic theory of natural selection, later dubbed 'survival of the fittest', it is the random scrambling and mutation of genes that makes possible variation, diversity and complexity.

Another Cage protégé, the Fluxus artist George Brecht, took the idea of a fairly open-ended 'score' out of its musical context and adopted for an instructional performance art. An early piece, *Motor Vehicle Sundown* (1960), was dedicated to Cage and involved many participants in parked cars doing various car-related actions all at once. However, his work developed in the direction of minimal verbal instructions or 'event scores' for performance pieces which were presented on cards in precise graphic form. For example, his spare design for *Word Event* (1961) has a large bullet point centred on the card and then the word EXIT. Performing the piece might be accomplished by isolating and attending to that familiar sign with fresh eyes, either on the card or *in situ* or as a readymade sign offered for sale in Fluxus magazines – or by simply leaving the room. A piece by La Monte Young, a Fluxus composer, *Composition 1960 #2* ('Build a fire in front of the audience ...'), as minimally performed by Brecht, involved lighting a book of matches. Another Young 'composition,' *Composition 1960 #10*, dedicated to Robert Morris, consists of the instruction, 'Draw a straight line and follow it.' The instruction is terse and open to any number of realizations. In 1961, Morris and Young collaborated on a performance of this piece in which they laboriously traced and retraced a line on stage 29 times. Nam June Paik, the Korean Fluxus artist, later performed a version of the work using his head dipped in ink and tomato juice as a brush to make a line on a long scroll laid on the floor (1962).

Performing Chance Procedures

The combination of verbal instruction, performativity and chance can be seen in the work of many artists following in this tradition. In his *Following Piece* (1969), for example, Vito Acconci set himself the task of following a randomly selected stranger walking in the street while remaining himself unobserved. Signalling the refusal of authorial control and corresponding receptivity, he called this activity 'Performing myself through another agent'.[5] Ten years later, during the month of February 1979, the French artist Sophie Calle initiated her own following piece, *Suite vénitienne* (1980). In some ways it resembles Acconci's since it involved following someone and documenting the activity with a camera.[6] Calle decided to travel to Venice, track down a man she had met once at a party in Paris, and follow him. Because the choice of Henri B., like Acconci's subjects, was more or less arbitrary, her activity lacks the character of a stalking. Rather, Calle puts herself at the mercy of another. Sounding very like a latter day André Breton, she says: 'I see myself at the labyrinth's gate, ready to get lost in the city and in this story. Submissive.'[7]

Calle's openness to chance events in this work and elsewhere qualifies her for inclusion here, but there is a slight element of risk in this piece, especially when Henri B. finally confronts her, and this connects the work to a whole genre of performance art that involves the artist subjecting him or herself to danger or harm. Some signal examples of this genre are Carolee Schneemann's orgiastic *Meat Joy* (1964), Yoko Ono's *Cut Piece* (1964), Chris Burden's *Shoot* (1971) and Marina Abramovic's *Rhythm 10* (1973), which involved her rhythmically stabbing a knife between the splayed fingers of her hand. In these cases, and many more one could mention, attention is focused on the bodily experience of the artist and the tension produced in the viewer.[8] The emphasis is on the immediate presence, visibility and vulnerability of the body enduring the performance of a strange ritual. As a result they have an existential or phenomenological quality quite alien to work using chance procedures. In addition, the participatory character of some of these works adds a dimension of indeterminacy which I will not pursue here, for I am mainly concentrating on chance at the moment of composition rather than reception.[9]

Writing in 1971 on the work of Eva Hesse and 'process' art more generally, Lucy Lippard observed that 'risk', a favourite term in the 1950s, implied at that time 'a determined mindlessness, even sacrifice, in the heat of creation.' For her, process art altered the role of the artist:

> Now the risk, or the gesture, rather than being made by the artist from the inside out, as a direct expression of himself, is an 'act' of the sculpture, almost independent of the creator, its scale and meaning deriving from its materials,

context and situation rather than any psychological necessity. Serra uses gravity, weight ... as pure physical risk.[10]

Robert Morris was the key apologist for this kind of work and he characterized process art as 'chance, contingency and indeterminacy'.[11] Allowing materials to succumb to the force of gravity has more in common with the kind of chance procedures detailed here than the 'sacrificial' risks taken by some performance artists. Gravity was, after all, the force at work in *3 Standard Stoppages* and falling turns out to be an important chance procedure. In fact, the etymology of chance is traceable to the Latin verb '*cadere*', to fall. (The French word, *le hazard*, stems from the Arabic name for a dice game.) The fall can be actual or potential. For example, Fischli and Weiss' *Equilibrium* series of photographs of precariously arranged found objects suggest imminent collapse.

The distinction I've sketched between chance and risk is helpful, but not absolute. The work of Los Angeles based Dutch conceptualist Bas Jan Ader is a case in point, since his staged accidents, such as riding a bike into a canal or falling from his roof, or climbing out on a branch over a stream and then letting go, exposed him not just to chance (and gravity) but to physical harm and even death. His final performance, *In Search of the Miraculous II* (1975), was a failed attempt to cross the Atlantic solo in his twelve and a half foot sail boat. His body was never found. This work points to the connection between the sea and chance which is also a recurrent motif in the discourse and art of chance. It goes back to Mallarmé's famous poem 'A throw of the dice will never abolish chance' which involves a shipwreck in a stormy sea, and forward to several of Tacita Dean's works. In Horace's *Odes* (1: 35) and in some visual representations of the capricious goddess Fortuna (Luck or Chance) who bestows her favours so randomly, she is given a rudder and billowing sail or a model ship.

The untimely death of Bas Jan Ader also raises the issue of the connection between chance and mortality. One of the most affecting works that turns on this link is Felix Gonzalez-Torres' *Untitled (March 5) #2* of 1991. The piece consists of two burning, wall-mounted light bulbs in porcelain sockets attached to intertwined wires. The date in the work's subtitle is the birth date of his partner who had recently died. The simple light bulbs allude to their close relationship and the impossibility of knowing in advance which life was to burn out first.

The continuing productivity of chance procedures in recent art can be seen in the work of a many of contemporary artists. Gabriel Orozco, for example, a prominent Mexican artist, is clearly interested in performative chance procedures. His *Yielding Stone* (1992) is a ball of soft, grey plasticine that he has rolled through the streets gathering whatever fragments and marks it encountered. Benjamin Buchloh notes that this is an example of 'transforming a surface into a purely passive receptacle of merely accidental pictorial and indexical marks'.[12] Plasticine, Orozco has said, is hardly ever used for the definitive version of a work ... Its malleability and vulnerability make it unsuitable for permanent forms in a finished piece.'[13] The surface of the ball has the sensitivity of skin, or light sensitive paper. This permanently malleable ball remains vulnerable to pokes and kicks when it is displayed in the gallery. Many of Orozco's video works, such as *From Dog Shit to Irma Vep*, also have an aleatory openness to whatever presents itself while he strolls along the street with his camera. This receptive mood is related to his interest in Zen – an interest which suggests that his photograph, *Extension of Reflection*, is a Zen circle performed in the street with a bicycle for a brush and a puddle for ink. The work makes canny reference to Robert Rauschenberg's twenty foot long *Automobile Tire Print* (1953) – a work which involved making a straight line with a Model A Ford driven slowly by John Cage across pieces of typewriter paper glued together to form an extended scroll, while Rauschenberg poured black house paint on the tire.

The Belgian-born artist, Francis Alÿs, takes walks through Mexico City and elsewhere which are undertaken in the spirit of harnessing chance occurrences. In one such performance, *The Collector* (1991–92), he drags a make-shift toy dog on wheels after him; it has been magnetized so it picks up metallic detritus in the street. Alÿs' note on the work is, in effect, an instruction: 'For an indeterminate period of time, the magnetized collector takes a daily walk through the streets and gradually builds up a coat made up of any metallic residue in its path.' Both Orozco and Alÿs are obviously interested in taking their art-making into the street and making contact with a reality beyond the studio through chance. There is also an element of play in their work, evident in the materials, whether it be modelling clay or a child's toy. It is Alÿs, however, who has most consistently taken to the street and its opportunities for chance encounters, or what he calls 'accidents'.

Alÿs takes as his point of departure a surrealist technique, the chance encounter, and transforms it so that the encounter is with some social reality rather than with an objective correlate of some unconscious fear or desire; he engineers an encounter with a social unconscious. Alÿs' strategy is to literalize a surrealist trope, defamiliarize it, and so make it poetic again. His *Seven Levels of Garbage*, for example, was an experiment that involved placing small metal sculptures in the garbage bags throughout Mexico City and then searching flea markets for years afterwards to find them. (Apparently only two have surfaced to date.) Whereas Breton and his friends sought out objects in flea markets that might hold a clue to unconscious desire, Alÿs is interested in the underworld of garbage-pickers and stall holders and in tracking their marginal economy.

The uses of chance in the examples I have cited are a way of introducing an element of uncertainty and contingency into the work, but it is not a matter of unbridled spontaneity or sheer chaos. On the contrary, in these cases the operation of chance occurs only in the context of certain predetermined conditions, much like a deck of cards or pair of dice. Within those constraints, a process is set in motion that has unpredictable results. Yet chance procedures vary from the highly systematic to the more intuitive and informal. They can be tied to instructional or mechanical systems or generated simply by letting scraps of paper fall. Jean Arp, one of the founders of Zurich Dada, was a master of this type of chance procedure. Beginning in 1916, he made a number of collages of torn bits of paper glued to a paper ground 'arranged according to the laws of chance'. The collages are so perfectly composed, however, that they call into question how scrupulous he was about relinquishing control and fixing the chance result. Nevertheless, Arp was an extremely articulate advocate of chance. Central to his insight is the connection between chance and the precariousness of life. For him, perfection and finish have the look of death, while accident, transience or withering show an openness to what happens, 'what befalls us'.[14]

Jackson Pollock let paint fall, but his drip technique cannot be called a chance procedure. The heightened spontaneity of expressionist brushwork or skeins of wet paint dropped and flung on a horizontal canvas certainly introduces accidental and unexpected effects. But there is an effort in this type of work to push painting to its limit, to risk painting, and master it. It is quite different in spirit to the work under discussion here. Perhaps 'improvisation' captures the mood of this work better. Consider the difference between Pollock's powerfully active technique and Duchamp's strategy of allowing dust and other airborne debris to collect on the lower register of the *Glass*. In 1920, Duchamp affixed a sign to his studio wall that read 'Dust Breeding: To Be Respected.' Taking a photograph of the dusty surface, Man Ray respected this procedure by leaving the shutter open for an hour, while he and Duchamp went to lunch.

Alÿs' performance called *The Leak* (1996), seems designed to highlight both the continuity and the difference between a procedure that involves risk and mastery and one that employs chance: he strolled through the streets of São Paulo, dribbling blue paint from a can. Pollock's drip technique is here stripped of all gestural expression and taken into the street. The principle of what might be termed weak intentionality is crucial, but Alÿs is alert to the limits of this principle. In the video *If you are a Typical Spectator what you are really doing is waiting for the accident to happen (bottle)* (1996), Alÿs trained his camera on an empty plastic bottle as it blew around the square. It strays into the street, Alÿs in hot pursuit, until bang, crash, the world turns upside down as he is hit by a car. This points to the difference between intentionally harnessing chance and retrospectively incorporating an accident – a distinction that also applies to Duchamp's planned chance events that make up the motifs of the *Large Glass* and its accidental shattering. In this work, Alÿs seems to be poking fun at his own openness to chance encounters which, in this case, literally knocks him down. Like Jacques Lacan in his anecdote about the discomfiture he felt at being the butt of a fisherman's joke, he is no longer observing a picture. He is suddenly in the picture.[15] The traumatic side of the chance encounter is perfectly understood here.

Psychoanalysis, Photography and Chance

The mentions of 'trauma' and 'chance encounter' signal that it is now time to circle back and consider another tradition of chance imagery that has its origin in psychoanalysis.[16] The role of psychoanalysis is of key importance in the modern understanding of the meaning of chance and the Surrealists readily responded to it. In his remarkable pamphlet, *Chance Imagery* (1957/1966), George Brecht makes a useful distinction between two species of chance. One sort of chance event is described as such because it results from 'consciously unknown causes'; the other type results from some mechanical operation where human agency is bypassed. Consequently, the origin of one kind of image 'is unknown because it lies in deeper-than-conscious levels of the mind'. The other kind derives from 'mechanical processes not under the artist's control. Both of the processes have in common a lack of conscious design.' The first understanding of chance, developed by psychoanalysis, governs surrealist automatism and the gestural abstraction of Jackson Pollock. The Surrealists were particularly drawn to Sigmund Freud's book, *The Psychopathology of Everyday Life* (1901), in which a range of common everyday accidents such as forgetting, slips of the pen, losing things, bungled actions, are shown to be ways of allowing unconscious thoughts and desires to attain some form of compromised expression. As Freud put it, 'Certain shortcomings in our psychical functioning ... and certain seemingly unintentional performances prove, if psychoanalytical methods of investigation are applied to them, to have valid motives and to be determined by motives unknown to consciousness.'[17] This three-hundred page book of anecdotes is thus dedicated to the explanation of the sort of phenomena that are normally brushed off as meaningless accidents.

André Breton took up and elaborated Freud's theory in his ideas of the chance encounter and the '*trouvaille*' or lucky find spotted amidst the detritus of the flea market: these sorts of occurrence, by virtue of their apparently fortuitous, accidental character, bypass one's consciousness and intentionality, thereby giving access to an otherwise inaccessible reality. As Breton said of the found objects described in *Mad Love*, such as the famous slipper-spoon, 'It is really as if I had been lost and they had come to give me news about myself.'[18]

While the encounter is sometimes interpreted as a happy coincidence of desire and reality, Breton offered another, 'modern materialist' definition of chance which brings it closer to a reactivation of trauma: 'Chance would be the form taken by external reality as it traces a path in the human unconscious.'[19] Traumatic events bypass what Freud refers to as the protective crust of consciousness leaving an indelible trace. Chance encounters touch on that raw nerve. The Czech conceptual artist, Jirí Kovanda, who was active during the period of post-Prague Spring 'normalization', makes use of this Freudian idea in his actions. His *Contact* piece of 1977 is particularly telling, for it mimics the psychical evasion of censorship: a purposive act is disguised as an 'accident'. The artist walks along the pavement, and seemingly without intent bumps into passers-by or just misses them, failing to make the contact he desires.[20]

The conjunction of chance, trace and trauma raises the issue of photography, at least as it is imagined in Walter Benjamin's 'Little History of Photography' (1931) and in Roland Barthes' *Camera Lucida* (1980). Photography has a special place in the history of chance procedures since it involves a mechanical device and photochemical or digital processes that function to some extent automatically. This bypassing of intention and artistic convention has made it important for those interested in chance. It might even be argued that the snapshot is the model for the work under discussion here, for there is a hiatus, even now with digital technology, between clicking the button and the resulting image. Stanley Cavell has written of 'inner opacity' and 'suspense' as essential features of the medium. David Campany has suggested that one way of understanding photography is 'as a trap for the incidental'.[21]

Although Duchamp's *Large Glass* only marginally involved photography, he referred to it as 'a delay in glass', suggesting that he was fully aware of the significance of the camera with its glass plates as an apparatus apparently designed to generate automatic or chance procedures. Even though sophisticated cameras are designed to produce predictable pictures in the hands of a skilled photographer, the automaticity of the process lends itself to unintended happy (or unhappy) accidents and even the most skilled photographers value this. As Walker Evans so eloquently put it, the camera excels at 'reflecting swift chance, disarray, wonder and experiment'.[22] There is an intrinsic connection, then, between the instructional means of short-circuiting authorial agency, of ensuring non-interference, and a certain use of the medium of photography.[23] Photography, or at least this particular snapshot use of photography, brings together authorial abnegation, indexicality and openness to chance. Ruscha refers at one point to its 'inhuman aspect', as it records without making qualitative judgements.[24]

Artists associated with Dada and Surrealism were the first fully to realize the potential of this characteristic of the medium. In the 'First Manifesto of

Probably one of the worst things to happen to photography is that cameras have viewfinders

John Baldessari, Interview with Nancy Drew, 1981

Surrealism' (1924), Breton said of automatic writing, 'to you who write, these elements are, on the surface, *as strange to you as they are to anyone else*.'[25] And this holds true for the experimental techniques used by Surrealist artists. Man Ray's more experimental photography, for example, might be understood as aiming at the 'the look of chance'. If one can take his word for it, the techniques of solarization and the Rayograph were discovered by chance. The doubly exposed portrait of *La Marquise Casati* (1922) was, he claims, also an accident. In 'Photography is not an Art', Man Ray listed what he considered his ten best photographs. Topping the list is 'an accidental snapshot of a shadow between two other carefully posed pictures of a girl in a bathing suit'.[26] A photographer of great technical mastery, Man Ray could quip that he had learned 'to produce accidents at will'.[27] In my view, photography was one of the many techniques the Surrealists used to circumvent intentionality, allowing the agency of chance to bring about the unexpected. As with André Masson's automatic drawings or Max Ernst's *frottages* or the *Involuntary Sculptures* photographed by Brassaï, the process precedes and determines the image. Photographic automatism is exemplary of chance procedure. Ann Banfield has discussed this mind-independent aspect of the medium, noting that 'what the photograph is sensible of can be outside the ego, a thought unthought, unintended, involuntary and without meaning'.[28]

In *Camera Lucida*, Roland Barthes called for a photographic practice that would cut through the generalized image repertoire, the de-realizing simulacra, to touch the absent real. This is made possible by the camera's capture of the unintended, chance occurrence, which is then registered by the observer as the punctum of the photograph. 'For punctum is also sting, speck, cut, little hole – and also a cast of the die. A photograph's punctum is the accident which pricks me.'[29] The camera lens is often imagined as an eye wide open, without the buffer against shock that we call consciousness. Salvador Dalí, for example, indicated this vulnerability when he praised 'the anaesthetic gaze of the naked, lashless eye of Zeiss' – imagining the camera as incapable of censorship, naked.[30] Breton conjured up this defenceless quality by referring to the 'blindness' of the camera, that gives it access to unconscious material normally only accessible to automatism and dream.[31] 'Blindness' I take to be metaphor calling attention to its mechanical character, but it also recalls the fact that the Classical goddess Fortuna was represented blind and even eyeless, because of the way she often rewards the unworthy and even wicked. The themes or blindness and its correlates, darkness and night, are recurrent in work involving chance. Both Robert Morris and William Anastasi, for instance, made blind drawings. Bruce Nauman's remarkable video installation *Mapping the Studio I (Fat Chance John Cage)* (2001), was made by filming his mouse and moth-infested studio at night using infra-red light and a specially adapted camera.

Hal Foster extended the sense of Barthes' photographic punctum to cover Warhol's technique in his 'Death in America' series. The works are based on repeated photographic readymades, but each one is crossed in the silkscreen process by an accidental, but unique, tear or 'pop'. Foster also mentions in this context Gerhard Richter's blurred photo paintings, but doesn't elaborate.[32] Richter is, however, an artist patently drawn to the depersonalization that both the readymade and chance procedures offer. His abstract painting using a squeegee or plank on wet paint recall the 'decalcomania' experiments of Max Ernst, and his colour chart paintings are arranged randomly by a computer, as were some of Ellsworth Kelly's abstract paintings in the early 1950s.

In those artists who value chance we recognize 'the replacement of the desire to do something with the desire to see what will happen'. I take this phrase from a chapter in a book by Walter Benn Michaels. Titled 'Action and Accident: Photography and Writing', it contains some of the most interesting reflections on chance I've found.[33] Although the context is mainly literary, Benn Michaels sees the relevance of his work for art theory. For example, he mentions in passing Harold Rosenberg's 'compensatory' effort to re-establish action in an automatic world. 'Action Painting' is a way of retrieving spontaneity and resisting the depersonalization of mechanism. Rosenberg does not value the gap between intention and outcome, although he does value risk. But what would it be like to live in an accident-free world? Is it not a more attractive prospect to inhabit a world 'where not only the consequences of one's actions but the very identity of those actions may be unpredictable and unstable'.[34] As Benn Michaels acknowledges, psychoanalysis has a pivotal place in the history of this debate, for it teaches that there is a gap between conscious intention and action. The unconscious is an interference apparatus that produces slips of the tongue, mistakes, sudden failures of recall, and so on. As we've seen, in analysis all these mistakes can supposedly be interpreted as having unconscious intentions, so they are not really mistakes at all. Nevertheless, Freud's vision of the mind stressed its internal division and opacity. Lacan, following Freud, located that internal split in the subject's relation to language: language precedes the self and exceeds its control, so language is also a major interference apparatus. This insight has led literary theorists, including Barthes, Paul de Man, Jacques Derrida and Michel Foucault to think of the literary text in the same way, that is, as exceeding its author's control. Stéphane Mallarmé's way of scattering lines of poetry of various font sizes across the ground of a white page is often invoked in this context, for this arrangement encourages an infinity of possible readings. This is what is meant by 'the death of the author' which, as Barthes notes, implies the birth of the reader. It is worth noting that Barthes' essay of that title was first published in a special double issue of the American avant-garde art magazine, *Aspen* (1967) that was dedicated to Mallarmé.[35]

We are perhaps nearing an understanding of the meaning of chance in art. It would, of course, be unbearable if our intentions were regularly frustrated. Yet there is something terribly arid, not to say mechanistic, in the idea of a world where all our purposes result in predictable consequences, where we are completely transparent to ourselves and where intentions always result in expected actions. We value the degree of interference in human intentional activity offered by the unconscious, by language, by the apparatus of the camera or computer, by the instruction performed 'blind.' In short, we desire to see what will happen.

1 The phrase is in Rosalind Krauss, 'Notes on the Index: Seventies Art in America', *October*, no. 3 (Spring 1977) 70.

2 Edward Ruscha, email to the author, August 2009.

3 See my 'Ruscha and Performative Photography', in special issue on 'Photography after Conceptual Art', ed. Diarmuid Costello and Margaret Iversen, *Art History*, vol. 32, no. 5 (2009).

4 John Cage, *Silence: Lectures and Writings* (Middletown, Connecticut: Wesleyan University Press/London: Marion Boyars, 1967) 1.

5 Vito Acconci, 'Notes on Photography', in *The Last Picture Show: Artists Using Photography, 1960–1982*, ed. Douglas Fogle (Minneapolis: Walker Art Center, 2003) 184. See also special issue on Acconci: *Avalanche*, no. 6, (Fall 1972).

6 In conversation with me and in other interviews, Calle has insisted that she was unaware of Acconci's *Following Piece* when she made *Suite vénitienne*. However, after she'd taken the photos a friend told her about it. She made a trip to New York to visit Acconci who 'gave her his blessing'. See the account of this episode in Cécile Camart, 'Sophie Calle, 1978–1981: Genèse d'une figure d'artiste', *Les Cahiers du Musée national d'art moderne*, no. 85 (Autumn 2003) 64.

7 Sophie Calle, *Suite vénitienne* (Paris: Éditions de l'Étoile, 1983); translated edition (Seattle: Bay Press, 1988) 6. Also relevant is André Breton's account of his trailing of Jacqueline Lamba through the streets of Montmartre in *L'Amour fou* (Paris, 1937); trans. Mary Ann Caws, *Mad Love* (Lincoln, Nebraska: University of Nebraska Press, 1987) 43.

8 See John C. Welchman, ed., *Aesthetics of Risk* (conference proceeding of Southern California Consortium of Art Schools, 2006) (Zürich: JRP/Ringier, 2008).

9 See Claire Bishop, ed., *Participation*, Documents of Contemporary Art series (London: Whitechapel Gallery/Cambridge, Massachusetts: The MIT Press, 2006).

10 Lucy R. Lippard, 'Eva Hesse: The Circle' (1971), in Lippard, *From the Center: Feminist Essays on Women's Art* (New York: E.P.Dutton, 1976) 165.

11 Robert Morris, 'Notes on Sculpture. Part 4', *Artforum* (April 1969); reprinted in *Continuous Project Altered Daily: The Writings of Robert Morris* (Cambridge, Massachusetts: The MIT Press, 1993) 67.

12 Benjamin H.D. Buchloh, 'Cosmic Reification: Gabriel Orozco's Photographs', *Gabriel Orozco* (London: Serpentine Gallery/Cologne: Verlag der Buchhandlung Walther König, 2004) 51.
13 Gabriel Orozco, *Photogravity* (Philadelphia: Philadelphia Museum of Art, 1999) 103.
14 Jean/Hans Arp, 'Looking', in *Arp*, ed. James Thrall Soby (New York: The Museum of Modern Art, 1958) 15.
15 Jacques Lacan, *Le Séminaire de Jacques Lacan, Livre XI: 'Les quatre concepts fondamentaux de la psychanalyse'* (Paris: Éditions du Seuil, 1973); trans. Alan Sheridan; ed. Jacques-Alain Miller, *The Four Fundamental Concepts of Psychoanalysis* (London: Penguin Books, 1977) 95.
16 For a study of the impact of theories of trauma and the death drive on art and theory see my *Beyond Pleasure: Freud, Lacan, Barthes* (University Park, Pennsylvania: The Pennsylvania State University Press, 2007).
17 Sigmund Freud, *The Psychopathology of Everyday Life* (1901); *The Standard Edition of the Complete Psychological Works of Sigmund Freud*, vol. VI (London: The Hogarth Press/Institute of Psychoanalysis, 1960) 239.
18 André Breton, *Mad Love*, op. cit., 8.
19 Ibid., 25.
20 Vit Havránek, ed., *Jirí Kovanda 2005–1976, Actions and Installations* (Zurich: Tranzit/JRP/Ringier, 2006) 106.
21 David Campany, 'Man Ray and Marcel Duchamp: Dust Breeding', in Sophie Howarth, ed., *Singular Images: Essays on Remarkable Photographs* (London: Tate Publishing, 2005) 51.
22 Walker Evans, 'The Reappearance of Photography' (1931); in Alan Trachtenberg, ed., *Classic Essays in Photography* (New Haven: Leete's Island Books, 1980) 185.
23 See Benjamin Buchloh's interview with Robert Morris for Morris' comments on his exactly contemporary attraction to the idea of instructional sculpture: Buchloh, 'Three Conversations in 1985: Claes Oldenburg, Andy Warhol and Robert Morris', *October*, no. 70 (Fall 1984) 33–54.
24 Edward Ruscha, *Leave Any Information at the Signal: Writings, Interviews, Bits, Pages*, ed. Alexandra Schwartz (Cambridge, Massachusetts: The MIT Press, 2003) 170–71.
25 André Breton, 'Manifesto of Surrealism' (1924); trans. Richard Seaver and Helen R. Lane in *Manifestos of Surrealism* (Ann Arbor: The University of Michigan Press, 1969) 24.
26 Man Ray, 'Photography is not an Art,' in Lucy Lippard, ed., *Surrealists on Art*, (Englewood Cliffs, New Jersey: Prentice-Hall, 1970).
27 Neil Baldwin, *Man Ray: American Artist* (New York: Da Capo Press, 1988) 158.
28 Ann Banfield, '*L'imparfait de l'objectif*: The Imperfect of the Object Glass', *Camera Obscura*, no. 24 (September 1990) 85. For more on involuntary photography see my essay of that title and one by Anna Dezeuze: 'Richard Wentworth's *Making Do, Getting By* and the Elusive Everyday', in Anna Dezeuze and Julia Kelly, eds, *Found Sculpture and Photography from Surrealism to Contemporary Art* (London: Ashgate, 2010).
29 Roland Barthes, *La Chambre claire* (Paris: Cahiers du Cinéma/Gallimard/Seuil, 1980); trans. Richard Howard, *Camera Lucida: Reflections on Photography* (New York: Hill and Wang, 1980) 27.
30 Salvador Dalí, 'Photography: Pure Creation of the Mind', *L'Amic de les Arts*, no. 18 (30 September

1927); reprinted in Salvador Dalí, *Oui: the Paranoid-Critical Revolution*, ed. Robert Descharnes (Boston: Exact Change, 1998) 13.

31 André Breton, 'Max Ernst', in *What is Surrealism?: Selected Writings*, ed. Franklin Rosemont (London: Pluto Press, 1978).

32 Hal Foster, 'The Return of the Real', *The Return of the Real*, (Cambridge, Massachusetts: The MIT Press, 1996) 134. See also Foster, 'Death in America', *October*, no. 75 (Winter, 1996) 37–60.

33 Walter Benn Michaels, 'Action and Accident: Photography and Writing', in *The Gold Standard and the Logic of Naturalism, American Literature at the Turn of the Century* (Berkeley and Los Angeles: University of California Press, 1987) 223.

34 Ibid., 232.

35 The translation by Michael Howard was published in *Aspen*, no. 5–6, guest-edited by Brian O'Doherty (Aspen, Colorado, Fall/Winter 1967). Barthes' essay was first published in France as 'La Mort de l'auteur' in *Manteia*, no. 5 (Paris, 1968).

Yoko Ono, from *Snow Piece (Tape Piece III)*, 1963

PERFORMANCE, PROCESS, POSSIBILITY

Georges Bataille
Chance//1944

[...] The human mind is set up to take no account of chance, except in so far as the calculations that eliminate chance allow you to forget it: that is, *not take it into account*. But going as far as possible, reflection on chance strips the world bare of the entirety of predictions in which reason encloses it. Like human nakedness, the nakedness of chance – which in the last resort is definitive – is obscene and disgusting: in short, *divine*. Since the course of the things of the world hangs on chance, this course is as depressing for us as a king's absolute power.

My reflections on chance are *in the margin of* thought's development.

All the same, we can't make them more radical (decisive). Descending as far as possible, they pull the rug out from under us when we think that the development of thought allows sitting down, allows rest.

A part of what applies to us can be – must be – reduced to reason or (through knowledge or science) to systematic understanding. We can't suppress the fact that at one point everything and every law was decided according to the whims of chance – or *luck* – without reason entering the picture, except when the calculation of probabilities allowed it to.

It's true, the omnipotence of reason limits luck's power. This limitation in principle suffices, and in the long run the course of the world obeys law. And since we're rational we see this; but the course of things escapes us at the extremes.

At the extremes, there's freedom.

At the extremes, thought ceases to be!

At least within the limits of possibilities that pertain to us, thought can only be present in two ways:

1 Thought is allowed to catch sight of and (in fascination) meditate on the open expanses of catastrophe. The calculus of probabilities limits the scope of this catastrophe, but as death makes us subjects of its empire, the meaning (or non-meaning) of catastrophe isn't to that extent 'humanly' cancelled.

2 Part of human life escapes from work and reaches freedom. This is the part of play that is controlled by reason, but, within reason's limits, determines the brief possibilities of a leap beyond those limits. Play, which is as fascinating as catastrophe, allows you positively to glimpse *the giddy seductiveness of chance*.

I grasp the object of my desire. I tie myself to this object, live in it. It's as sure as light, and like the first hesitant star in the night sky, it's a marvel. In order to know this object with me, someone would have to accommodate my darkness. This distant object is unfamiliar, but familiar too – every flowery exhalation of a young girl, the hectic flush of her cheek, touches it. And it's so transparent a breath will tarnish it, a word dissipate it.

A man betrays chance in a million ways, and in a million ways he betrays 'what he is'. Can you claim you'll never give in to repressive frowning rigidity? The mere fact of not giving in is itself a betrayal. In the fabric of chance, dark interlinks with light. It was only to pursue and mutilate me on a path to horror, depression and denial (as well as to licence and excess) that chance touched me in airy lightness, in utter weightlessness (slow down, dawdle, grow sluggish even for an instant, and chance will disappear). I'd have never found it by looking. Speaking, I've surely betrayed it already. Only if I don't care about betraying myself or about other people's betrayal of me do I escape treachery. I'm dedicated to chance with everything in me, my whole life, all my strength – and there's only absence and inanity in me ... laughter, such *light* laughter! Chance: I imagine, in the gloom of night, a knife-tip entering my heart, a happiness beyond limits, unbearable happiness ...

the light too much joy too much heaven too much
the earth too vast a fast-moving horse
I hear the waters I'm weeping for light

the earth turns beneath my eyelids
stones roll in my bones
the anemone and glow-worm
help me to unconsciousness

in a shroud of roses
an incandescent teardrop
proclaims the day.

Two opposing impulses seek out chance. One of these is predatory, inducing dizziness; the other promotes harmony. One requires violent sexual union – bad luck sinks voraciously on luck, consumes it or at least abandons it and marks it with the sign of doom. There's a flaring up and bad luck takes its course, ending in death. The other is divination, the wish to read chance, be its reflection, be lost in its light. Mostly the opposing movements reach an understanding, each with the other. But if we seek the kind of harmony that's found in turning away from violence, chance is cancelled out as such, it's set on a regular and monotonous path. Chance arises from disorder, not regularity. It demands randomness – its light sparkles in dark obscurity. We fail it when we shield it from misfortune, and its sparkle abandons it when failed.

Chance is more than beauty, but beauty derives its sparkle from chance.

The huge majority (bad luck) drags beauty down to prostitution.

All chance is sullied. Beauty can't exist without a flaw. Perfect, chance and beauty have stopped being what they are: they're the rule. The desire for chance is inside us like a sore tooth, and at the same time it's the opposite – it wants misfortune's unfocused cosiness.

The consummation of chance in a burst of lightning and the fall that follows the consummation can't be – painlessly – imagined by anyone.

The gossamer-like lacerating idea of chance!

Chance is hard to bear. Commonly it's destroyed and the bottom of things drops out. Chance wants to be *impersonal* (or it's vanity, a bird in a cage), hard to put your hands on, melancholy, slipping out into night like a song ...

I can't imagine a *spiritual* way of life that isn't impersonal, dependent on chance, never on efforts of the will.

On a roof I saw large, sturdy hooks[1] placed halfway up. Suppose someone falls from a rooftop ... couldn't he maybe *catch hold* of one of those hooks with an arm or leg? If I fell from a rooftop, I'd plummet to the ground. But if a hook was there, I'd come to a stop halfway down!

Just a little later I might say to myself: 'Once an architect planned this hook, and without it I'd be dead. I should be dead, but I'm not at all – in fact, I'm alive. A hook was put there.'

Let's say my presence, my life, are inescapable. Something impossible and incomprehensible would still be its principle.

I understand now – picturing the momentum of falling – that there's nothing in this world unless it meets up with a *hook*.

Usually we avoid seeing a hook. We confer an aspect of necessity on ourselves, on the universe, on the earth, on people.

With a hook arranging the universe, I plunged into an infinite play of mirrors. This play had the same principle as a fall blocked by a hook. Can anyone get more into the core of things? I shook. I couldn't go on. Rapture within me, emotion welling up to the point of tears, rituals of darkness that defy description, every orgy in the world and all times blending in this light. [...]

If it didn't stop along the way, art would exhaust the movement of chance. It would become something else and more.[2] Chance, though, isn't capable of dawdling, and its lightness of foot protects it from this 'more'. It wants to have its success incomplete and quickly emptied of meaning, one success is soon left behind for another. Hardly does the success appear than its light is extinguished, and another is called forth. Success wants to be gambled, gambled again, wagered endlessly whenever the cards are dealt in a new game.

Personal luck hasn't much to do with luck. Mostly it's a sorry blend of conceit and anguish. Chance is only chance provided that impersonality, or a game of communication that never ends, can be glimpsed.

The light of chance is dimmed by artistic success. As a matter of fact, chance is a woman who wants to be undressed.

Bad luck or anguish sustains the possibility of luck. The same cannot be said of vanity or reason (or, generally, of whatever impulses lead a person to give up playing – gambling, that is).

A fleeting, stifling beauty, embodying chance in a woman's body, is attained through love. But possession of chance requires fingers as light as chance itself. You have to have fingers that don't grasp. Nothing is more contrary to chance (to love) than endless questioning or anxious trembling or the need to exclude unfavourable chance developments; nothing is more pointless than exhausting reflection. I come to love with an enchanted lack of concern, which in its folly is the reverse of a lack of concern. Ponderousness excludes passion so thoroughly you might as well not consider it. In its single-mindedness, love is weakness, melodrama, a need to suffer. Chance summons a chaos through which its links are forever and continuously forged. Affectation, a closed mind and conventional love feelings represent a negation *in spite of which* love is intense, passionate (but we reply to chance by *intentionally* setting the odds against ourselves).

– Even momentarily, ponderousness is a destruction of chance. – All philosophy (all of knowledge makes chance into an exception) is reflection on a lifeless residue, on a regular process that allows neither chance nor mischance. To recognize chance[3] is a suicide of knowledge, and chance, concealed in a philosopher's despair, bursts out in the frothings of the demented. – I base my conviction on the folly of my fellow human beings (or on the intensity of my pleasure). If I hadn't previously exhausted and measured the possibilities of the mind, turning them upside down, what would I have to say? One day I'll *try chance out*, and, moving across eggs like a sprite, I'll let it be understood I'm walking, and my wisdom will seem magical. Possibly this excludes other people – assuming that my attaining chance demands *knowing nothing about them*! Man reads the possible outline of chance in his 'customs', an outline that is himself, a state of grace, an arrow let fly. Animals were a wager, and so is man, we're an arrow released into air. Where it will fall, I can't say. Where I'll fall, I can't say. [...]

From chance to poetry, the distance derives from the inanity of so-called poetry. A calculated use of words, the negation of poetry, destroys chance and reduces things to what they are. Using words poetically involves a perversion akin to the hellish beauty of faces or bodies – which death reduces to nothing.

The absence of poetry is the eclipse of chance.

Chance is like death: 'the harsh embrace of a lover, desired, feared'.

Chance is the painful place of overlap of life and death – in sex and in ecstasy, in laughter and in tears.

Chance has the power to love death. But this desire destroys death too (less certainly than hatred of death or fear of it). The path to chance is hard to follow; it's threatened by, but also inseparable from, horror and death. Without horror and death or without the *risk* of them, where would the magic of chance be? [...]

1 [Hooks like these are used to hold poles on roofs to prevent the snow from sliding off in the winter. – Tr.]

2 In fact, art escapes. On principle artists mostly limit themselves to their speciality. If they exceed it, this is sometimes to further a truth that is even more important, in their eyes, than art itself. Most artists refuse to see that art encourages them to create a god-like (that is, in our times, a God-like) world.

3 This has nothing to do with a calculus of possibilities [note added in 1959 edition].

Georges Bataille, extracts from the 'Games of Chance' chapter of *Le Coupable* (Paris: Éditions Gallimard, 1944); trans. Bruce Boone, *Guilty* (San Francisco: The Lapis Press, 1988); reprinted in *The Bataille Reader*, ed. Fred Botting and Scott Wilson (Oxford: Blackwell, 1997) 39–42; 43–44; 46.

George Brecht
Chance Imagery//1957

Chance

The word 'chance' (with a Latin root relating to the falling of dice) can conveniently be taken to mean that the cause, or system of causes, responsible for a given effect is unknown or unlooked for, or at least that we are unable completely to specify it. Of course, in the real world, causes are also effects, and effects causes. The fall of a die, for example, is the effect of an infinite number of (largely unknown) causes (among which we can imagine resilience of the die, hardness of the table, angle of contact to be included), and this effect, in turn, may be the cause of my winning a certain amount of money.

It is sometimes possible to specify only the universe of possible characteristics which a chance event may have. For example, a toss of a normal die will be expected to give a number from one to six. Any particular face will be expected to turn up in about one-sixth of a great many throws. But the outcome of any one toss remains unknown until the throw has been made. It is often useful to keep in mind this 'universe of possible results', even when that universe is hypothetical, for this clarifies for us the nature of our chance event as a selection from a limited universe. We should note here that events are defined as due to chance in a relative way. There is no absolute chance or random event, for chance and randomness are aspects of the way in which we structure our universe. These are elementary considerations with many ramifications, but I hope they will serve as a conceptual base line for the discussion to follow, which should clarify the nature of chance. We shall later discuss the random event, as a special type of bias-free chance event.

In connection with art, and the affective image, we shall indicate two aspects of chance, one where the origin of images is unknown because it lies in deeper-than-conscious levels of the mind, and the second where images derive from mechanical processes not under the artist's control. Both of these processes have in common a lack of conscious design.

Dada and Surrealism

In the sense that there is a certain lack of conscious control in everything we do, the use of chance in art could be traced (academically) to the cave drawings of prehistoric man; but the first explicit use of chance in painting seems to come shortly before World War I. If we admit automatism as chance, then the improvisations of Kandinsky (1911), painted 'rather subconsciously in a state of strong inner tension', would take precedence over Picasso's first *papiers collés* (1912), in which were incorporated fortuitous scraps of newspaper and cardboard.

(The question of the chance nature of automatism might be endlessly debated. It seems to me that the answer lies in the distinction between our seeking immediate causes or ultimate causes of automatic actions. It takes little reflection to see that ultimate causes might readily and reasonably be ascribed to chance, but psychoanalytic theory has taught us to expect 'conscious ignorance and unconscious knowledge of the motivation of psychic accidentalness',[1] and it does not always take very deep or lengthy probing to reveal immediate causes for the psychically accidental. At any rate, it is practical to consider chance as being defined by *consciously* known causes, and by this definition, at least, automatism is a chance process.)

Since we are restricting ourselves to the generation of chance-images, and not to their appreciation, we shall indicate only the place of the unconscious (including the subconscious, or fore-conscious) as a source of significant images. The importance of chance to the unconscious has manifold facets, not only in modern psychology, but also (and particularly) in Oriental thought (such as that manifested in the I-Ching or in Zen).

The Dadaists considered the unconscious to be a source of images free from the biases engrained in us by parents, social custom and all the other artificial restrictions on intellectual freedom:

'We are now in a position to formulate the problem of art, more accurately the problem of expression, as it appeared to the writers of the *Litterature* group [Aragon, Breton, Soupault]: only the unconscious does not lie, it alone is worth bringing to the light. All deliberate and conscious efforts, composition, logic, are futile. The celebrated French lucidity is nothing but a cheap lantern. At best the "poet" can prepare traps (as a physician might do in treating a patient), with which to catch the unconscious by surprise and to prevent it from cheating ...' (Marcel Raymond)[2]

'The unconscious is inexhaustible and uncontrollable. Its force surpasses us. It is as mysterious as the last particle of a brain cell. Even if we knew it, we could not reconstruct it.' (Tristan Tzara)[3]

As far as affective form is concerned, chance is an aspect of the universe made significant by unconscious interactions, but it is not the only aspect. When the largely iconoclastic displays of Dada were superseded by the more systematic researches of the Surrealists, Breton, for one, in the *First Manifesto of Surrealism* (1924), made this general interest in the unconscious explicit:

'During the course of Surrealist development, outside all forms of idealism, outside the opiates of religion, the marvellous comes to light within *reality*. It comes to light in dreams, obsessions, preoccupations, in sleep, fear, love, chance; in hallucinations, pretended disorders, follies, ghostly apparitions, escape mechanisms and evasions; in fancies, idle wanderings, poetry, the supernatural and the unusual; in empiricism, in *super-reality*.'[4] (This statement, written in 1924, followed Freud's *The Interpretation of Dreams* by 24 years and *Pyschopathology of Everyday Life* by 20.)

It is useful practically to include automatism in a consideration of chance in art, and it is only our viewpoint that makes it a chance process, but there is actually no reason why the others of Breton's categories could not also be included. We exclude them arbitrarily from this discussion only to preserve a certain tightness in our consideration of the methodological resources of the contemporary research 'artist', which we will take up further on. Automatism is also an aspect of chance in the sense that we accept its product as something which it really is not. In all of Breton's manifestations of the marvellous (a handy summary) we read into phenomena characteristics which they do not possess in an absolute way. Duchamp called this 'irony' ('a playful way of accepting something'), and the concept is a critical one in understanding the vector through Dada, Pollock, the present-day chance-imagists, and the future. The idea will appear again in the section on Pollock, and shows up particularly as a method I've called the 'irrelevant process' (also discussed later).

We are more interested, though, in the mechanically chance process, and here Duchamp did the pioneer work. In 1913 he undertook what seems to be the first explicit use of chance for the creation of an affective image, in the *3 stoppages étalon* [*3 Standard Stoppages*]. He made these images by holding a thread one metre long, 'straight and horizontal', one metre above a blank canvas. After letting it fall onto the canvas, it was fixed with a trickle of varnish into the chance convolution in which it fell. This process was repeated to give three such canvases.

Duchamp seems to consider three phenomena basic to his exploitation of chance: wind, gravity and aim. (This discussion is based largely on an article about Duchamp by Harriet and Sidney Janis.)[5] The *3 stoppages étalon* illustrates gravity; wind was used to create the cloud formations for *La Mariée mise à nu par ses célibataires, même* [*The Bride Stripped Bare by Her Bachelors, Even*, or 'Large Glass', 1915–23]: 'Air currents blowing a piece of mesh gauze against a screen, imprinted a limpid rectangle upon it. The experiment repeated three times gave three chance images, variations on the square ... The third device in allowing shapes to create themselves and thus void the responsibility of the hand, is termed by Duchamp *adresse*, that is, skill in aiming. Nine marks were made upon the glass by the impact of shots of matches dipped in paint, from a toy cannon ... Aiming nine shots at a given point, these formed a polygram as a result of variation in the aim-control and accompanying conditions. He then converted the flat polygram or floor plan into an elevation plan. Here the nine points became the locations for the nine malic forms in perspective.'[6]

Duchamp's theories on the use of chance seem highly developed. But not exhaustive. Other Dadaists, especially Arp, Ernst and Tzara, later developed other important applications of chance: Arp composed collages by picking up chance scraps of paper, shuffling them, and glueing them down just as they fell (example: the 'Squares arranged according to the laws of chance', a collage of 1916). Ernst developed the 'decalcomania of chance',[7] wherein, for example, ink was spread between two sheets of paper, which were then pulled apart. [...] Tzara composed poems by drawing words from a hat. ('To make a dadaist poem/Take a newspaper./Take a pair of scissors./Choose an article as long as you are planning to make your poem./ Cut out the article./ Then cut out each of the words that make up this article and put them in a bag./ Shake it gently./ Then take out the scraps one after the other in the order in which they left the bag./ Copy conscientiously./ The poem will be like you./ And here you are a writer, infinitely original and endowed with a sensibility that is charming though beyond the understanding of the vulgar.'[8]

Frottage was a 'semi-automatic process for obtaining patterns of designs by rubbing canvas or paper which has been placed over a rough surface such as planking, embossing, a brick wall, etc.'[9] [...] This is an example of a technique for which we shall later have a more general term: 'the irrelevant process'. A very interesting technique of the Surrealists, which permitted the cause of an event to be lost, so to speak, in multiplicity, was that of the *cadavre exquis* ['exquisite corpse'] wherein several persons each made part of a picture, folding the paper to cover each addition, before passing the drawing to the next participant. [...]

The ability of the unconscious to reconcile opposites is nowhere so evident as in Dada, for within a periphery of nonsense the ridiculous and the profound were made to evince each other: 'Dada wished to destroy the reasonable frauds of men and recover the natural, unreasonable order. Dada wished to replace the logical nonsense of the men of today with an illogical nonsense. That is why we beat the Dadaist bass drum with all our might and trumpeted the praises of unreason ... Dada like nature is without meaning, Dada is for infinite meaning and finite means.' (Gabrielle Buffet-Picabia, 1949)[10] Within such a (frameless) framework, chance played a major part, as testified by Arp himself: 'Chance opened up perceptions to me, immediate spiritual insights. Intuition led me to revere the law of chance as the highest and deepest of laws, the law that rises from the fundament. An insignificant word might become a deadly thunderbolt. One little sound might destroy the earth. One little sound might create a new universe.'[11] The almost incredibly incisive mind of Tristan Tzara, as early as 1922, even recognized the relationship of all this to Oriental philosophy (in one of the most convincing of Dada documents, the 'Lecture on Dada'). 'Dada is not at all modern. It is more in the nature of a return to an almost Buddhist religion of indifference.'[12] Such aspects of reality as Oriental thought – scientific thought – Dada – chance become somewhat clearer in such a light. Perhaps chance is the most allusive of the phenomena studied by the Dadaists and Surrealists because it is capable of being most widely generalized. We shall see.

The Second World War helped to disperse the European Dadaists and Surrealists, and many of the most original artists – Breton, Ernst, Tanguy, Masson – regrouped in New York, particularly around two New York galleries, the Julien Levy Gallery and Peggy Guggenheim's Art of This Century.

Jackson Pollock

Jackson Pollock's first show was held at Peggy Guggenheim's gallery in 1943. Here he was able to associate with the proponents of that 'sacred disorder' which was later to become the key to his own original style. 'To them Pollock owed his radical new sense of freedom, and he spoke more than once of his debt to their unpremeditated and automatic methods. By elevating the appeal to chance and accident into a first principle of creation, the Surrealists had circumvented the more rigid formalisms of modern art.'[13] It is not difficult to find their influence in Pollock's paintings of the war years (for example, *Guardians of the Secret*, 1943). Pollock achieved a profound, sustained and irrational synthesis of all the principles which had preceded him in Dada, and in a way consistent with his contemporary world. His paintings seem much less manifestations of one of a group of techniques for releasing the unconscious (as the Dada experiments seemed), than they do of a single, integrated use of a chance as a means of unlocking the deepest possible grasp of nature in its broadest sense.

Not to get lost in conjecture, let us briefly give evidence for two points: first that Pollock's calligraphy was truly automatic and second that there is a considerable element of chance in the ultimate arrangement of pigment in the chance-paintings of roughly 1947–51.

First, part of a statement by Pollock made in 1947:

'When I am *in* my painting, I'm not aware of what I'm doing. It is only after a sort of "get acquainted" period that I see what I have been about.'[14]

Again, from an earlier statement:

'... the fact that good European moderns are now here is very important, for they bring with them an understanding of the problems of modern painting. I am particularly impressed with their concept of the source of art being the unconscious. This idea interests me more than these specific painters do ...'[15]

Aside from the lack of conscious control of paint application in these paintings, there are technical reasons for looking at this complex of interdependent forms as predominantly chance events. For one thing, the infinite number of variables involved in determining the flow of fluid paint from a source not in contact with the canvas cannot possibly be simultaneously taken into account with sufficient omniscience that the exact configuration of the paint when it hits the canvas can be predicted. Some of these variables, for example, are the paint viscosity, density, rate of flow at any instant; and direction, speed and configuration of the applicator, to say nothing of non-uniformity in the paint. Even if we deny automatism, and claim omniscience for an unconscious moulded by a long learning period, it is obvious that in some of Pollock's paintings of this period (in *One, 1950*, for example) differently-coloured streams of paint have flowed into each other after application, resulting in a commingling completely out of the artist's hands. Never before Pollock were chance processes used with such primacy, consistency and integrity, as valuable sources of affective imagery.

Paintings get to be what they are physically through an interaction of method and material, and they have their effect in an interaction between painting and observer. As far as the observer is concerned, Pollock has demonstrated that the ability of humans to appreciate complex chance-images is almost unlimited. Here I would I like to introduce the general term 'chance-imagery' to apply to our formation of images resulting from chance, wherever these occur in nature. (The word 'imagery' is intentionally ambiguous enough, I think, to apply either to the physical act of creating an image out of real materials, or to the formation of an image in the mind, say by abstraction from a more complex system.) One reason for doing this is to place the painter's, musician's, poet's, dancer's chance images in the same conceptual category as natural chance-images (the configuration of meadow-grasses, the arrangement of stones on a brook bottom), and to get away from the idea that an artist makes something 'special' and beyond the world of ordinary things. An Alpine peak or an iris petal can move us at times with all the subtle power of a *Night Watch* or one of the profound themes of [Beethoven's late string quartet] *Opus 131*. There is no a priori reason why moving images should originate only with artists.

This leaves 'art' to mean something *constructed*, from a starting point of preconceived notions, with the corollary that as art approaches chance-imagery, the artist enters a oneness with all of nature. This idea has in essence been well expressed by D.T. Suzuki:

'There is something divine in being spontaneous and not being hampered by human conventionalities and their artificial hypocrisies. There is something direct and fresh in this lack of restraint by anything human, which suggests a divine freedom and creativity. Nature never deliberates; it acts directly out of its own heart, whatever this may mean. In this respect Nature is divine. Its "irrationality" transcends human doubts of ambiguities, and in our submitting to it, or rather accepting it, we transcend ourselves.'[16] 'Our inner life is complete when it merges into Nature and becomes one with it.'[17]

When an artist achieves this essential oneness with all of nature, everything he creates illuminates nature, as well as himself.

'*Reason has cut man off from nature*.' (Hans Arp)[18] [...]

Randomness

Chance images are characterized by a lack of conscious design. When these images are 'handmade', and conscious thought is evaded, so that the images have their source in deeper-than-conscious areas of the mind, we will prefer the Surrealists' term 'automatic' to the word 'random', though 'random', in the way it is used in everyday speech, might seem appropriate (as meaning, for example, 'without definite aim, direction, rule, or method').[19] We will prefer this usage in order to restrict 'random' to a technical meaning which it has more commonly in statistics, where it applies to special techniques for eliminating bias in sampling. The term 'strict randomness' is useful for ensuring that the word random is understood in this technical sense, but, in general, we shall merely say random, and it should always be understood here that the technical meaning is implied. Chance is sometimes used in painting in such a way that the images are neither clearly automatic nor random, and here we can only refer to chance-images or chance-processes.

It remains to indicate, then, what this technical meaning comprises, recognizing that in general, the reason for the importance of randomness for purposes of scientific inference will be the same as the reason for its importance in the arts, that is, the elimination of bias. It is not intuitively obvious that strict randomness is difficult to achieve; therefore let us indicate the general presence of bias where human choice or ordinary mechanical systems are involved. This will give us an intuitive insight into approaches capable of eliminating bias, and will lead finally to a working definition of randomness itself.

Concerning a general bias in human choice, Kendall and Smith have made the following interesting statement:

'It is becoming increasingly evident that sampling left to the discretion of a human individual is not random, although he may be completely unconscious of the existence of bias, or indeed actively endeavouring to avoid it. House-to-house sampling, the sampling of crop yields, even ticket-drawing have all been found to give results widely divergent from expectation.'[20]

Yule and Kendall[21] have given an example of human bias which was detected in the course of agricultural experiments carried out in England. The heights of wheat plants were to be measured at two stages in their growth. Of the sets of eight plants sampled for measurement at each of the two stages, two were selected 'at random' by eye, and the other six were selected by strictly random methods. Analysis of the measurements showed clearly that, in the samples selected by eye, there was a clear bias toward selecting taller shoots in May, before the ears of wheat had formed, while in June, after further maturation, another bias toward selecting plants of more like average height, and avoiding the extremely tall or short plants, was evidenced.

I have attempted some one-hand typing of series of random digits, and found not only a bias toward a greater frequency of higher digits (regardless of the hand used for the typing), but also peculiar patterns in the series; digits being followed unusually often by certain other digits, for example. (For an interesting discussion of chance numbers, and further references on this subject, see section 12 of Freud's *Psychopathology of Everyday Life.*)

One might expect to avoid human bias by using mechanical systems, but experience has shown that it is not easy to find simple unbiased mechanical systems. Perfectly balanced coins and roulette wheels, like perfectly cubical and homogenous dice, seem to occur rarely in nature, if at all. Weldon,[22] for example, threw twelve dice 4,096 times. For unbiased dice the probability of a 4, 5 or 6 is Ω, so that he should have obtained one of these faces 24,576 times. These three faces actually occurred 25,145 times, which is a statistically significant bias. Even an electronic analogue of a roulette wheel, built by the RAND Corporation for the generation of random digits, after careful engineering and re-engineering to eliminate bias, was found again to have statistically significant biases, after running continuously for a month, in spite of the fact that tests showed the electronic equipment itself to be in good order.[23]

How can bias be avoided? First, it can be reduced by resorting to compound chance events, and, formally, it can be eliminated by the use of random numbers. By making the chance-event a compound of two or more independent events, elements in the compound event can be made more nearly independent of each other, and thus biases can be avoided. For example, in the Surrealist *cadavre exquis*, it was made impossible for any one person to foresee the overall result of combining the independently contributed parts of the drawing, so that bias in the relationship of elements in the compound chance-event (drawing) was avoided. John Cage has also used this technique in his *Music for Four Pianos*, wherein four pianists play independently of each other, the resulting rhythmic and melodic pattern being thus freed of personal bias. In fact, this technique has been used, in a much-refined way, to generate a table of strictly random numbers (those published by the Interstate Commerce commission).[24] Independent columns of digits from waybills received by the commission deriving from numerical data such as shipment weight, revenue, car serial number, etc., were used as a basic set from which the final set was derived.

Tables of random numbers provide a convenient and reliable means of avoiding bias in selection; convenient because they allow random selection of anything which can be numbered, reliable because they can be verified to be statistically random. Tests for randomness in random number tables are described in Kendall and Smith[25] and G. Udny Yule.[26] The use of tables of random numbers is briefly described in the following section on methodology.

Randomness, then, implies an independence of each individual choice from every other choice, plus an aggregate impartiality toward the characteristic being sampled. In tables of random digits, for example, a state of randomness implies both that the occurrence of any particular digit at a particular point in the table is independent of the occurrence of all the other digits, and that the proportional occurrence of that digit in the long run is arbitrarily close to some pre-established value. Practically speaking, this means that in a table such as the RAND table, the digit 5 in a certain place is just as likely to be followed by a 6, 7, 8 or 9 as it is to be followed by a 0, 1, 2, 3 or 4, and also that in the table as a whole, the proportion of digits 5 should be reasonably close to one-tenth ...

Coda

Chance in the arts provides a means for escaping the biases engrained in our personality by our culture and personal past history, that is, it is a means of attaining greater generality. The result is a method of approach with wide application. The methods of chance and randomness can be applied to the selection and arrangement of sounds by the composer, to movement and pace by the dancer, to three-dimensional form by the sculptor, to surface form and colour by the painter, to linguistic elements by the poet. Science tells us that the universe is what we conceive it to be, and chance enables us to determine what we conceive it to be (for the conception is only partly conscious). The receptacle of forms available to the artist thus becomes open-ended, and eventually embraces all of nature, for the recognition of significant form becomes limited only by the observer's self. It must be obvious too that the infinite range of application of these methods is compounded when the matter of materials is also considered, and this is a subject we have only incidentally touched on here. [...] I doubt that an increase in our ability to recognize significance in the chance-images which nature presents all about us will mean an end of the personal activities which we have been calling art. The artist will probably continue to make significant images, both because some such images rarely occur in nature, and because of a personal release which comes about from such activity:

'The painter makes paintings in the urgent need to discharge his own emotions and visions. (Pablo Picasso)[27]

'Pictures are vehicles of passion, of all kinds and orders, not pretty luxuries like sports cars. In our society, the capacity to give and to receive passion is limited. For this reason, the act of painting is a deep human necessity, not the production of a hand-made commodity. (Robert Motherwell)[28]

But it seems to me that we fall short of the infinite expansion of the human spirit for which we are searching, when we recognize only images which are artefacts. We are capable of more than that.

An After-Note

In 1957, when this article was written, I had only recently met John Cage and had not yet seen clearly that the most important implications of chance lay in his work rather than in Pollock's. Nor could I have foreseen the resolution of the distinction between choice and chance which was to occur in my own work.

We are eight years farther on the spiral, and I prefer work to re-work. 'Chance-Imagery' is presented in the form in which it was originally written. (November 1965)

1 ['reference 2' in source] Sigmund Freud, *Psychopathology of Everyday Life. The Basic Writings of Sigmund Freud*, trans. A.A. Brill (New York: Random House, 1938) 164.

2 [3] Marcel Raymond, *From Baudelaire to Surrealism;* quoted in Robert Motherwell, ed., *The Dada Painters and Poets: An Anthology* (New York: Wittenborn, Schultz, 1951) xix.

3 [1] Tristan Tzara, Lecture on Dada' (1922), in *The Dada Painters and Poets*, op. cit., 248.

4 André Breton, *First Surrealist Manifesto*; quoted by Georges Hugnet in one of his two introductory essays for *Fantastic Art, Dada, Surrealism*, ed. Alfred H. Barr, Jr. (New York: The Museum of Modern Art) 1947.

5 Harriet and Sidney Janis, 'Marcel Duchamp: Anti-Artist' (1945), in *The Dada Painters and Poets*, op. cit., Appendix C, 306.

6 Ibid.

7 Ibid.

8 [6] Tristan Tzara, 'manifesto on feeble love and bitter love', in *The Dada Painters and Poets*, op. cit., 92.

9 [7] Alfred H. Barr, Jr, 'A list of devices, techniques, media', *Fantastic Art, Dada, Surrealism*, op. cit., 65.

10 [8] Gabrielle Buffet-Picabia, 'Some Memories of Pre-Dada: Picabia and Duchamp' (1949), in *The Dada Painters and Poets*, op. cit., 266.

11 [9] Jean (Hans) Arp, 'Dada Was Not a Farce' (1949), in *The Dada Painters and Poets*, op. cit., 294.

12 [10] Tristan Tzara, 'Lecture on Dada' (1922), in *The Dada Painters and Poets*, op. cit., 247.

13 [11] Sam Hunter, catalogue of the 1956 Pollock retrospective show, *Bulletin*, vol. XXIV, no. 2 (New York: The Museum of Modern Art).

14 [12] Jackson Pollock, 'My Painting', *Possibilities*, no. 1:79 (New York, Winter 1947–48) 78–83.

15 [13] Jackson Pollock, 'Jackson Pollock' (a questionnaire), *Arts and Architecture*, vol. 61, no. 2 (February 1944) 14.

16 [14] D.T. Suzuki, 'Zen Buddhism', *Selected Writings of D.T. Suzuki*, ed. William Barrett (New York: Doubleday & Co., Inc., 1956) 234.

17 [15] Ibid., 256.

18 [16] Jean (Hans) Arp, 'Notes from a Dada Diary', in *The Dada Painters and Poets*, op. cit., 222.

19 [20] *Webster's New International Dictionary*, second edition (1959).

20 [21] M.G. Kendall and B. Babington Smith, 'Randomness and Random Sampling Numbers', *Journal of the Royal Statistical Society*, vol. CI, pt. 1 (London, 1938) 147–66.

21 [22] G. Udny Yule and M.G. Kendall, *An Introduction to the Theory of Statistics*, 14th edition (New York: Hafner Publishing Co., 1950).

22 [23] Cited in M.G. Kendall, *The Advanced Theory of Statistics*, vol. I, fifth edition (New York: Hafner Publishing Co.) 199.

23 [24] The RAND Corporation, *A Million Random Digits with 100,000 Normal Deviates* (Glencoe, Illinois: The Free Press, 1955). A description of the method used for production of the random digits is contained in the introduction.

24 [25] Interstate Commerce Commission, Bureau of Transport Economics and Statistics, *Table of*

105,000 Random Decimal Digits (Washington, D.C., May 1949) Statement no. 4914, File no. 261–A–1.

25 [20] Kendall and Babington Smith, op. cit.

26 G. Udny Yule, 'A Test of Tippett's Random Sampling Numbers', *Journal of the Royal Statistical Society*, vol. CI, pt. 1 (1938) 167.

27 [29] Quoted by Frank Elgar, in Elgar and Maillard, *Picasso* (New York: Frederick A. Praeger, Inc., 1956).

George Brecht, extracts from *Chance Imagery* (1957), A Great Bear Pamphlet (New York: Something Else Press, 1966) 4–12; 16–19; 23–5.

Ann Temkin
Ellsworth Kelly: *Colors for a Large Wall* (1951)//2008

Ellsworth Kelly's *Colors for a Large Wall* (1951) appears to be a fully self-evident work, a masterpiece whose narrative begins and ends with its square grid of sixty-four individual monochrome panels. On the contrary, however, it represents the culmination of a long adventure begun in Paris in early 1951 and continuing in Sanary, in the south of France, at the end of that year. For several months in Paris, Kelly had immersed himself in creating a suite of eight large collages, each titled *Spectrum Colors Arranged by Chance* (1951). They were composed of hundreds of small squares of coloured paper distributed across a supporting sheet in predetermined patterns, with the placement of individual colours assigned randomly. *Colors for a Large Wall* is based on an 8 x 8 inch collage made with 36 coloured squares over from that ambitious project (1951).[1]

The bold means used in all of these works – chance operation, ready-made colour – were instrumental to Kelly's invention of himself as an artist during those years in Paris. He was well versed in colour theory; it was only six years earlier, at Pratt Institute in Brooklyn, that he had trained in Albert Munsell's colour system. Yet his decision to go to Paris in 1948 was a decision to leave that and the rest of his education behind. To qualify for funds from the G.I. Bill of Rights, Kelly enrolled at the École des Beaux-Arts, but he rarely attended class. His allergy to dogma also distanced him from the geometric abstraction of the Salon des Réalités Nouvelles, the dominant artistic force in postwar Paris. Kelly needed new masters and found them in artists who advocated the use of chance rather than relational rules and deliberated composition. In Paris he struck up friendships with John Cage and Jean Arp, both of whom provided liberating inspiration in their unorthodox methodologies for finding and making art.[2]

The Spectrum collages were made with the French coloured papers that Kelly had been working with during the previous year.[3] The front of the sheets was bright and glossy, and the back was gummed for adhesion. Kelly was delighted by his fortuitous discovery of these papers at a local art-supply store, and he purchased a wide variety of colours. He initiated the Spectrum project when he realized that his collage and paintings primarily juxtaposed a single colour with white; he decided he 'wanted to find out about colour' anew.[4]

'Canned chance', a phrase from one of Marcel Duchamp's fragmentary notes from the 1910s, aptly describes Kelly's approaches to these works.[5] The first one was based directly on his painting *Seine* (1950); like the painting, the collage suggests a shimmering reflection on the water. Subsequent collages all featured distinct mathematical systems for the distribution of squares in the composition. Each enabled the mapping of the numbers one through eighteen onto the hundreds of square units Kelly had outlined on the supporting sheet of paper. After randomly assigning numbers to the eighteen colours that comprised his palette, he went about glueing the coloured squares onto the places dictated by their numbers. He worked with one colour at a time, filling all the squares for each number before going on to the next, so that the overall result would remain a mystery until the end. Using this process he created eight collages, the first a horizontal rectangle and the others approximately 3 feet square (except for the eighth, which is larger, at 44 x 44 inches).[6] The first three collages are on a white ground, the next three are on a black ground, and the last two have no black or white exposed at all.

When Kelly left Paris to join friends in Sanary, in November 1951, he brought along the leftover squares in an envelope. Shortly after his arrival he used them to make two collages: first what was to become a study for *Sanary*, and then *Colors for a Large Wall*. For the latter, he pencilled a grid of 64 units, a structure he chose for its chessboard-like neutrality, onto a sheet of paper and arrayed the squares 'very, very quickly, without thinking'. Because only 36 coloured squares remained, 28 spaces remained empty and white.[7] Each row has three to six colours, with several repeating (black appears ten times), although squares of the same colour are never adjacent.

Kelly's great gambit was to convert this tiny collage into the largest painting he had yet made, with the square-inch papers translated into square-foot canvases painted with oils to match the paper colours. He had not intended the collages to be studies for the paintings, and the 64-unit one, in particular, perplexed him. After he made the collage, it was several days before he decided to ask the cabinetmaker who worked downstairs to make him 64 stretchers. The resulting painting's modular format – a grid of individual paintings comprising a whole – was an extraordinarily bold innovation, yet it was in part a practical decision: Kelly did not have the means to store or ship a large-scale canvas.

Kelly's move to such a large painting was based on his ambition to invent a public art for the modern era. More than a year earlier he had written to Cage:

> My collages are only ideas for things much larger – things to cover walls. In fact all the things I've done I would like to see much larger. I am not interested in painting as it has been accepted for so long – to hang on the walls of houses as pictures. To hell with pictures – they should be the wall – even better – on the outside wall – of large buildings.[8]

The same month that he made *Colors for a Large Wall*, he applied to the Guggenheim Foundation for a grant to produce a small book he called *Line Form Color* (its mock-up employed the same gummed papers found in the Spectrum collages). The book, he said, would 'be an alphabet of plastic pictorial elements, aiming to establish a new scale of painting, a closer contact between the artist and the wall, providing a way for painting to accompany modern architecture.'[9] The statement spoke less to the book, which the foundation declined to sponsor, then to *Colors for a Large Wall*, the painting that laid out the path for the artist's future. Kelly considered it his *Demoiselles d'Avignon*, a pivotal work in his oeuvre.[10] The painting was both the culmination of his close involvement with chance procedure and ready-made materials and the point of departure for his ongoing exploration of colour and form in the following decades.

1 Ellsworth Kelly, 'Notes of 1969', in *Ellsworth Kelly* (Amsterdam: Stedelijk Museum, 1980) 34.

2 This period of Kelly's work has been the object of intensive study. See, for example, Yve-Alain Bois, Jack Cowart and Alfred Pacquement, *Ellsworth Kelly: The Years in France. 1948–1954* (Washington, D.C.: National Gallery of Art, 1992), and Bois, *Ellsworth Kelly: The Early Drawings, 1948–1955* (Cambridge, Massachusetts: Harvard University Art Museums, 1999).

3 Most of the Kelly literature links the use of these colours to his job teaching art to children at the American School, Paris, in 1950–51. Kelly recalls that he discovered the papers before that time, however; Kelly, telephone conversation with Ann Temkin, 31 August 2007.

4 Kelly, conversation with Temkin, Spencertown, New York, 9 January 2006.

5 See *Salt Seller: The Writings of Marcel Duchamp (Marchand du Sel)*, ed. Michel Sanouillet and Elmer Peterson (New York: Oxford University Press, 1973) 33.

6 *Spectrum VI* is the only collage that was translated into a painting: *Spectrum Colors Arranged by Chance* (1951–53), in the San Francisco Museum of Modern Art.

7 Kelly, conversation with Temkin, 9 January 2006.

8 Kelly, letter to John Cage, 4 September 1950, quoted in Yve-Alain Bois, Jack Cowart and Alfred

Pacquement, *Ellsworth Kelly: The Years in France*, op. cit., 188.

9 Kelly, 'Project for a Book: Line, Form and Color', in *Line Form Color*, 1951 (Cambridge, Massachusetts: Harvard University Art Museums, 1999) n.p.

10 Kelly, conversation with Temkin, 9 January 2006.

Ann Temkin, extract from 'Ellsworth Kelly', in *Color Chart: Reinventing Color, 1956 to Today* (New York: The Museum of Modern Art, 2008) 46–7.

John Cage
Experimental Music//1958

Formerly, when anyone said the music I presented was experimental, I objected. It seemed to me that composers knew what they were doing, and that the experiments that had been made had taken place prior to the finished works, just as sketches are made before paintings and rehearsals precede performances. But, giving the matter further thought, I realized that there is ordinarily an essential difference between making a piece of music and hearing one. A composer knows his work as a woodsman knows a path he has traced and retraced, while a listener is confronted by the same work as one is in the woods by a plant he has never seen before.

Now, on the other hand, times have changed; music has changed; and I no longer object to the word 'experimental'. I use it in fact to describe all the music that especially interests me and to which I am devoted, whether someone else wrote it or I myself did. What has happened is that I have become a listener and the music has become something to hear. Many people, of course, have given up saying 'experimental' about this new music. Instead, they either move to a halfway point and say 'controversial' or depart to a greater distance and question whether this 'music' is music at all.

For in this new music nothing takes place but sounds: those that are notated and those that are not. Those that are not notated appear in the written music as silences, opening the doors of the music to the sounds that happen to be in the environment. This openness exists in the fields of modern sculpture and architecture. The glass houses of Mies van der Rohe reflect their environment, presenting to the eye images of clouds, trees or grass, according to the situation. And while looking at the constructions in wire of the sculptor Richard Lippold, it is inevitable that one will see other things, and people too, if they happen to be there at the same time, through the network of wires. There is no such thing as an empty space or an empty time. There is always something to see, something to hear. In fact, try as we may to make a silence, we cannot. For certain engineering purposes, it is desirable to have as silent a situation as possible. Such a room is called an anechoic chamber, its six walls made of special material, a room without echoes. I entered one at Harvard University several years ago and heard two sounds, one high and one low. When I described them to the engineer in charge, he informed me that the high one was my nervous system in operation, the low one my blood in circulation. Until I die there will be sounds. And they will continue following my death. One need not fear about the future of music.

But this fearlessness only follows if, at the parting of the ways, where it is realized that sounds occur whether intended or not, one turns in the direction of those he does not intend. This turning is psychological and seems at first to be a giving up of everything that belongs to humanity – for a musician, the giving up of music. This psychological turning leads to the world of nature, where, gradually or suddenly, one sees that humanity and nature, not separate, are in this world together; that nothing was lost when everything was given away. In fact, everything is gained. In musical terms, any sounds may occur in any combination and in any continuity.

And it is a striking coincidence that just now the technical means to produce such a free-ranging music are available. When the Allies entered Germany towards the end of World War II, it was discovered that improvements had been made in recording sounds magnetically such that tape had become suitable for the high-fidelity recording of music. First in France with the work of Pierre Schaeffer, later here, in Germany, in Italy, in Japan, and perhaps, without my knowing it, in other places, magnetic tape was used not simply to record performances of music but to make a new music that was possible only because of it. Given a minimum of two tape recorders and a disk recorder, the following processes are possible: 1) a single recording of any sound may be made; 2) a re-recording may be made, in the course of which, by means of filters and circuits, any or all of the physical characteristics of a given recorded sound may be altered; 3) electronic mixing (combining on a third machine sounds issuing from two others) permits the presentation of any number of sounds in combination; 4) ordinary splicing permits the juxtaposition of any sounds, and when it includes unconventional cuts, it, like re-recording, brings about alterations of any or all of the original physical characteristics. The situation made available by these means is essentially a total sound-space, the limits of which are ear-determined only, the position of a particular sound in this space being the result of five determinants: frequency or pitch, amplitude or loudness, overtone structure or timbre, duration and morphology (how the sound begins, goes on, and dies away). By the alteration of any one of these determinants, the position of the sound in sound-space changes. Any sound at any point in this total sound-space can move to become a sound at any other point. But advantage can be taken of these possibilities only if one is willing to change one's musical habits radically. That is, one may take advantage of the appearance of images without visible transition in distant places, which is a way of saying 'television', if one is willing to stay at home instead of going to a theatre. Or one may fly if one is willing to give up walking.

Musical habits include scales, modes, theories of counterpoint and harmony, and the study of the timbres, singly and in combination of a limited number of sound-producing mechanisms. In mathematical terms these all concern discrete steps. They resemble walking – in the case of pitches, on stepping stones twelve in number. This cautious stepping is not characteristic of the possibilities of magnetic tape, which is revealing to us that musical action of existence can occur at any point or along any line or curve or what have you in total sound-space; that we are, in fact, technically equipped to transform our contemporary awareness of nature's manner of operation into art.

Again there is a parting of the ways. One has a choice. If he does not wish to give up his attempts to control sound, he may complicate his musical technique towards an approximation of the new possibilities and awareness. (I use the word 'approximation' because a measuring mind can never finally measure nature.) Or, as before, one may give up the desire to control sound, clear his mind of music, and set about discovering means to let sound be themselves rather than vehicles for man-made theories or expressions of human sentiments.

This project will seem fearsome to many, but on examination it gives no cause for alarm. Hearing sounds which are just sounds immediately sets the theorizing mind to theorizing, and the emotions of human beings are continually aroused by encounters with nature. Does not a mountain unintentionally evoke in us a sense of wonder? Otters along a stream a sense of mirth? Night in the woods a sense of fear? Do not rain falling and mists rising up suggest the love binding heaven and earth? Is not decaying flesh loathsome? Does not the death of someone we love bring sorrow? And is there a greater hero than the least plant that grows? What is more angry than the flash of lightning and the sound of thunder? These responses to nature are mine and will not necessarily correspond with another's. Emotion takes place in the person who has it. And sounds, when allowed to be themselves, do not require that those who hear them do so unfeelingly. The opposite is what is meant by response ability.

New music: new listening. Not an attempt to understand something that is being said, for, if something were being said, the sounds would be given the shapes of words. Just an attention to the activity of sounds.

Those involved with the composition of experimental music find ways and means to remove themselves from the activities of the sounds they make. Some employ chance operations, derived from sources as ancient as the Chinese *Book of Changes*, or as modern as the tables of random numbers used also by physicists in research. Or, analogous to the Rorschach tests of psychology, the interpretation of imperfections in the paper upon which one is writing may provide a music free from one's memory and imagination. Geometrical means employing spatial superimpositions at variance with the ultimate performance in time may be used. The total field of possibilities may be roughly divided and the actual sounds within these divisions may be indicated as to number but left to the performer or to the splicer to choose. In this latter case, the composer resembles the maker of a camera who allows someone else to take the picture.

Whether one uses tape or writes for conventional instruments, the present musical situation has changed from what it was before tape came into being. This also need not arouse alarm, for the coming into being of something new does not by that fact deprive what was of its proper place. Each thing has its own place, never takes the place of something else; and the more things there are, as is said, the merrier.

But several effects of tape on experimental music may be mentioned. Since so many inches of tape equal so many seconds of time, it has become more and more usual that notation is in space rather than in symbols of quarter, half and sixteenth notes and so on. Thus where on a page a note appears will correspond to when in a time it is to occur. A stop watch is used to facilitate a performance; and a rhythm results which is a far cry from horse's hoofs and other regular beats.

Also it has been impossible with the playing of several separate tapes at once to achieve perfect synchronization. This fact has led some towards the manufacture of multiple-tracked tapes and machines with a corresponding number of heads; while others – those who have accepted the sounds they do not intend – now realize that the score, the requiring that many parts be played in a particular togetherness, is not an accurate representation of how things are. These now compose parts but not scores, and the parts may be combined in any unthought ways. This means that each performance of such a piece of music is unique, as interesting to its composer as to others listening. It is easy to see again the parallel with nature, for even with leaves of the same tree, no two are exactly alike. The parallel in art is the sculpture with moving parts, the mobile.

It goes without saying that dissonances and noises are welcome in this new music. But so is the dominant seventh chord if it happens to put in an appearance.

Rehearsals have shown that this new music, whether for tape or for instruments, is more clearly heard when the several loud-speakers or performers are separated in space rather than grouped closely together. For this music is not concerned with harmoniousness as generally understood, whether the quality of harmony results from a blending of several elements. Here we are concerned with the coexistence of dissimilars, and the central points where fusion occurs are many: the ears of the listeners wherever they are. This disharmony, to paraphrase Bergson's statement about disorder, is simply a harmony to which many are unaccustomed.

Where do we go from here? Towards theatre. That art more than music resembles nature. We have eyes as well as ears, and it is our business while we are alive to use them.

And what is the purpose of writing music? One is, of course, not dealing with purposes but dealing with sounds. Or the answer must take the form of paradox: a purposeful purposelessness or a purposeless play. This play, however, is an affirmation of life – not an attempt to bring order out of chaos nor to suggest improvements in creation, but simply a way of waking up to the very life we're living, which is so excellent once one gets one's mind and one's desires out of its way and lets it act of its own accord. [...]

John Cage, extract from 'Experimental Music', address to the convention of the Music Teachers' National Association, Chicago, winter 1957, first printed in 1958; reprinted in John Cage, *Silence* (Middletown, Connecticut: Wesleyan University Press, 1961) 7–12.

Allan Kaprow
Assemblage, Environments and Happenings//1966

[...] Accident, as a trigger of the unconscious and, occasionally, of real freedom, is a common enough feature in much of the art of the twentieth century – but within limits. In current art it looms very large. An artist ostensibly involved with Change may actually be tangling with chance. Change is closely bound up with Chance but it is not the same thing; for while Chance may palpably reveal some aspect of Chance, the latter may also be regularized to exclude the former. If employing Change in one's work is risky at this time because of a probably high percentage of artistic failure due to nothing more than a lack of cooperation from a public invited to participate in the activity of transformation, a conscious use of chance bypasses failure by building non-control into the work as a desideratum. Whatever happens by definition happens as it should. Theoretically, every occurrence is as 'good' as every other.

Chance technique has a number of clear applications, which we shall illustrate. But before doing so, I should place them in perspective within this essay. In the foregoing, organicist principles have been primary. In the uses to which Chance has been put, the analytic tradition characteristic of Western thinking since the Greeks seems to govern its methodology. Art is broken down into basic elements or universals which are believed to hold true for all time. There are hues, shapes, positions, movements from one position to another; sounds in which may be distinguished amplitude, frequency, duration, timbre, attack-decay and where in space they originate; there are heat and cold by degrees, and kinds of touch from rough to smooth; there are also the specific materials comprising these, the relationships between them and, finally, certain very basic meanings that are evoked by them according to cultural training.

Such categorizing may seem antithetical to an ongoing, extensional point of view, and one temperamentally inclined to the latter may be averse to it. Clearly, these categories have been at the heart of all the form-content, ego-society, body-soul conflicts that have filtered from the past to our day. Yet in the present case, if we *assume* that all elements have an equal status, whether or not we actually believe this, then the chance operations (John Cage's expression for techniques designed to produce an indeterminate situation in music) applied to the above elements, if followed diligently, appear to have been able to provide a result close in spirit to the values espoused in the foregoing. The product is something which appears to be on its own, whole and separated from our anxieties, to be brought back into contact with us as though for the first time.

This is the only reason for using highly procedural techniques. It is paradoxical that to achieve a wholeness, self-evident and easy in its being, complicated and apparently unnatural means are sometimes necessary. If chance operations were merely an ingenious way of atomizing art into even more categories than history has accustomed us to, there would be no reason to discuss them. That they have in fact been liberating compels us to understand their use.

Chance, then, is meant to be a purposive following of rules, whereas Change is the following of intuition and wisdom. The rules of Chance are external to persons and history, while Change (even systemized into rules derived from, say, the Chinese *I Ching: The Book of Changes*) is dependent upon human experience. Chance operations are means to an end in which they are not necessarily inherent, but Change operations reflect a view of nature held by the artist, and as such are revealed in the transformations of the art.

Chance may be applied broadly to four areas comparable to Aristotle's 'four causes': the efficient, material, formal and final causes required of any being. The four areas are: the creator or creators (including nature as a creator), the materials used (including their life expectancy), the form that the work shall have (including its scale), and its function or purpose in life. As for the last, in most cases the implicit purpose will be an artwork constructed for someone's perusal, but we shall have something more to say about this shortly. The other three can be discussed in order.

The Creator(s)

The artist determines, by roulette wheel or dice throws, how many persons in addition to himself will be part of the compositional activity. The maximum number is fixed in the beginning by how many persons are actually available for the work. Nature, as a co-creator, may be included or not by the fall of a coin: heads it is in; tails it is out. Nature's role will in any case depend on practical considerations, namely, the particular locale, the weather conditions, and the plant- and wildlife prevalent there. Nature cannot be asked, even by the roulette wheel, to furnish icy blasts at the Equator. Taking advantage of what *is* possible, it is not hard to imagine a rain storm making a marvellously soggy shapeliness of blotters, rags and papers composed within an apple grove laden with ripe fruit. Long-term chances, only approximately foreseeable, can be brought about by insects, rotting, heat and cold, seeds dropped by birds and blown by winds, and so forth. Here again, duration in its protracted form becomes as much an uncertainty as physical constitution and appearance. Nature invited as a chance process could produce a painting on the ground merely by dropping leaves; passing cloudscapes could be viewed through plastic film or other structures built against the sky; rabbits and similar garden foes could eat their way right into a masterpiece if it seemed like a vegetable patch to them ... Finally, having allowed for nature's proclivities, each human creator is assigned a number within the total number of potential collaborators. Besides the initial artist, further turns of the roulette wheel decide exactly who shall execute the work, and when.

The Materials

Materials may be obtained by cutting up all the items listed in a random selection of pages from the telephone company's 'Yellow Pages'. These are stirred into a pot and are picked out one after the other, blindfold, up to that number fixed by a previous chance operation. *Clothes, gas, spiderwebs, sky, river* and *boxes* are examples. While I alone have just derived these as though in preparation for a work, this may be done by more than one person. The only limit to observe is, once again, the practicability of any choice. If the selection includes 20 tons of gold dust or three hermaphrodites with red hair, it may be quite difficult to come by them, and so in such instances, one must pick some more slips of paper from the pot.

Nature as a source of relatively inert materials – such as tree stumps, dirt and rocks – rather than as an active agent of events, can be part of one's list, but on its own terms. If rocks and dirt are not readily available, then the creator(s) should go to where they are normally found: the country. The advantage is that an Environment (or Assemblage) can be constructed anywhere in the world without restriction to conventional exhibition places.

Furthermore, the life span of natural materials will decide the life span of the Environment just as much as nature's more palpable movements will decide it. (Here the materials as subject matter function also as quasi creators and the line between the categories blurs. But this is true for any organically conceived art.) If, on the other hand, chance moves decide that the work should be destroyed earlier, this must be done; if a longer life is called for – say, a continuous supply of green pine needles – then replenishing the perishables is in order.

Composition

The ways in which the materials may be arranged can be spelled out for each material: in pattern (A), casually juxtaposed (B), or blended (C). In the previous section, six materials were listed. That means that each would be written as 1A, 1B or 1C; 2A, 2B or 2C, and so on. How many times each material is to be treated as A, B or C will have been previously established by turns of the roulette wheel, throws of the dice, or other equivalent methods. Let us say there are twenty moves for *clothes*, seventeen for *gas*, two hundred and eleven for *spiderwebs*, three for *river*, none for *sky*, and fourteen for *boxes*. Six graphs are drawn on large sheets of paper and the proper number of A, B or C treatments for each of the six materials are indicated thereon by corresponding squares. The graphs are put face up on the floor and a coin is tossed, without particular aim, onto each graph the appropriate number of times, to decide in what sequence each material is to be manipulated. These moves are listed on a sheet of paper. Then the six lists are combined by further chance operations on a single list in order to tell how, say *boxes* are to be combined with some other material(s). Now the second material(s) is listed without a qualifying letter A, B or C, because the first material already tells what is to be done with it. If it comes out that *boxes* (6) are to be arranged in pattern A with *river* (5), then we do not yet know exactly how to do this. For this information another list is compiled by the same chance methods, to tell specifically how the materials are to be arranged in pattern, casually juxtaposed, or blended with respect to each of the six materials' very considerable number of possible combinations. Now, the instruction for the compound *boxes* (A) *river* might specify:

Ten suspended boxes of river water are clustered above eighteen boxes half-submerged in the river just offshore. The space between the boxes above and below, and between each other, will be twice the measurement of the largest member of each.

There are now two more times for the *boxes* to interact with the *river*, as determined earlier; but the *boxes* have eleven more times to interact with the other materials. Toward the end of the preparations, it may be that not all of a material's possible combinations are used up. At such a point the creator or creators simply stop and go on to the remaining materials, until all the possibilities are exhausted. The Environment is then executed according to plan. The scale of the work, large or small, is thus automatically decided.

The methods described above have hardly been precise; plenty of margin for the exercise of personal whim was left in the details. Moreover, in all cases the initiating artist remained essentially at the controls, either exclusively or as co-creator and, thereafter, as overseer. Some artists, however, may wish to be more disciplined. They may wish to subdivide the categories into many more parts and tighten up the whole process of chance operations by analysing the controls, so that the last shred of artistic bias and mere habit will be eliminated and the unforeseeable made more likely.

The artist can determine (1) that the decisions as to whether a work of art shall be made or not is left to chance; (2) whether or not the initial artist shall execute it at all; (3) who, if anyone, shall be involved with it thereafter; (4) whether or not it shall be designated as art in fact, that is whether it should not be called a dry-goods store, for instance, and opened for regular business.

At this point the 'artist' as such is no longer a real entity. He has eliminated himself (and for one who has genuinely concerned himself with self-renunciation, the decision to do so must be respected). But its great poignancy is that it can never be a total act, for others must be made aware of the artist's disavowal of authorship if its meaning is not to be lost. It is just this which has been the dramatic lesson of the 'inactivity' of Marcel Duchamp. And it is the lesson of monastic life in general. This is the threshold upon which aesthetics, ethics, religion and life per se become indistinguishable. It is probably at the centre of ultimate philosophy, and to that extent goes beyond the proper subject of this book [*Assemblage, Environments and Happenings*], which has to do with *making* something.

But in so far as all art is, by implication, a discrimination of some values over others, it becomes the equivalent of philosophical activity. And thus the threshold must not be lost sight of. Any artist working with the main issues of current art must see it clearly. It is essential to know what Change and Chance are, where the one leaves off and the other begins, when to use one, when the other, and when neither; and it is most essential to know that the use of Chance can become a vehicle for the *denial* of art and self, as much as for their realization.

In any case, using Chance is a personal act no matter how much it attempts to be otherwise, for *a priori*, it is used, not simply given in to. Used responsibly, that is to say, with the artist acting as censor when an impossible or impractical instruction turns up and, above all, staying awake to what is taking place, the results can often be astonishing. Used stupidly, Chance will reduce to another confining academism. After all the shock of playing around with chance operations wears off, they seem much like using an electronic computer: the answers are always dependent on what information and biases are fed into the system in the first place. If dullness is built in, the chances are that dullness will come out. John Cage, who is chiefly responsible for making available to other artists the values and techniques of Chance in art, has gone to elaborate lengths to allow such methods to separate his and others' tastes from the music produced – to make it, in short, indeterminate. Yet the music is always recognizably Cage and often of very high quality. Others, imitating his approach, sound exactly like imitators and their work is dead, while still a few others, using the methods in their own way (and sometimes to the displeasure of Cage), make music which is live and obviously individual.

Hence, as a point of view and a technique, Chance methodology is not only refreshing in the best sense of the word; it is extremely useful in dispersing and breaking up knots of 'knowables', of groupings, relationships and larger structures which have become obsolete and habitual through over-use. Everything, the stuff of art, of daily life, the working of one's mind, gets thrown into sudden and startling patterns, so that if old values are destroyed, new experiences are revealed. Chance, therefore, is a dramatic affair involving both our need for security and our need for discovery or risk. [...]

Allan Kaprow, extract from *Assemblage, Environments and Happenings* (New York: Harry N. Abrams, 1966) 174–81.

Allan Kaprow
Interview with Susan Hapgood//1992

Susan Hapgood Dore Ashton once called your work 'Neo-Dada'. Do you remember what the context was?

Allan Kaprow She reviewed my last real exhibition, two environments that I had in succession at the Hansa Gallery in 1958. A number of the sculptures were assemblages made out of a variety of things – light bulbs flashing on and off, things that moved, paintings whose surfaces were broken up into literally separate planes in space. In other words, they were prototypes for the next step, the environmental. Her review called my work 'Neo-Dada'. I took exception to that because I really had none of the sociopolitical attitudes of the Dadaists. I remember one thing Ashton said in the review: 'Methinks he doth protest too much.' But I wasn't protesting at all. I think that's what I objected to. I was really just having fun.

Hapgood You said in your essay for the *New Forms–New Media* catalogue that critics made erroneous references to Neo-Dada to describe objects, environments and Happenings. Can you elaborate?

Kaprow Dada was a common reference point. To the extent that people would comment on what we were doing in that particular show or elsewhere, they would speak about Dada. It was mainly in conversation. Frequently, I thought, we were wrongly associated with Dada. Anti-art isn't something the Dadas invented. There's a whole thread of 'life is better than art' dating at least to the time of Wordsworth, right through Emerson and Whitman, to John Dewey and beyond, emphasizing art as experience, trying to blend art back into life – this tradition influenced me very much. But anti-art is an old Western theme.

Hapgood What about the cynical side of Dada?

Kaprow The cynical side was not present. If you talk about freedoms – for example, the freedom to employ open processes or the freedom to use a variety of objects and materials from the everyday world – these were derived from the prototypes of Dada. But to ascribe to me protest and cynicism – not at all.

Hapgood How else was the term 'Neo-Dada' used?

Kaprow Well, it was generally thrown around as a criticism. No one said, 'Oh, isn't it wonderful that you're a Neo-Dadaist.' It was a criticism, not a joyous utterance.

Hapgood Did the active role of the audience as participants in Happenings bear any comparison to Duchamp's insistence that the viewer creates the meaning of a work?

Kaprow Well, Duchamp gave that speech in Texas in 1957, I think. That's where he made the famous statement that the work of art is essentially a composite of meanings added to by posterity, whatever the artist may have put down first. I didn't read it until somewhat later. Then he gave a talk at the Museum of Modern Art where he also spoke more on the same lines, if I remember rightly. I did not attend, but it was recorded and published. But he also said something else about the rash of neo-Duchampian shows. He said, 'When I selected my first objects, I did not have in mind whole shows of shovels and bottle racks, because that would have killed the point.' And he implied that younger artists who were just buying out hardware stores were doing the wrong thing; they would overdo it. I think we all learned from those little hints from Duchamp. A key feature was discreetness, a timing and restraint that many of us didn't learn well enough.

Duchamp was personally very helpful to us, no question. He came to our Happenings, most of them. He certainly came to mine, and he brought his friends, Ernst and Richter and Huelsenbeck. And, in my case, Duchamp later acted as a referee in my getting a number of grants. So he was very helpful, both practically and intellectually.

Hapgood In a 1967 interview, you said that Schwitters conceived Happenings but never did them. Were you referring to his descriptions of Merz theatre?

Kaprow What I learned about Schwitters was simply what was available to me through books: about his plans for theatre, about his performances, about his wordplay. But I never heard or saw any of them. So, as far as I knew, most of them were cabaret-style performances, not Happenings. As much as they may have been capable of being Happenings, they never evolved to that point.

Hapgood Why do you believe artists used detritus and junk in their art?

Kaprow It was clearly part of transforming reality. It gave everyone a sense of instant involvement in a kind of crude everyday reality, which was quite a relief after the high-art attitude of exclusion from the real world. It also allowed us to give up a certain kind of seriousness that traditional art-making required. What's more, the materials were available everywhere on street corners at night. And if you didn't sell these environmental constructions, you'd just throw them back into the garbage can. Why not just throw them out? At once, the process in its fullest would be enacted. It was very liberating to think of oneself as part of an endlessly transforming real world.

Hapgood The element of getting away from tradition, couldn't that be called an anti-art gesture?

Kaprow Yes. *Now* I know it could be, but I didn't then. At that time, I didn't like the idea of giving up a sense of art.

Hapgood In retrospect, there does seem to be some subtle protest.

Kaprow But the protest was not against society, it was against traditionalism in art. You might remember that this was during the Eisenhower years, and there was a powerful conservatism operating that began to repudiate Abstract Expressionist attitudes and anything attached to the European tradition of art. Even *ARTnews* and editor Tom Hess were going all out to celebrate a return to the figure and the 'sanity-in-art' movement. 'Sanity' meant reverting, not only to the figure, but to European prototypes of painting and sculpture; supposedly, this would reinstate humanitarianism and the great traditional values that had been forgotten. That was what we were implicitly protesting against. Under the aegis of de Kooning, even many of the Hofmann students who had been abstract artists were reverting. Matisse and German Expressionism were recalled again. To me, that seemed less interesting than experimental work. So you could say we were protesting, some of us.

Hapgood Did Rauschenberg's comment about working in the gap between art and life reflect a prevalent attitude at the time? Was this a prescription that artists followed?

Kaprow No, that comment became famous later on; I would be very surprised if anybody even knew about it when it was first uttered. It was basically a prevalent attitude. I've tried to rephrase the attitude myself, not wishing to act in that gap, if there is one, but pushing it more toward the life side. I'm not too interested in gaps. [...]

Hapgood Do you remember when you first read Motherwell's Dada anthology?

Kaprow Yes. I was at Columbia in 1951 and 1952, taking classes with Meyer Schapiro. I was most interested in Mondrian at the time; and we were just getting used to Abstract Expressionism, which had peaked by then. Dada wasn't particularly interesting to most artists. Motherwell's anthology, *The Dada Painters and Poets*, came out in 1951, but I didn't read it immediately. It was a little later before I was really very immersed in it. Probably within the year. And once I read it, of course, I found Dada, as presented by Motherwell, to be much more interesting than Surrealism. Then there followed a whole lot of publications and artists' revived interest in Dada.

I didn't meet Rauschenberg until 1952, but he was another important link to Dada. As was George Brecht, who was my neighbour in the early 1950s. I was teaching at Rutgers at that time, and George Brecht was working for the Personal Products Division of Johnson & Johnson, in New Brunswick [New Jersey]. And Bob Watts was part of the Art Department at Douglass College, the Women's College of Rutgers. George Segal was also a neighbour. All of us lived in the New Brunswick area.

Hapgood Did you talk to Brecht about Motherwell's anthology?

Kaprow Well, he had an earlier interest in Dada. He was doing work at that time – which I remember very vividly – that encouraged chance operations. For example, he once brought an 8 x 4 foot masonite panel and several boxes of wooden matches over to the farm where I was living. He laid out this panel on the driveway and casually threw matches over the surface. Then he tossed a lit match among them and they all burst into flame in some kind of random pattern. Then we lifted up the panel and the matchsticks fell off, leaving burn marks. This was his way, one of many, of trying to produce paintings that dealt concretely with what he felt Pollock was all about. He even wrote an essay on chance, which dealt with his interpretation of Pollock, essentially saying that Pollock was interested in giving up organizational techniques. But Brecht was more interested in a kind of randomized dispersion principle. I remember him showing me tables of random numbers. For him, Dada was a celebration of chance, or the appearance of chance.

Hapgood This is before John Cage's class.

Kaprow Right. He joined Cage's class just a bit before I did. In fact, we used to drive into New York City together. But I had known Cage earlier. Not well, but over the years I'd met him here and there and was part of the periphery of his circle, because I was familiar with Jasper [Johns] and Bob [Rauschenberg] and a lot of the musicians that Cage knew, like composer Morton Feldman. It was a very small group of people in those days. I attended Cage concerts as early as 1948, when he was diddling around with the prepared piano, and all kinds of toys and gadgets to make noise. I made a decision then to concretize my work by having a real action or activity take place. For example, hammering a nail or blowing your nose would be self-evident. It wouldn't just be the isolated feature of one sense being recorded.

Cage's teaching was sophisticated philosophically. From his own sensibility and from Zen Buddhist readings, he learned that the experience of the present is a combination of receptivity and action. For Cage, concreteness wasn't the isolation of one feature of a situation, framed out of context; it was actually an experience, like that [hits table]. That sense of the experiential moment was a clarifier for me. Once I realized how simple the whole thing was, it was only a matter of taking off as fast as I could in the direction of Happenings. (I did my earliest ones in his classes in 1957–58).

Hapgood Did Cage talk directly about Dada in the class?

Kaprow He mentioned it now and again. I know that he was familiar with all of those people and certainly he knew Duchamp.

Hapgood Is it fair to say that by the latter half of the 1950s there was a major shift of interest among artists from Surrealism to Dada?

Kaprow Surrealism was interesting to the previous generation of New York School painters, and we sort of 'got it' through over-saturation. But it was their thing, and very European. When Dada came along, there were few objects to see, it all seemed really very far-out, although we didn't necessarily understand its sociopolitical programmes. We did not think, as the Dadaists did in 1916, that the world had gone crazy and there was no redemption in sight – its current of cynicism. Rather, we felt that here was freedom to put the real world together in weird ways. It was a discovery, a heady kind of appetite for debris, for cheap throwaways, for a new kind of involvement in everyday life without the judgements about it, either social or personal.

Hapgood Did John Cage's ideas about chance develop directly out of his knowledge of Dada and Marcel Duchamp?

Kaprow No. He claimed that his interest in chance derived from his study of Zen Buddhism, even though Zen Buddhism has no tradition of chance whatsoever. I think for Cage it was the open sense of an unwilled grander design in the universe, one in which an experience is more important than knowledge of the grand design. For me, Cage's teaching was a real gift, an opening-up rather than a prejudice or a gimmick. But it was threatening to a lot of people because it meant losing control.

Hapgood Did everyone read books on Zen? And which books were the most widely read?

Kaprow The grand message-bearer of Asiatic philosophy and religion to the Western world was Daisetzu Suzuki, a transcendentalist and former student of John Dewey. He was an admirer of Ralph Waldo Emerson and all the American [transcendentalist] philosophers, and he felt their work represented a kind of analogy to the Japanese view of the world. Suzuki was really the bridge, more than anybody else. Cage attended Suzuki's lectures on Zen Buddhism in the Philosophy Department at Columbia University. Those lectures and readings certainly helped Cage clarify his own point of view. Now I didn't attend those lectures. In Cage's case, the whole notion of chance was a result of putting together a lot of readings: Thoreau, Emerson, anarchism, as well as Asiatic philosophy and the *I Ching*.

So the answer to your question about how the chance operations evolved is: through Cage, as well as an awareness of Dada. He was very informed about Dada, a real intellectual. I'm sure he was aware of Duchamp's use, and Arp's use, of chance operations. I remember reading in Motherwell's Dada anthology, and also in the Lebel book, how Duchamp made part of the *Large Glass* by shooting paint-dipped matches out of a toy cannon: where they landed was where their marks went. In any case, the question is a complex one that, to my knowledge, has never been asked – how did the system of chance operations evolve? All I know is that by the time I met Cage, I mean when I was going to the class, it had already been worked into a system.

Hapgood Wasn't your interest in the Gutai Group related to this idea of chance? Do you remember how your heard about the Gutai activities?

Kaprow Alfred Leslie told me about an article he had read in the *New York Times* [Ray Falk, 'Japanese Innovators', *New York Times* (8 December 1957) 24 ff]. It was in the Sunday paper, but I hadn't read the *Times* that particular Sunday. Leslie saw I was moving into a kind of wild spatialized collage/assemblage mode, and he said, 'Hey, did you read about this?'

Hapgood So the article was sort of a passing curiosity, then?

Kaprow Oh, it was a prominent article! Brecht must have heard about it, because the work he was doing paralleled the various Gutai environmental and action-type pieces. He must have read the article in the *Times*, and I would guess that Bob Watts would have, too.

Hapgood Your own article, 'The Legacy of Jackson Pollock' [*ARTnews* (October 1958)], was published the following year and also created something of a stir, didn't it?

Kaprow Well, I got some feedback from people in my circle, like my editor, Tom Hess, who took a rather dim view of my very eccentric interpretation of Jackson Pollock as someone whose work led to conventional repetition or to what many felt was a kind of Dada junk.

It was written in its entirety after Pollock died in 1956, but then I reworked it slightly later. I gave it to Hess in 1958, within a month of finishing the rewrite. But he held onto it for reasons of caution before he published it. Then he finally made up his mind to publish it, and I asked for it back to correct a few errors.

Hapgood I think the part about art employing any materials necessary is very impressive considering that it was written in 1956. Were you familiar with Schwitters' work by this point?

Kaprow Yes. What was unusual was the jump that I made from quasi-painting work, like Schwitters', in which the common metaphor of art and the world was closure, to a kind of environmental phenomenon, open to everything because it was so big. That was a really extreme leap. Painting seemed unnecessary to anyone who wanted to experiment. I didn't, of course, say that it was over; it certainly wasn't. So in the Pollock article, I proposed that artists could go in one of two directions: to further develop action painting, or to work environmentally in lifelike situations. [...]

Allan Kaprow and Susan Hapgood, extract from interview (Encinitas, California, 12 August 1992) in *Neo-Dada: Redefining Art, 1958–62* (American Federation of Arts in association with Universe Publishing, 1994) 115–16.

La Monte Young
Compositions//1960

Composition 1960 #2

Build a fire in front of the audience. Preferably, use wood although other combustibles may be used as necessary for starting the fire or controlling the kind of smoke. The fire may be of any size, but it should not be the kind which is associated with another object, such as a candle or a cigarette lighter. The lights may be turned out.

After the fire is burning, the builder(s) may sit by and watch it for the duration of the composition; however, he (they) should not sit between the fire and the audience in order that its members will be able to see and enjoy the fire.

The composition may be of any duration.

In the event that the performance is broadcast, the microphone may be brought up close to the fire.

Composition 1960 #3

Announce to the audience when the piece will begin and end if there is a limit on duration. It may be of any duration.

Then announce that everyone may do whatever he wishes for the duration of the composition.

Composition 1960 #4

Announce to the audience that the lights will be turned off for the duration of the composition (it may be any length) and tell them when the composition will begin and end.

Turn off all the lights for the announced duration.

When the lights are turned back on, the announcer may tell the audience that their activities have been the composition, although this is not at all necessary.

La Monte Young, *Compositions* (1960), in *An Anthology of Chance Operations*, artist's book (Bronx, New York: La Monte Young and Jackson Mac Low, 1963) n.p.

George Brecht
Motor Vehicle Sundown (Event)//1960

Any number of motor vehicles are arranged outdoors.

There are at least as many sets of instruction cards as vehicles.

All instruction card sets are shuffled collectively, and 22 cards are distributed to the single performer per vehicle.

At sundown (relatively dark/open area incident light 2 foot-candles or less) the performers leave a central location, simultaneously counting out (at an agreed-upon rate) a pre-arranged duration 1 1/2 times the maximum required for any performer to reach, and seat himself in, his vehicle. At the end of this count each performer starts the engine of his vehicle and subsequently acts according to the directions on his instruction cards, read consecutively as dealt. (An equivalent pause is to be substituted for an instruction referring to non-available equipment.) Having acted on all instructions, each performer turns off the engine of his vehicle and remains seated until all vehicles have ceased running.

Instruction Cards (44 per set):

1 Head lights (high beam, low beam) on (1–5), off.
2 Parking lights on (1–11), off.
3 Foot-brake lights on (1–3), off.
4 (Right, left) directional signals on (1–7), off.
5 Inside light on (1–5), off.
6 Glove-compartment light on. Open (or close) glove compartment (quickly, with moderate speed, slowly). Glove-compartment light off.
7 Spot-lamp on (1–11), move (vertically, horizontally, randomly), (quickly, with moderate speed, slowly), off.
8 Special lights on (1–9), off.
9 Sound horn (1–11).
10 Sound siren (1–15).
11 Sound bell(s) (1–7).
12 Accelerate motor (1–3).
13 Wind-shield wipers on (1–5), off.
14 Radio on, maximum volume, (1–7), off. Change tuning.
15 Strike hand on dashboard.
16 Strike a window with knuckles.
17 Fold a seat or seat-back (quickly, with moderate speed, slowly). Replace.
18 Open (or close) a window (quickly, with moderate speed, slowly).

19 Open (or close) a door (quickly, with moderate speed, slowly).
20 Open (or close) engine-hood, opening and closing vehicle door, if necessary.
21 Trunk light on. Open (or close) trunk lid (if a car), rear-panel (if a truck or station-wagon), or equivalent. Trunk light off.
22 Operate special equipment (1–15), off.
23-44 Pause (1–13).

A single value from each parenthetical series of values is to be chosen, by chance, for each card. Parenthetic numerals indicate duration in counts (at an agreed-upon rate). Special lights (8) means truck-body, safety, signal, warning lights, signs, displays, etc. Special equipment (22) means carousels, ladders, fire-hoses with truck-contained pumps and water supply, etc.

George Brecht, *Motor Vehicle Sundown (Event)* (1960) (East Brunswick, New Jersey: Contingent Publications, 1960) n.p.

Siegfried Kracauer
Theory of Film//1960

[...] The fortuitous being a characteristic of camera-reality, film no less than photography is attracted by it. Hence the major role assigned to it in a truly cinematic genre, the American silent film comedy. To be sure, the minor triumphs of Buster Keaton or Chaplin's Tramp over destructive natural forces, hostile objects and human brutes were sometimes due to feats of acrobatic skill. Yet unlike most circus productions, film comedy did not highlight the performer's proficiency in braving death and surmounting impossible difficulties; rather, it minimized his accomplishments in a constant effort to present succesful rescues as the outcome of pure chance. Accidents superseded destiny, unpredictable circumstances now foreshadowed doom, now gelled into propitious constellations for no visible reason. Take Harold Lloyd on the skyscraper [in *Safety Last*, 1923]: what protected him from falling to his death was not his prowess but a random combination of external and completely incoherent events which, without being intended to come to his help, dovetailed so perfectly that he could not have fallen even had he wanted to. Accidents were the very soul of slapstick.[1]

The affinity of film for haphazard contingencies is most strikingly demonstrated by its unwavering susceptibility to the 'street' – a term designed to cover not only the street, particularly the city street, in the literal sense, but also its various extensions, such as the railway stations, dance and assembly halls, bars, hotel lobbies, airports, etc. If the medium's descent from and kinship with photography needed additional confirmation, this very specific preference, common to both of them, would supply it. Within the present context the street, which has already been characterized as a centre of fleeting impressions, is of interest as a region where the accidental prevails over the providential, and happenings in the nature of unexpected incidents are all but the rule. Startling as it may sound, since the days of Lumière there have been only a few cinematic films that would not include glimpses of a street, not to mention the many films in which some street figures among the protagonists.

It was D.W. Griffith who initiated this tradition. For prototypes of cinematically significant imagery one will always have to revert to him. He featured the street as an area dominated by chance in a manner reminiscent of Lumière's shots of crowded public places. In one of his early films, which bears the suggestive title of *The Musketeers of Pig Alley* (1912), much of the action is laid in dingy houses, a New York East Side street teeming with nondescript passers-by, a low dive and a small yard between cheap tenements where teenagers forever loiter about. More important, the action itself, which revolves around a thievery and ends on a pursuit, grows out of these locales. They offer opportunities to the criminal gang to which the thief is committed; and they provide the adventitious encounters and promiscuous gatherings which are an essential element of the intrigue. All this is resumed on a broader scale in the 'modern story' of Griffith's *Intolerance* (1916). There the street takes on an additional function reserved for it: it turns into the scene of bloody clashes between striking workers and soldiers sent out against them. (The sights of the crowds of fleeing workers and the corpses left behind foreshadow the Russian films of the Revolution.)

Yet if the street episodes of the 'modern story' involve depicting mass violence, they by no means exhaust themselves in it. Eisenstein praises them for something less glaring – the way they impress upon the spectator the fortuitous appearances and occurrences inseparable from the street. In 1944, all that he remembered of these episodes was an ephemeral passer-by. After having described him, Eisenstein continues: 'As he passes he interrupts the most pathetic moment in the conversation of the suffering boy and girl. I can remember next to nothing of the couple, but this passer-by who is visible in the shot only for a flashing glimpse stands alive before me now – and I haven't seen the film for twenty years!' 'Occasionally', he adds, 'these unforgettable figures actually walked into Griffith's films almost directly from the street: a bit-player developed in Griffith's hands to stardom; the passer-by who may never again have been filmed.[2] [...]

Eisenstein also remarks that 'Griffith's inimitable bit-characters ... seem to have run straight from life onto the screen.'[3] Inadvertently he thus equates life with the street. The street in the extended sense of the word is not only the arena of fleeting impressions and chance encounters but a place where the flow of life is bound to assert itself. Again one will have to think mainly of the city street with its ever-moving anonymous crowds. The kaleidoscopic sights mingle with unidentified shapes and fragmentary visual complexes and cancel each other out, thereby preventing the onlooker from following up any of the innumerable suggestions they offer. What appears to him are not so much sharp-contoured individuals engaged in this or that definable pursuit as loose throngs of sketchy, completely indeterminate figures. Each has a story, yet the story is not given. Instead, an incessant flow of possibilities and near-intangible meanings appears. The *flâneur* is intoxicated with life in the street – life eternally dissolving the patterns which it is about to form.[4]

The medium's affinity for the flow of life would be enough to explain the attraction which the street has ever since exerted on the screen. Perhaps the first deliberately to feature the street as the scene of life was Karl Grune in a half-expressionist, half-realistic film which significantly bears the title of *The Street* (*Die Strasse*, 1923). Its hero is a middle-aged *petit bourgeois* possessed with the desire to escape from the care of his lifeless wife and the prison of a home where intimacy has become deadening routine. The street calls him. There life surges high and adventures are waiting for him. He looks out of the window and sees – not the street itself but a hallucinated street. 'Shots of rushing cars, fireworks and crowds form, along with shots taken from a roller coaster, a confusing whole made still more confusing by the use of multiple exposures and the insertion of transparent close-ups of a circus clown, a woman and an organ-grinder.'[5] One evening he walks out into the real street – studio-built, for that matter – and gets more than his fill of sensations, what with card sharpers, prostitutes and a murder to boot. Life, an agitated sea, threatens to drown him. There is no end of films in this vein. If it is not a street proper they picture, it is one of its extensions, such as a bar, a railway station, or the like. Also, life may change its character; it need not be wild and anarchic as with Grune. In Delluc's *Fievre* (1921) or Cavalcanti's *En Rade* (1927) a mood of *fin de siècle* disenchantment and nostalgic longing for faraway countries lingers in crowded sailor hangouts. And in Vittorio De Sica's *The Bicycle Thief* (1948) and *Umberto D* (1952) the omnipresent streets breathe a *tristesse* which is palpably the outcome of unfortunate social conditions. But whatever its dominant characteristics, street life in all these films is not fully determined by them. It remains an unfixable flow which carries fearful uncertainties and alluring excitements. [...]

1 [footnote 3 in source] Cf. Kracauer, 'Silent Film Comedy', *Sight & Sound*, vol. 21, no. 1 (August–September 1951) 31.

2 [4] Sergei Eisenstein, *Film Form: Essays in Film Theory* (New York: Harcourt Brace, 1949) 199.

3 [18] Ibid., 199.

4 [19] Walter Benjamin, 'Über einige Motive bei Baudelaire' ['On some Motifs in Baudelaire'], *Zeitschrift für Sozialforschung*, vol. VIII, no. 1–2 (1939) 60n; 67; 88.

5 [20] See Kracauer, *From Caligari to Hitler: A Psychological History of the German Film* (Princeton: Princeton University Press, 1947) 121.

Siegfried Kracauer, extracts from *Theory of Film: Redemption of Physical Reality* (London/Oxford/New York: Oxford University Press, 1960) 62–3; 72–3.

Gilles Deleuze
The Dice Throw//1962

The game has two moments which are those of a dice throw – the dice that are thrown and the dice that fall back. Nietzsche presents the dice throw as taking place on two distinct tables, the earth and the sky. The earth where the dice are thrown and the sky where the dice fall back: 'if ever I have played dice with the gods at their table, the earth, so that the earth trembled and broke open and streams of fire snorted forth; for the earth is a table of the gods, and trembling with creative new words and the dice throws of the gods' (*Thus Spoke Zarathustra* [hereafter *Z*], III, 'The Seven Seals', 3; 245). 'O sky above me, you pure and lofty sky! This is now your purity to me, that there is no eternal reason-spider and spider's web in you; that you are to me a dance floor for divine chances, that you are to me a god's table for divine dice and dicers.' (*Z*, III, 'Before Sunrise', 186) But these two tables are not two worlds. They are the two hours of a single world, the two moments of a single world, midnight and midday, the hour when the dice are thrown, the hour when the dice fall back. Nietzsche insists on the two tables of life which are also the two moments of the player or the artist; 'We temporarily abandon life, in order then temporarily to fix our gaze upon it.' The dice throw affirms becoming and it affirms the being of becoming.

It is not a matter of several dice throws which, because of their numbers, finally reproduce the same combination. On the contrary, it is a matter of a single dice throw which, due to the number of the combination produced, comes to reproduce itself as such. It is not that a large number of throws produce the repetition of a combination but rather the number of the combination which produces the repetition of the dice throw. The dice which are thrown once are the affirmation of *chance*, the combination which they form on falling is the affirmation of *necessity*. Necessity is affirmed of chance in exactly the sense that being is affirmed of becoming and unity is affirmed of multiplicity. It will be replied, in vain, that thrown to chance, the dice do not necessarily produce the winning combination, the double six which brings back the dice throw. This is true, but only in so far as the player did not know how to *affirm* chance from the outset. For just as unity does not suppress or deny multiplicity, necessity does not suppress or abolish chance. Nietzsche identifies chance with multiplicity, with fragments, with parts, with chaos: the chaos of the dice that are shaken and then thrown. *Nietzsche turns chance into an affirmation*. The sky itself is called 'chance-sky', 'innocence-sky' (*Z*, III, 'Before Sunrise'); the reign of Zarathustra is called 'great chance' (*Z*, IV, 'The Honey Offering' and III, 'Of Old and New Law Tables'; Zarathustra calls himself the 'redeemer of chance'). '*By chance*, he is the world's oldest nobility, which I have given back to all things; I have released them from their servitude under purpose ... I have found this happy certainty in all things: that they prefer to *dance* on the feet of chance' (*Z*, III, 'Before Sunrise', 186); 'My doctrine is "Let chance come to me: it is as innocent as a little child!"' (*Z*, III, 'On the Mount of Olives', 194). What Nietzsche calls *necessity* (destiny) is thus never the abolition but rather the combination of chance itself. Necessity is affirmed of chance in as much as chance itself affirmed. For there is only a single combination of chance as such, a single way of combining all the parts of chance, a way which is like the unity of multiplicity, that is to say number or necessity. There are many numbers with increasing or decreasing probabilities, but only one number of chance as such, one fatal number which reunites all the fragments of chance, just as midday gathers together the scattered parts of midnight. This is why it is sufficient for the player to affirm chance once in order to produce the number which brings back the dice throw.

To know how to affirm chance is to know how to play. But we do not know how to play, 'Timid, ashamed, awkward, like a tiger whose leap has failed. But what of that you dice throwers! You have not learned to play and mock as a man ought to play and mock!' (*Z*, IV, 'Of the Higher Man', 14; 303). The bad player counts on several throws of the dice, on a great number of throws. In this way he makes use of causality and probability to produce a combination that he sees as desirable. He posits this combination itself as an end to be obtained, hidden behind causality. This is what Nietzsche means when he speaks of the eternal spider, of the spider's web of reason, 'A kind of spider of imperative and finality hidden behind the great web, the great net of causality' – we could say, with Charles the Bold when he opposed Louis XI, 'I fight the universal spider'

(*Genealogy of Morals*, III, 9). To abolish chance by holding it in the grip of causality and finality, to count on the repetition of throws rather than affirming chance, to anticipate a result instead of affirming necessity – these are all the operations of a bad player. They have their root in reason, but what is the root of reason? The spirit of revenge, nothing but the spirit of revenge, the spider. *Ressentiment* in the repetition of throws, bad conscience in the belief in a purpose. But, in this way, all that will ever be obtained are more or less probable relative numbers. That the universe has no purpose, that it has no end to hope for any more than it has causes to be known – this is the certainty necessary to play well. (*The Will to Power*, III, 465) The dice throw fails because chance has not been affirmed enough in one throw. It has not been affirmed enough in order to produce the fatal number which necessarily reunites all the fragments and brings back the dice throw. We must therefore attach the greatest importance to the following conclusion: for the couple causality-finality; probability-finality, for the opposition and the synthesis of these terms, for the web of these terms, Nietzsche substitutes the Dionysian correlation of chance-necessity, the Dionysian couple chance-destiny. Not a probability distributed over several throws but all chance at once; not a final, desired, willed combination, but the fatal combination, fatal and loved *amor fati*; not the return of a combination by the number of throws, but the repetition of a dicethrow by the nature of the fatally obtained number. [...]

Gilles Deleuze, extract from *Nietzsche et la philosophie* (Paris: Presses Universitaires de France, 1962); trans. Hugh Tomlinson, *Nietzsche and Philosophy* (New York: Columbia University Press, 1983); reprinted edition (London: Continuum, 2006) 23–6 [footnotes not included].

Anna Dezeuze
Origins of the Fluxus Score: From Indeterminacy to 'Do-It-Yourself' Artwork//2002

'Events' as Raw Materials

An intriguing document embodies the dialogues between artists, composers, poets and dancers which led to the creation of Fluxus: *An Anthology of chance operations, concept art, anti-art, improvisation, indeterminacy, meaningless work, natural disasters, stories, diagrams, poetry, essays, compositions, dance constructions, music, plans of action, mathematics.* Initially assembled by composer La Monte Young for a planned issue of a periodical called *Beatitude East* from 1960 but only published in 1963, *An Anthology* included works by artists, composers, poets and dancers who can be loosely classified in four groups: artists such as Simone Forti and Walter De Maria, who had known Young in California before he moved to New York in 1960;[1] New York-based experimental composers John Cage, Earle Brown, Christian Wolff and Richard Maxfield;[2] Cage's and Maxfield's students at the New York School of Social Research, who included Jackson Mac Low, Dick Higgins, George Brecht and Toshi Ichiyanagi, then married to Yoko Ono;[3] and three poets living in Europe: Emmett Williams, Claus Bremer and Diter Rot [Dieter Roth's name 1959–68].[4] As is by now well known, Maciunas volunteered to design *An Anthology* as a book when the issue of *Beatitude East* was cancelled, and used it as a model to plan his first Fluxus publication.

In its title and format *An Anthology* is characterized by a blurring of the boundaries between poetry, music and dance. As each work is presented by type, in addition to its title and author, it emerges, for example, that Mac Low's and Joseph Byrd's works include both 'music' and 'poetry', while Brecht's works are listed as 'indeterminacy, music, compositions' and Higgins' as 'dance, mathematics and compositions'. This blurring was made possible by a new conception of musical composition summarized by Higgins in 1964 when he wrote that '[m]usical activity takes place in time, and ... anything that just breaks up time by happening in it, absorbing it, is musical.' (Higgins, *Postface and Jefferson's Birthday* [1964] 42.) For Higgins, dance, poetry and drama are only so many specific types of 'musical activities' with different emphases, whether it be bodily movement in dance or words for poetry. (Ibid., 42.) Duration was one of the five dimensions of sound which John Cage had listed in the first class in his course on experimental composition. (See Brecht, 'Notebook I, June–September 1958' in *Notebooks I–III* [1991] 3.) Cage had developed musical structures based on duration rather than harmony in order to use all types of what he called 'events in sound-space' including sounds as well as silence, which has no pitch. (Ibid., 4.) Two 1952 pieces by Cage embody this model of a structure based on duration: the well-known 4'33" in which a music performer is asked to remain without playing for 4 minutes and 33 seconds, signalling three distinct sections within this duration; and *Water Music*, in which actions such as blowing a siren whistle, pouring water or playing the radio are juxtaposed with musical sounds according to precise durations indicated in minutes and seconds. In these pieces, Cage shifted from the metronome to the stopwatch as a means to measure duration as the framing element for the 'events' occurring within it.

According to Mac Low, this 'time-structure' was favoured by most students in Cage's class. 'The term time-structure', explains Mac Low, 'emphasizes that the structure of such works depends on the relative durations of juxtaposed passages rather than on their contents'. ('How Maciunas Met the New York Avant-Garde', in *Fluxus Today and Yesterday* [1980] 47.) This model of a fixed structure to be filled with varying contents opened the space for an extended conception of an 'event' which could include not only musical but also everyday sounds. Cage encouraged his students to use non-conventional sounds during the classes by having them play on toy instruments and compose pieces using everyday objects such as radios. The 'events' which occur in Brecht's *Motor Vehicle Sundown (Event)*, reproduced in *An Anthology*, are drawn from a repertory of activities which can be performed in a vehicle, including turning on and off headlights, glove compartment lights, spot-lamps and trunk lights, sounding horns, opening windows or operating the windscreen wipers. By using cars and placing the performance outside the conventional space of music concerts, Brecht expanded the concept of the 'event' to create a show involving visual and olfactory sensations as well.

For Higgins and Mac Low, Cage's music became a paradigm for poetry, and Higgins saw himself as 'a composer who uses words'. (Higgins, conversation with Jacques Donguy, in *Poésure et peintrie, d'un art et l'autre* [1993] 419.) Even before attending Cage's classes Mac Low was exploring in his poems a kind of equivalent of what Cage was searching for in music, by giving silences the same weight as words.[5] In his *Asymmetries* composed from September 1960 and published in *An Anthology*, the white spaces between the words stand for silences 'equal in duration to the time it would take to read aloud the words printed anywhere above or below them'. (Mac Low, 'Methods for Reading Assymetries', in *An Anthology*, 1963/1970.) As silence becomes equal in importance to sound, the empty spaces only come to life if the poem is read out loud, and in *Thanks – A Simultaneity for People* (dated December 1960 to February 1961) and also reproduced in *An Anthology*, the poetic text is no longer given, as performers are invited to choose freely the 'utterances' which they will perform in alternation with silences of varying lengths. The instructions allow performers to select as 'utterances' not only words, phrases, syllables and phonemes but also 'non-vocal sounds', thus adding a musical dimension. (Mac Low, 'Thanks: a Simultaneity for People', in *An Anthology*, 1963/70.)

Simone Forti first discovered Cage's works during a dance workshop led by Cage student Robert Dunn. In the first class, Dunn gave his students a score by Cage in which pages of clear plastic with dots were to be dropped on a graph by the performer. 'Where the dots fell determined where and when the "events" were to be performed.' But, Simone Forti recalls, 'the nature of events to be performed in those time and spatial relationships, was left completely up to the choice of the performer. Such an event could be the sound of a bell, it could be falling off a cliff, it could be anything'. (Forti, *Handbook in Motion* [1974] 35–6.)[6] Like Cage's students, Forti thus seems to have conceived the possibilities of Cage's conception of the sound 'event' beyond those realized by the composer himself: from musical sound, the 'event' came to include 'anything', from everyday movements favoured by the dancers in Dunn's workshop to the dramatic act of 'falling off a cliff'.

Chance and Choice

The point-drawing system used by Cage in some of his scores was one of his many methods to 'let the sounds be themselves, rather than vehicles for manmade theories, or expressions of human sentiments'. (Cage, 'Indeterminacy' [1957], in *Silence* [1961/73] 10.) Two main compositional devices were used in experimental music and poetry in the 1950s to avoid choices and hierarchies on the part of the artist. The one favoured by European serial composers such as Pierre Boulez and Karlheinz Stockhausen was based on mathematical processes, chosen at the start of the composition and applied in a systematic way throughout. (See Michael Nyman, *Experimental Music: Cage and Beyond* [1974/99].) This is comparable to the processes used by Emmett Williams and Claus Bremer in their poems in *An Anthology* such as Williams' 1958 *Cellar Song for Five Voices* which is the produce of the systematic permutation of five phrases (somewhere/bluebirds are flying/high in the sky/in the cellar/even blackbirds are extinct), creating over a hundred combinations. The very form of the work reflects the process by which it was created. 'The aim was to eliminate the subjective point of view of the author, and present poetic material that the reader could do with as he saw fit', explained Daniel Spoerri about the periodical *Material*, in which he published works by Williams and Rot in the late 1950s. (Williams, *Anthology of Concrete Poetry* [1967].)

The other main means 'to eliminate the subjective point of view of the author' was to introduce random chance processes. For example, to determine the organization of sound 'events' within a time structure, Cage used to list in a chart all the 'event' materials which he wanted to use and then would throw dice in order to determine their characteristics and order, sometimes using the Chinese book of changes, the *I Ching*. (See Pritchett, *The Music of John Cage* [1993].) George Brecht's 1957 essay on 'chance imagery', written before he studied with Cage, reveals a shared interest in the use of chance techniques within creative processes and reads retrospectively like a guidebook to the compositional processes used by many other artists included in *An Anthology*. For example, Brecht suggests the technique of numbering elements and using a table of random numbers to select them – a method used by La Monte Young to determine all the compositional choices in his 1960 *Poem for Chairs, Tables and Benches etc., or Other Sound Sources*, and by Mac Low to obtain the title, the number and names of the characters in his 1958–9 play *The Marrying Maiden – A Play of Changes*, as well as the words of their speeches and the way they should be delivered. In Mac Low's later *Asymmetrics* the performer is invited to throw a pair of dice to select the method by which to read the poem, while the instruction cards in Brecht's *Motor Vehicle Sundown* are shuffled and dealt amongst the performers. Both cards and dice are listed by Brecht in *Chance Imagery*, along with coins, the roulette wheel, and drawing from a bowl, as random methods to be used when there is only a limited number of elements available for selection.[7]

If the use of systematic or random methods allowed composers and poets to 'eliminate the subjective point of view of the author' in order to let the sounds, words or any kind of 'events' 'be themselves', there are, however, crucial differences in the ways in which the reader/performer can relate to these 'events'. In Williams' *Cellar Song for Five Voices*, in Brecht's *Motor Vehicle Sundown* or in Mac Low's determinate *Asymmetrics*, performers follow strict instructions, having been given a list of 'events' to realize in relation to specific cues, whereas Mac Low's *Thanks*, for example, allows performers to choose the 'events' and the moment in which they will utter them. This distinction between chance and 'choice' procedures, as Earle Brown termed them,[8] poses the question of who is given the task to choose and organize the 'events' as 'raw materials': is the composer or the performer? However complex, Cage's compositions before 1957 involve chance procedures at the level of *composition* but allow only limited choices to the performer, while his colleagues of the 'New York School', Earle Brown, Morton Feldman and Christian Wolff, were actually much more involved in introducing indeterminate elements in the *performance* of their works, as Cage pointed out in his 1958 lecture on 'Indeterminacy', which focuses specifically on the role of the performer.

'The function of the performer or of each performer' in a piece by Earle Brown, Cage writes, 'is that of making something out of a store of raw materials'.

(Cage, 'Composition as Process, II – Indeterminacy' [1958], in *Silence*, 38.) From 1952 Earle Brown delineated two approaches to introducing choices for performers: firstly, 'a "mobile" score subject to physical manipulation of its components, resulting in an unknown number of different, integral and "valid" realizations', and secondly, a *conceptually* "mobile" approach to basically fixed graphic elements; subject to an infinite number of performance realizations through the involvement of the performer's immediate responses to the intentionally ambiguous graphic stimuli relative to the conditions of performance'. (Brown, prefatory notes in *Folio (1952/3) and 4 Systems (1954)* [1961].) Brown's *December 1952*, a one-page score reproduced in *An Anthology*, consisting of vertical and horizontal segments of varying lengths and widths scattered on the page, embodies both these approaches, It is 'mobile' in its orientation because it can be read from any of the four sides of the score, and it is 'conceptually mobile' because its notation is so extremely ambiguous that the performer must decide the source, pitch, timbre and intensity of all the sounds as well as their relative durations.

The notation of Christian Wolff's 1960 *Duet I*, also reproduced in *An Anthology*, is less ambiguous than Brown's *December 1952*, but is 'conceptually mobile' by making the players' choice dependent on each others' performances. The fragments that fill the page can be played in any order and 'what section on a page is played depends on a cue (the initial sound of the section), given by whoever starts by a section which can be started by him. The other player must immediately decide what section is being played and join in where his part requires it'. (Wolff, 'Duet I'.) The molecule-like structures which constitute the fragments indicate the coordinations in the attacks and releases of the sounds in a unique 'cue-answer' system, as Brecht called it in his 1958 notebook.[9]

Writing about a work of this period by Brown, Brecht expressed the range of performer-choice on a scale of what he called 'situation participation'. (Brecht, *Notebooks I–III*, 67.) The scale starts from 'the magnetic tape and sound reproduction system at one end' through conventional nineteenth- and twentieth-century scores where there is little or no performer choice, and 'abstract scores' such as Bach's *Art of the Fugue*, where the speed and instrumentation are left open. At the other end of the scale of 'situation participation' Brecht positioned folk music, blues and jazz, whose forms traditionally leave space for performer improvisation. Significantly, Brown, unlike the other American experimental composers, had a jazz background. 'I couldn't understand why classical musicians couldn't improvise, and why so many looked down on improvisation', he recounts. (Brown, conversation with John Yaffe, in CD booklet, *Music for Piano(s) 1951–1995* [1996].) The series of works including *December 1952* was, according to him, a way of 'progressively trying to get them free of having to have every little bit of information before they had confidence enough to play'. (Ibid.)

Similarly, the turn in Jackson Mac Low's work towards increased performer-choice occurred through his contact with theatre improvisation during the rehearsals for his play *The Marrying Maiden* at the Living Theatre in June 1960. Mac Low had written out action directions for the actors on about 1,400 playing cards, such as 'walk forward ten paces' or 'do something romantic'. (Mac Low, interview with Nicholas Zurbrugg, in *Crayon* [1991] 275.) When some actors started to use the cards to improvise scenes with each other, performing tasks independent from the actual play, it was a revelation. 'It made me realize', Mac Low recounts, 'that I could allow performers ordinary freedom of choice within a non-intentionally determined situation (one constrained by such means as chance operations and systematically random selection and/or by a score composed by such means)'. (Ibid., 275.) This new tendency, developed for December 1960 in *Thanks – A Simultaneity for People*, would in fact be 'profoundly reinforced' by Mac Low's own performance in Brown's *December 1952* at the Living Theatre in 1962. (Mac Low, 'How Maciunas Met the New York Avant-Garde' [1980] 43.)

From Experimental Notation to the Word Score

An Anthology offers many examples of experimental notation in music and poetry. In the most 'conceptually mobile' works, notation is reduced to the relation between graphic marks on an empty background which suggest 'events' to be interpreted freely within the time and space of performance. For example, composer Toshi Ichiyanagi's 1960 *Mudai no. 1* consists of calligraphic paint marks without any instructions, in the same way as Diter Rot's undated poem, *White Page with Holes*, is quite literally what its title indicates. In the first edition of *An Anthology* of 1963, however, the title of the same work is given as *Black Page with Holes*, which adds another conceptual dimension to it. My thanks to Jon Hendricks for pointing this out to me. Stéphane Mallarmé's experiments with the typographical arrangement of words on the white space of the page in his 1897 *Un Coup de dès jamais n'abolira le hazard* [A throw of the dice will never abolish chance] was an inspiration for many concrete poets such as Rot and Williams.[10] The typography of Mac Low's *Asymmetries* is similar to that of *Un Coup de dès*, while his untitled poem and Williams' *Beatitude from the Gospel according to Saint Matthew*, both in *An Anthology*, explore the spacing and order of typewritten signs on the page, creating visually arresting objects. In fact, without the instructions for performance in Williams' *Cellar Song for Five Voices* and Mac Low's *Asymmetries*, the visuality of the poems would predominate over their performative dimension, encouraging the reader to look at them rather than using them as scores for performance. This ambivalence was in fact already suggested in Mallarmé's *Un Coup de dès,* which the author significantly defined as a kind of musical 'score'. (Mallarmé, 1914 preface to the poem in *Oeuvres,* 424.)

'[T]he problem of graphics ... is not a superficial matter but a concern with how to indicate the technical complexity that is conceivable now, in terms that communicate unverbal and unhistorical intentions to a performer or a group of performers'. (Brown, 'Some Notes on Composing' [1963], in G. Chase, ed., *The American Composer Speaks* [1966] 304.) Earle Brown's explanation points to two main reasons for developing new types of notation: in terms of composition, new symbols were needed to score sounds that were being used for first time, as well as the complex relations between them; in terms of performance, new notations allowed the composer to emphasize what she or he saw as the most important elements, leaving the performer to develop these key features in ways more complex than a fully notated score could have suggested. With these new notations, verbal instructions were often necessary, like keys to a map or instruction manuals for a new machine, sometimes filling many pages, as in Mac Low's 'Methods for reading the *Asymmetries*' or Wolff's instructions for *Duet I.* 'Learning a new piece', composer and music critic David Behrman remarked in 1965, had become 'like learning a new game, or a new grammar'. (Behrman, 'What Indeterminate Notation Determines', in *Perspectives in New Music* [Spring–Summer 1965] 58.)

In the word or 'event' scores, these verbal instructions are no longer associated to a graphic poem or a musical score. The score for La Monte Young's *Composition* 1960 #7 visually embodies this transition from musical to verbal notation in its juxtaposition of a single notated B-F sharp chord with the simple verbal instruction 'to be held for a long time'. This composition came out of Young's interest in exploring the effects of prolonging sounds over long durations, first developed in his *Two Sounds* of April 1960. In fact, the verbal instruction seems to have been introduced for similar reasons to those listed by Brown. Firstly, words are the most economical way to transcribe a duration which is not specified. Secondly, leaving the performer to decide what 'a long time' is emphasizes the main focus of the work as the subjectivity of temporal experience, in the same way as Earle Brown developed a new type of proportional notation to encourage performers to explore a new 'interior time sense'. (Brown, 'Some Notes on Composing', 304.)

Similarly, Brecht's 1959–62 *Drip Music (Drip Event),* which simply indicates that 'a source of dripping water and an empty vessel are arranged so that the water falls into the vessel', echoes Cage's verbal instruction to the performer of his *Water Music* to 'pour water from one receptacle to the another.' Instead of transcribing into notes the exact sound of water being poured, Cage '[l]et the notations refer to what is to be done, not to what is heard, or to be heard'. (Nyman, *Experimental Music: Cage and Beyond*, 21–2.) A 1959 note by Brecht emphasizes this shift from 'the idea of an "ideal" eighth-note', for example, to the conception of 'a notational eighth-note', for example, to the conception of 'a notational eighth-note' as 'a direction for an action' which has 'an operational definition'. (Brecht, *Notebook III*, 123.) Whereas Cage's *Water Music* combined the sound of pouring water with other musical sounds, *Drip Music* is literally reduced to a 'direction for an action': by indicating only the task to be performed, the score focuses the performer's attention on the process rather than the result, which becomes 'incidental', in Brecht's own words.[11]

'One man is told that he must lie on the floor during the entire piece. The other man is told that he must tie the first man to the wall.' Simone Forti's minimal *Instruction for a Dance* published in *An Anthology* can be seen as an 'incidental' dance in the same way as Brecht composed 'incidental music', as the actual visible result – or lack of visible result – will be the direct outcome of the tasks given to each of the performers. Forti's interest in task-based performances, which started with the dance exercises developed in Ann Halprin's and Robert Dunn's workshops, was also encouraged by her participation in a 'happening' by Robert Whitman in 1960: 'it struck me that most of my actions were done not in order that the movement be seen, but so that the particular task could be accomplished', she recalls. (Forti, *Handbook in Motion*, 35.) While Whitman's happenings involved many performers accomplishing unrelated tasks simultaneously, Forti focused on one or more related tasks. Indeed, as Liz Kotz has pointed out, both Brecht and Forti went through a similar process of adapting task-based exercises from their teachers – Cage, and Ann Halprin/Robert Dunn, respectively – isolating as works in themselves what were meant as preparations for more complex arrangements. (Kotz, 'Post-Cagean Aesthetics and the "Event" Score', *October* [Winter 2001] 74.) A comparison between the two-page-long instructions for Brecht's *Motor Vehicle Sundown* and his two-word-long *Two Vehicle Events* of Summer 1961 clearly shows the shift to single-focus word scores in Brecht's work around Spring 1961: the same 'instrument' is used in both cases, but instead of the *mise en scène* with performers in motor vehicles going through a great range of 'events' simultaneously, the instructions in *Two Vehicle Events* are reduced to two nouns/verbs, 'start' and 'stop', each preceded by a bullet point, without any indication of the exact sound-source, sequence or duration. Brecht's desire for an increasing simplification of these task-based instructions is obvious in the evolution in the notation of *Drip Music* which in a 'second version' of 1962 is pared down to a single word: 'dripping'.

If, as Earle Brown explained, performer choice could only occur when information was withdrawn from the score, it certainly reached a peak in

Brecht's minimal and enigmatic notations. But for Brown, when performer choice is left free to the extent that the content of a work is entirely different from one performance to the other, as in his own *December 1952*, it is no longer a music 'piece': it becomes a 'musical activity'.[12] The idea of a task-based 'activity' lies at the heart of the conception of the score as a 'direction for an action'. Higgins' series of *Danger Musics*, which he started to write in 1961, are a most extreme embodiment of what he called 'provocation notation', defined as 'a situation in which the maker of a thing provokes some sort of activity'. (Higgins, 'Postface', 42.) *Danger Musics* are generally characterized by the sole act that in them 'one answers the question or followed the principle, any way, and by doing something that seems relevant to this, the performance takes place'. (Ibid., 42.) They instruct readers to perform actions ranging from the everyday, such as *Danger Music 15*, which reads 'work with butter and eggs for a time', to the physically perilous, as in *#1*'s invitation to 'spontaneously catch hold of a hoist hook and be raised up at least three storeys', and the downright life-threatening, as in *#9*'s order to 'volunteer to have your spine removed'.

In contrast to these often dramatic actions, other early word scores explore '[s]ounds barely heard, sights barely distinguished' – activities 'at the point of imperceptibility', according to Brecht. (Brecht, 'Events (assembled notes)', in unpublished letter to George Maciunas [1961].) For example, in La Monte Young's *Composition 1960 #5* the performer's task is to 'turn a butterfly (or any number of butterflies) loose in the performance area'. '[I]t didn't seem to me that anyone or anything should have to hear sounds ... [I]t is enough that they exist for themselves', explained by La Monte Young in 1960.[13] Silence thus becomes full of inaudible sounds which only word scores can transmit, from butterflies flying to the earth turning, which Yoko Ono invites us to listen to in her 1963 *Earth Piece*.[14] With this shift to perceptual activities, the 'event' score becomes as much an invitation to find an 'event' as to perform it: listening to a dripping tap, for example, could be a possible realization of *Drip Music*. 'For the virtuoso listener', Brecht observed in 1959, 'all sound may be music'. (Brecht, *Notebook III*, 123.)

Whether 'provocation notations' or invitations to listen to the barely audible, these word scores based on the 'discovery' or 'observation' of phenomena are fully removed from the traditional space of musical composition and performance and enter the space of everyday experience. Just as Brown was aware of the 'simultaneous existence and non-existence' as music of 'activities' such as *December 1952* (Brown, 'On Form', in *Source*, I [1965] 50), Brecht defined the word score as 'an art verging on the non-existent; dissolving into other dimensions, or becoming dimensionless, having no form'. (Brecht, 'Events [assembled notes]'.) Writing about Fluxus 'event' scores, Ina Blom has convincingly discussed this new relation between score and performance as 'a dynamic between two radical extremes, when the extremity of one position (i.e. the extreme generality of an instruction for an event) by necessity pushes into the opposite position (i.e. the extreme specificity of the realization of the instruction)'. (Blom, 'The Intermedia Dynamic', in *Fluxus Virus, 1962–1992* [1992] 216.) The notation engenders a process, whether imaginative or physical, which will always be 'too specific to approach in retrospect by any other person or narrator than the one who submerges herself into the process'. (Ibid., 216.) Blom sees the evolution both of specific artists such as Brecht or Young, and of Fluxus as a whole, as a shift towards extreme generality. 'By this logic', she concludes, the status of the score as a work 'can never be fixed, because it can only be seen through this continual movement, this dynamic between seemingly opposite forces'. (Ibid., 216.)

Performer Choice and Spectator Participation

This unique dynamic movement not only characterizes Fluxus' score, it is also a crucial feature of early object-based works by Brecht and Ono. In his first solo exhibition, entitled 'Towards Events', at the Reuben Gallery, New York, in 1959, Brecht showed three-dimensional works such as *The Cabinet*, a wall cabinet with a glass door containing a clock, a mug, a cup, a yoyo, a bell, a word puzzle, a bottle filled with red liquid and other objects.[15] The invitation to the exhibition provided the visitors with 'instructions' to remove, use the objects 'in ways appropriate to their nature' and then put them back. (Brecht, 'Invitation', in *Towards Events* [1959].)

'The aspect of this work which (to me) is of most interest', Brecht explained in 1960:

> Is not the object-like part, that is, the cabinet and its contents, but rather what occurs when someone is involved with its object-like part. The work to me is more in the nature of a performance (music and dance) than of an object. It is therefore of greatest importance that the spectator, participant, be free to open and close the door and handle the objects freely. (Brecht, 'Notes on the shipping and exhibiting of MEDICINE CABINET' [1960])

As Bruce Altshuler has pointed out, while Brecht was 'primarily concerned with events to be created through engagement with his objects, the objects themselves being something like props for these events', Yoko Ono, on the other hand, 'would call for visitor participation in the creation of the objects themselves' in her series of *Instruction Paintings* first exhibited at the AG Gallery in New York in July 1961. (Altshuler, 'Instructions for a World of Stickiness: The Early Conceptual Works of Yoko Ono', in *Yes Yoko Ono* [2000]

66.) During this exhibition, Ono gave visitors verbal instruction to burn, cut up or step on different-shaped canvases hung on the walls, spread on a table or placed on the floor. A piece such as *Waterdrop Painting*, in which the viewer is incited to let water drip on a circular piece of canvas, seems to be the visual equivalent of Brecht's 1959–62 *Drip Music*: both are activities occurring in time, both are task-based, suggesting a process through which an 'incidental' aural and visual result will be achieved. A year later, Ono decided to dispense with the object altogether, exhibiting the instructions without the pieces of canvas at the Sogetsu Art Center, Tokyo, in May 1962. 'I think painting can be instructionalized', she would write 3 years later.

> Artist [sic] in this case, will only give instructions or diagrams for painting – and the painting will be more or less a do-it-yourself kit according to the instructions. The painting starts to exist only when a person followed the instructions to let the painting come to life. (Ono, 'Letter to Ivan Karp, 4 January 1965' in *Grapefruit* [1965])

In the same way as the increasingly important role of performer choice in experimental music and poetry radically modified the traditional definition of the score and the relation between composer and performer, the invitation to spectator participation in Brecht's and Ono's 'event-objects' disrupted the accepted attitudes of gallery visitors. 'At the end of the 1950s', recalled Brecht in an interview, 'to enter a gallery and put your thumb on a painting was sacrilege'. (Brecht, interview with Irmeline Lebeer [1973], in *An Introduction to George Brecht's Book of the Tumbler on Fire* [1978] 88.) Similarly, Ono's first *Instruction Painting of* 1960, *Painting to be Stepped on* – a piece of canvas placed on the floor along with this self-explanatory title – was a reaction against the Abstract Expressionist scene in New York, in which, she remembers, 'people used to worship pictures ceremoniously'.[16] Out of rebellion, Ono wanted to provoke these people: 'Why don't you then simply step on a picture,' she asked them, 'just to see what happens?'[17] Both Brecht and Ono introduced spectator participation 'in a spirit of liberation' [...][18]

1 [footnote 8 in source] Other artists whom Young met in California and invited to contribute to *An Anthology* were Terry Riley, Terry Jennings, Joseph Byrd, Robert Morris and Dennis Johnson.

2 [9] La Monte Young's first contacts with Cage, Brown and Wolff dated back to his participation in the 1959 New Music summer Course in Darmstadt, Germany, which was a very important centre for international contemporary music at the time. Nam June Paik attended this course as well.

3 [10] Young came to New York to study with Richard Maxfield who introduced him to Mac Low.

4 [11] They were contacted by Young after he had read their works in poetry magazines.

5 [12] In his 1955 *Five Biblical Poems* silences are represented by three-sided boxes, 'each equal in duration to any word and thus indeterminate in length' (See Williams, *Anthology of Concrete Poetry* [1967]).

6 [13] The work that Forti recalls may have been Cage's score for *Fontana Mix*. For a detailed description of Robert Dunn's workshop, see Sally Banes, *Democracy's Body – Judson Dance Theater, 1962–64* (Epping: UMI Research Press, 1980).

7 [14] Brecht used cards from the beginning of his classes in 1958, as in *The Artificial Crowd* of 2 July 1958, for example, in which cards are 'passed out to the audience', bearing instructions using clapping (for x times), shaking or not shaking milk bottles filled with various objects and saying words (see Brecht, *Notebook I* [1958], in *Notebooks I–III* [1991] 12).

8 [15] The distinction between 'chance and 'choice' procedures is discussed by Earle Brown in 'Interview with Richard Duffalo, Rye, New York, 1986', Duffalo, *Trackings: Composers Speak with Richard Duffalo* (New York: Oxford University Press, 1989) 113.

9 [16] See Brecht, *Notebook I* [1958] in *Notebooks I–III* (Cologne: Verlag der Buchhandlung Walther König, 1991) 42. Brecht was referring to Wolff's *Duo for Pianists II* which preceded *Duet I*. Wolff started to develop notations stressing the 'cue and answer' relations between the performers in 1957; see Christopher Fox, 'Music as Social Process: Some Aspects of the Work of Christian Wolff', *Contact*, no. 30 (Spring 1987).

10 [17] For more information about concrete poetry and its relation to Mallarmé, see Mary Ellen Solt, *Concrete Poetry: A World View* (Bloomington: Indiana University Press, 1968).

11 [18] In the score for Brecht's 1961 *Incidental Music* Brecht gives instructions to a pianist for tasks such as tilting the piano seat, piling blocks inside the piano, or dropping dried peas onto the keyboard. 'I don't tell you what to try for', explained Brecht to Michael Nyman in his interview with Nyman, *Studio International*, 192 (984) (November–December 1976) 256.

12 [19] '[I]n order to be called "open form", a work must have an identifiable content which can then be formed, as in *25 Pages* or the *Available Forms* works. By this definition, *December 1952* is not a piece of music at all; it is musical activity when performed' – Brown, 'On Form', *Source*, I (1) 1965) 50.

13 [20] La Monte Young's 'Lecture 1960' was first given at Ann Halprin's workshop in California in the summer of 1960, and was first published in the *Tulane Drama Review* in 1965.

14 [21] 'Listen to the earth turning', Yoko Ono, *Earth Piece*, Spring 1963 in Yoko Ono, *Grapefruit*, 1964 (Tokyo: Wunternaum Press, 1964). Douglas Kahn has shown that it was the appearance of recording and amplifying devices that made composers realize that sound events should not be limited to what is audible to the human ear; see Kahn, *Noise, Water, Meat – A History of Sound in the Arts* (Cambridge, Massachusetts: The MIT Press, 1999) 189–99.

15 [22] Brecht also showed in this exhibition some early paintings and collages and 'constructions to be hung upon a wall as a painting, but whose elements may be moved about by the viewer in a manner determined by the nature of the work', such as *Marbles and Blair* (see 'Brecht to Show Events at Reuben Gallery', press release for *Towards Events*, New York, Reuben Gallery, 1959).

16 [23] 'Yoko Ono: Jeder muss etwas dazu tun ... – ein Gresprāch von Andreas Denk', *Kunstforum International*, no. 125 (January–Februuary 1994) 278 (my translation).

17 [24] Ibid., 279, note 24.

18 [25] The work 'was done in a spirit of liberation: to let the spectators take part in what was happening' – Brecht, 'Interview with Irmeline Lebeer' (1973), in Henry Martin, ed., *An Introduction to George Brecht's Book of the Tumbler on Fire* (Milan: Multhipia Edizioni, 1978) 88.

Anna Dezeuze, extract from 'Origins of the Fluxus Score: From Indeterminacy to the "Do-It-Yourself" Artwork', *Performance Research*, vol. 7, no. 3 (2002) 79–92 [references abbreviated].

Branden W. Joseph
The Social Turn//2008

[...] Situated roughly between the *I-Ching*-derived chance techniques of the *Music of Changes* (1951) and the complete indeterminacy of *Variations II* (1961), [is the] period in John Cage's work [which] has long been recognized as central, indeed, fundamental, to the breakdown of the modernist project and the advent of postmodernism.[1] Despite its multidisciplinary importance, which had profound consequences for art, music, dance and film, Cage's impact on the period outside the discipline of music (and sometimes within) is more often minimized or dismissed than explored. Frequently, the idea of chance, aside from any specific understanding of Cage's deployment of it, is hypostatized as the sole content of his aesthetic and equated with an attitude of complete relativism. Caricaturing him as some type of holy fool, dismissing him as a mere imitator of Dada, or disparaging him as a religious reactionary on account of his invocation of Zen, critics consistently overlook the logical, self-reflexive and utterly consistent development of the first two decades of Cage's career. Individual quotes and compositions are routinely cited or analysed out of context (a practice, to be sure, abetted by Cage's decomposition of his own writings via chance procedures and typographic experiments), while the specifics of both his scores and his performances are usually simply ignored.

Such off-hand treatment by critics and historians, however, differs markedly from the reception of Cage by the artists (in the widest sense of the term) who interacted with him on an almost daily basis in New York or at Black Mountain College, encountered his work at Darmstadt (like La Monte Young), took his composition courses at the New School for Social Research, or studied his scores in Robert Dunn's choreography workshop, out of which the Judson Dance Theater would arise. While it would be impossible to chronicle the evolution of

Cage's project in detail here, it is nonetheless important to analyse certain of its most significant implications, for they formed the backdrop against which the aesthetic positions developed (variously) within the network of which Young and Tony Conrad were a part would play themselves out.[2]

The first implication of Cage's work is the production of an aesthetic of immanence. For the better part of two decades, Cage had pursued a thoroughgoing disarticulation of any and all abstract or transcendent connections between sound or between the individual components of a sound, such as frequency, amplitude, timbre, duration, or other morphology. In this, he opposed the direction of his European contemporaries, most notably Stockhausen and Boulez, who sought an aesthetic of integral serialism by which all aspects or parameters of a composition would be interrelated. Beginning with the investigation of chance procedures, Cage worked to detach sounds from traditional, illustrative or other pre-established meanings, as well as to disconnect composition (the arrangement of sounds) from continuity, whether produced by melody or by rhythm, and any form of structure: harmonic, atonal and eventally even the neutral time structures he himself had produced and lauded throughout the 1940s. 'It is thus possible', Cage argued, 'to make a musical composition the continuity of which is free of individual taste and memory (psychology) and also of the literature and "traditions" of the art. The sounds enter the time-space centred within themselves, unimpeded by service to any abstraction, their 360 degrees of circumference free for an infinite play of interpenetration.'[3]

Going beyond the disarticulation of a priori connections between sounds, Cage also sought to undercut the production of any determinate a posteriori interconnections between them, as well. Quickly realizing that, once fixed, a chance-derived score such as *Music of Changes* (which was indeterminate with regard to *composition*) was still as determinate upon *performance* as if it had been intentionally produced,[4] Cage sought to insert indeterminacy into the relation between composer and performer (by allowing, for example, for multiple realizations of any compositional notation) as well as into the relation between performer and listener (by means, for instance, of arranging loudspeakers and musicians around the audience so that no two listeners would hear the same 'mix' of sounds), so that there was no longer any 'best seat in the house' (one of the aspects of Cage's work that Henry Flynt replicated in 1959). Cage's goal, in all such endeavours, was to eliminate as much as possible from the acoustical experience the creation of any abstract form that could be received as existing on a level above, beyond or outside the immanent realm (what Deleuze and Guattari, when discussing Cage, among others, would term a 'plane of immanence').[5]

Such an embrace of immanence does not, as is often charged, amount to a quietistic acceptance of 'life' or 'nature' (two of Cage's favourite terms) as unchanging or eternal realms, or as ones that are identical to the actually existing social structure as it unreflexively appears from what Cage called an 'anthropomorphic' point of view. 'Nature', for Cage, or more properly, nature's 'manner of operation', was understood as an ongoing process of ateleological and non-hierarchical transformation. At his most specific, Cage described the purpose of music as 'an imitation ... of nature in her manner of operation as, in our time, her operation is revealed', further explaining that 'art changes because science changes – that is, changes in science give artists different understandings of how nature works'.[6] Always attentive to contemporary scientific and technological developments (the one-time futurist was famously the son of an inventor), Cage's notions of complexity and chaos ultimately, perhaps, have more resonances with cybernetics and chaos theory than with Eastern religion. For Cage, the idea of 'identifying with nature' was above all a reconfiguration of the avant-garde technique of estrangement, the most important aspect of which, arguably, was the disidentification with overly reductive (but not all) ideas of causality: 'The life situation from a natural, rather than anthropomorphic, view is more complex than art or putting arts together tastefully ... the really important problems require greater earnestness.'[7]

The second component of the Cagean aesthetic concerns the relation between the listener and the indeterminate musical production. Instead of confronting the composition as a totality – unified by its derivation from or representation of an abstract (non-immanent) structure or form – listeners were to encounter sonic events as a 'field' or 'constellation' that not only potentially surrounded them, but that opened onto and interpenetrated with random acoustical occurrences 'outside' and therefore beyond any single intentionality. (Hence Cage's quip that 'a cough or a baby crying will not ruin a good piece of modern music.')[8] Like a glass house, to use one of Cage's favourite metaphors, or an auditorium with the windows left open, Cage's compositions emulated a type of acoustical 'transparency' to external events that undermined their separation and autonomy. To this end, many of Cage's compositions could be performed simultaneously, allowing for a kind of superimposition or audio collage effect through which they melded into one another and further blurred their status as discrete works. With neither determinable formal nor 'spatial' limitations, Cage's compositions were to be grasped not as discrete, acoustical 'time-objects', but as temporally changing, yet ateleological ('purposeless') 'processes'.[9] The listener, then, instead of following pre-given structures or attempting to comprehend the work as a message (whether intentionally implanted or not), was to assume an attitude of attentiveness within a differentiated, but non-hierarchical field of sonic occurrences: 'to approach them as objects is to utterly miss the point.'[10] For Cage, this reconfiguration of the traditional subject-object/listener-work relation into an almost topographical situation of a listener within a multidimensional transformational field (i.e., a field of more than two dimensions) was an explicit challenge not only to abstraction but to dialectics:

> Where a single operation is applied to more than one notation, for example to those of both frequency and amplitude characteristics, the frequency and amplitude characteristics are, by that operation common to both, brought into relationship. These relationships make an object; and this object, in contrast to a process which is purposeless, must be viewed dualistically. Indeterminacy when present in the making of an object, and when therefore viewed dualistically, is a sign, not of identification with no matter what eventuality, but simply of carelessness with regard to the outcome.[11]

According to Cage, seeing the composition as an ateleological process, or focusless but differentiated field, produces an additional transformation in the listening relationship, which is the third relevant point of his aesthetic: Interpretation gives way to 'experimentation'. In place of the attempt to comprehend the meaning of a composition or any of the sounds in it as signs with unilaterally determinable (i.e., bi-univocal) meanings – whether pre-given or a posteriori and even if multiple or ambiguous – the listener was to experience the process as without ulterior signification, structure or goal. Cage sometimes groped for terms to describe this relationship: 'awareness', 'curiosity', 'use', even 'an entertainment in which to celebrate unfixity'.[12] Nevertheless, 'experimentation', as developed within the Cagean project, was the process of interpretation, of reading and receiving signs, in the absence of pre-given signifieds.[13] Such was not conceived by Cage as an embrace of negation (no received meaning whatsoever), or of irrationality or mystical oneness (though, combined with Zen, both were almost unavoidable receptions), but at least at its most radical, as a death of the composer that was also a liberating birth of the listener. As Liz Kotz has observed, the more celebrated notion of the 'death of the author' put forward by Roland Barthes in 1968 was likely a reimportation of the idea into literature and art from the context of contemporary music.[14]

In this reconfigured listening experience, neither the unavoidably *perceived* connections between sounds nor the listener's thoughts or feelings about them were denied or eliminated. 'Hearing sounds which are just sounds', Cage stated, 'immediately sets the theorizing mind to theorizing.'[15] However, the locus of the meaning of the acoustical experience is transferred to the listener, who is thereby allowed to 'become their own centre', rather than submit to the will or thoughts of either composer or performer. 'Of course, there are objects', Cage declared about the visual analogue of his aesthetic in Rauschenberg's Combines. 'Who said there weren't? The thing is, we get the point more quickly when we realize it is we looking rather than we may not be seeing it.'[16]

The dissolution or dismantling of transcendent structures was understood as a subversion of power. This was the fourth relevant point of Cage's aesthetic. For Cage, the traditional, determinate passages from composer to score, score to performer, and performer to listener, were understood in terms of power relations. Thus, to disarticulate them as necessary, bi-univocal relations meant that neither performer nor audience had to be subservient to the will of another; they could instead work from their own centres, not by doing whatever they want, but nonetheless without being 'pushed', as Cage put it, in any one direction.[17] As he explained about one such musical relation, 'Giving up control so that sounds can be sounds (they are not men: they are sounds) means for instance: the conductor of an orchestra is no longer a policeman.'[18] This (ultimately utopian) attempt to dissolve or to eradicate all forms or effects of power was essentially an anarchist position, and it would be explicitly labelled as such by Cage in 1960 in a brief statement published in *ARTnews*: 'Emptiness of purpose does not imply contempt for society, rather it assumes that each person, whether he knows it or not, is noble, is able to experience gifts with generosity, that society is best anarchic.'[19]

The final component of the Cagean legacy to be drawn out at this point is its challenge to the disciplinary status of the separate arts. Beginning with a quest to undermine the separation between music and noise in his futurist-inspired percussion work of the 1930s and 1940s, Cage moved, at the outset of the 1950s, to undo the distinction between sound and silence. Following upon his experience in an anechoic chamber at Harvard in 1951, Cage famously redefined silence as inherently and unavoidably filled with sounds, the production of which is simply unintended. There is thus no such thing as silence. Instead, there are only two kinds of sounds: 'those intended and those others (so-called silence) not intended.'[20] By 1954, Cage would go further, extending the progressive disarticulation of 'abstract' categories such as sound and silence to the distinction between the auditory and the visual. The inevitable combination of these two components in any and all performed actions, which implicitly questioned the distinction between the visual arts and music, Cage described as 'theatre'.[21] As he wrote in *45' for a Speaker* (a lecture carefully scripted to incorporate, via chance determinations, such activities as coughing, brushing his hair, blowing his nose, and banging his fist on the table), 'Music is an oversimplification of the situation we actually are in. An ear alone is not a being; music is one part of theatre. "Focus" is what aspects one's noticing. Theatre is all the various things going on at the same time. I have noticed that music is liveliest for me when listening, for instance, doesn't distract me from seeing.'[22]

All five aspects of Cage's aesthetic would have been available to an attentive student in 1959 and would become progressively more so up to the publication of *Silence*, the first volume of his collected writings, in 1961. [...]

1 [footnote 32 in source] This was actually the second major phase of Cage's development. The first revolved around percussion. Cage's work would transform again in the 1960s, a transformation that Henry Flynt suggests was, in part, brought forth by the developments in the circle around La Monte Young. Henry Flynt, 'La Monte Young in New York, 1960–62', in *Sound and Light: La Monte Young, Marian Zazeela*, ed. William Duckworth and Richard Fleming (Lewisburg, Pennsylvania: Bucknell University Press, 1996) 77.

2 [33] The best critical study of Cage's work remains James Pritchett, *The Music of John Cage* (Cambridge: Cambridge University Press, 1993). I have attempted to chronicle certain aspects of Cage's development in detail elsewhere. [...]

3 [34] John Cage, 'Composition: To Describe the Process of Composition Used in *Music of Changes* and *Imaginary Landscape No. 4*' (1952) in *Silence* (Middletown, Connecticut: Wesleyan University Press, 1961) 59.

4 [35] John Cage, 'Composition as Process II: Indeterminacy' (1958), in *Silence*, 36.

5 [36] Gilles Deleuze and Félix Guattari, *A Thousand Plateaus: Capitalism and Schizophrenia*, trans. Brian Massumi (Minneapolis: University of Minnesota Press, 1987) 266–7.

6 [37] John Cage, 'On Film' (1956), in *John Cage: An Anthology*, ed. Richard Kostelanetz (New York: Da Capo Press, 1991) 115; John Cage, 'Where Are We Going? And What Are We Doing?' (1961), in *Silence*, 194. [...]

7 [38] John Cage, 'On Film' (1956), in *John Cage: An Anthology*, 115.

8 [39] John Cage, '45' for a Speaker' (1954), in *Silence*, 161.

9 [40] John Cage, 'Composition as Process II: Indeterminacy', in *Silence*, 38.

10 [41] John Cage, 'Composition as Process I: Changes' (1958) in *Silence*, 31.

11 [42] John Cage, 'Composition as Process II: Indeterminacy', in *Silence*, 38. Cage comments further on dualism and dialectics in 'Program Notes' (1959), in *John Cage: Writer*, ed. Richard Kostelanetz (New York: Limelight Editions, 1993) 81–2.

12 [43] John Cage, 'Where Are We Going? And What Are We Doing?' (1961), in *Silence*, 237; and 'On Robert Rauschenberg, Artist, and His Work' (1961), in *Silence*, 98.

13 [44] Daniel Charles, *Gloses sur John Cage* (Paris: Union Générale d'Éditions, 1978) 91–109; and Gilles Deleuze and Félix Guattari, *Anti-Oedipus: Capitalism and Schizophrenia*, trans. Mark Seem, Robert Hurley and Helen R. Lane (Minneapolis: University of Minnesota Press, 1983) 370–71.

14 [45] Liz Kotz, 'Post-Cagean Aesthetics and the "Event" Score', *October*, no. 95 (Winter 2001) 59 and 59n10.

15 [46] John Cage, 'Experimental Music' (1957), in *Silence*, 10.

16 [47] John Cage, 'On Robert Rauschenberg, Artist, and His Work' (1961), in *Silence*, 108.

17 [48] John Cage, 'Where Are We Going? And What Are We Doing?' (1961), in *Silence*, 224–6.

18 [49] John Cage, 'History of Experimental Music in the United States' (1959), in *Silence*, 72.

19 [50] John Cage, 'Form is a Language', *ARTnews* (April 1960); reprinted in John Cage: An Anthology, 135. [...]

20 [51] John Cage, 'Experimental Music: Doctrine' (1955), in *Silence*, 14.

21 [52] Ibid., 12.

22 [53] John Cage, '45' for a Speaker', in *Silence*, 149.

Branden W. Joseph, extract from *Beyond The Dream Syndicate: Tony Conrad and the Arts after Cage* (New York: Zone Books, 2008) 76–82 [some footnotes abbreviated].

Alexandra Munroe
Cage Zen//2009

Cage's study and appropriation of Asian philosophy and aesthetics shaped his compositional practice and writings from the mid 1940s to at least the mid 1960s. He was open about his use of Taoist and Buddhist texts, haiku poetics and Indian mysticism as inspiration for his radical proposition 'to stop all the thinking that separates music from living.'[1] Increasingly, Cage's formal and philosophical insights became the foundation of his credo on art as an open field of experiential immediacy:

> We learned from Oriental thought that those divine influences are, in fact, the environment in which we are. A sober and quiet mind is one in which the ego does not obstruct the fluency of things that come in through the senses and up through one's dreams. Our business in living is to become fluent with the life we are living, and art can help this.[2]

Thoroughly identified with Japanese Zen, Cage is most revered as a modern American Zen master. 'I thought of John as a sort of teacher/preacher/soldier', Jasper Johns remarked.[3] His studies and friendship with Suzuki, whose Columbia University lectures he attended in the 1950s, stimulated this focus.[4] 'Since the forties and through my study with D.T. Suzuki of the philosophy of Zen Buddhism', he wrote, 'I've thought of music as a means of changing the mind ... an activity of sounds in which the artist found a way to let sounds be themselves.'[5] Cage's aesthetic statements, appropriating Zen terms, concepts and rhetorical devices such as paradox, shape such key writings as 'Lecture on Nothing' (1949–50), 'Julliard Lecture' (1952), 'Robert Rauschenberg' (1953), 'Experimental Music: Doctrine' (1955) and 'Composition as Process' (1958). His conception of Zen as a technique to activate perception also influenced such historic compositions as *4'33"*, *Haiki* and *Water Music* (all 1952). The mode of direct experience that impressed Cage is *zazen*, the basis of formal meditative practice that informs traditional Zen arts like archery, calligraphy, haiku and tea ceremony. But Cage was not concerned with ritual practices and disregarded their social and political history as an organized religion in modern Japan. Rather, his use and interpretation of Zen were strategic and creative. A key technique he aestheticized is the doctrine of dharma transmission. In monastic forms of Zen Buddhism, enlightenment passes through direct experience between the minds of master and student, without the mediation of religious texts or ritual. Cage's Zen-inspired experiential methods established mental, transformative interaction – a relational dynamic between the creator and recipient/viewer – as a crucial principle in neo-avant-garde art. In this formulation of Cage Zen, art is a catalyst for direct insight into nature, consciousness and being. Art, Cage remarked, is 'not self expression but self alteration'.[6]

For Cage, the formulation of space and emptiness as substantive essence, worthy of being material for art, refers to the central principle of void, or *sunyata*, in Mahayana Buddhist metaphysics. Cage contrasts traditional Western notions of silence to his own sensibility instilled with Zen philosophy in his influential treatise 'Composition as Process' (1958):

> What happens, for instance, to silence? That is, how does the mind's perception of it change? Formerly, silence was the time lapse between sounds, useful towards a variety of ends ... Where none of these or other goals is present, silence becomes something else – not silence at all, but sounds, the ambient sounds. The nature of these is unpredictable and changing. These sounds (which are called silence only because they do not form part of a musical intention) may be depended upon to exist. The world teems with them, and is, in fact, at no point free of them.[7]

Cage's concepts of space and emptiness informed his theory on the interactive relationship of art, the viewer, and what he calls 'the environment'. Here silence and emptiness are not the opposites of sound and form, as in Western thought, but rather contain in themselves the complete presence of duration and change. Requiring the artist's and viewer's focus, art abandons fixed form and becomes an indeterminate (or 'purposeless') process. Cage calls such events '*experimental* action', which are 'generated by the mind as empty as it was before it became one ... [It] sees things directly as they are: impermanently involved in an infinite play of interpenetrations.'[8]

As Branden Joseph argues, Cage's conception of emptiness influenced the interpretation and practice of neo-avant-garde production in the 1950s: Rauschenberg is a prime example.[9] In summer 1952 at Black Mountain, a laboratory for creative innovation where painters, composers, poets, architects and craft artists drew freely from Eastern and European traditions, Cage invited Rauschenberg to participate in the multimedia event *Black Mountain Piece*, in which he included Rauschenberg's *White Painting* (1951) as part of the set.[10] Rauschenberg's series of all white canvases, entirely devoid of any articulation or form, developed from his collage painting *Mother of God* (*c*. 1950), which presents a white circle, symbolic of the divine, on a background of city maps. Rauschenberg wrote to his dealer Betty Parsons:

> They are large white (1 white as 1 GOD) canvases organized and selected with the experience of time and presented with the innocence of a virgin. Dealing with the suspense, excitement and body of an organic silence, the restriction and freedom of absence, the plastic fullness of nothing, the point a circle begins and ends, they are a natural response to the current pressures of the faithless and a promoter of intuitional optimism. It is completely irrelevant that I am making them – *Today* is their creator.[11]

Cage saw in Rauschenberg's blank surfaces how the artless operation of site, process and durational time could constitute a work of art. This paradigm shift moved the definition of art as a fixed object *in* time and space to an intuitive experience *of* time and space. Impressed by Rauschenberg's idea that 'a canvas is never empty', the *White Paintings*, Cage mused, offer 'reflective surfaces changing what is seen by means of what is happening ... a painting constantly changing.'[12]

Proceeding from this epiphany, Cage wrote the celebrated score for *4'33"*, which David Tudor performed at Black Mountain that same summer. This structure of three movements of silence lasting four minutes and thirty-three seconds was Cage's manifesto presentation of silence as the absence of intentional sound: nothingness becomes manifest as full, and the random sounds of the environment emerge as the listening experience. In performance, the silent score is frequently indicated by the opening and closing of the piano lid. In the score (1952), the three movements of time are marked in proportional notation to space. Cage dedicated the score to Irwin Kremen, who later wrote on the radical nature of its notational structure: 'In effect, real time is here the fundamental dimension of music, its very ground. And where time is primary, change, process itself, defines the nature of things. That aptly describes the silent piece – an unfixed flux of sound through time, a flux from performance to performance.'[13]

One of Cage's model texts was 'The Doctrine of Universal Mind', a collection of sermons and dialogues by the ninth-century master Huang Po (d. *c.* 850). Cage read this text as a late-night performance at Black Mountain in summer 1952.[14] Huang Po's teachings are among the principal doctrines of Zen Buddhism and a founding text of the Rinzai school of sudden enlightenment. What Cage took from Huang Po's witty and colloquial writing is the need to drop rational, cognitive and deductive thinking in favour of an intuitive grasp of all that is present. As Huang Po teaches, 'avoid pondering things in your mind, thereby purging your bodies of discriminatory cognition ... If you can only rid yourselves of conceptual thought, you will have accomplished everything ... That which is before you is it.'[15] As if in response, Cage writes, 'Where these ears are in connection with a mind that has nothing to do, then the mind is free to enter into the act of listening, hearing each sound just as it is, not as a phenomenon more or less approximating a preconception.'[16]

From the late 1950s, the artists associated with Fluxus and Happenings expanded, challenged and radicalized the parameters of Cage's Asian rhetoric and methodology. They revelled in an increasingly eclectic inventory of Asian thought, traditions and contact with avant-garde artists of East Asia. Kaprow's event composition for *18 Happenings in 6 Parts* (1959) – with three simultaneous performances, eight overlapping sound tracks, and precise instructions for the audience – transformed central conditions of Cagean indeterminacy and interactive participation. By 1962, when Nam June Paik performed *Zen for Head* (1962) at the first Fluxus festival of new music in Wiesbaden, the value-shifts from intention to non-intention, from object to process, and from stasis to duration, reflected the broader application of what Paik called the 'old Zen-Cage thesis: "It is beautiful, not because it changes beautifully, but – simply – because it changes."'[17]

Zen for Head was Paik's enactment of La Monte Young's 1960 performance score, 'Draw a straight line and follow it.' Paik dipped his head, hands and necktie in a bowl of ink and tomato juice, and using his body as a brush, dragged himself along the entire length of a thirteen-foot-long sheet of paper. Paik's allusion to Zen in his title, and emulation of expressionist 'Zen calligraphy' to create a Dadaist hand scroll, inverted all that Cage Zen had come to represent. This irreverent and inelegant antic upended the virtues of contemplative experience with the wild force of unmediated action. Writing in 1963, artist Earle Brown described Paik as 'a kind of Oriental *Kammerkrieg* ... a place for war-surplus bravery, fear, heroics, aggression, hot and cold running sweat, cruelty, exhilaration, love'. Referring to Paik as a Zen teacher, Brown describes how it is 'very traditional in the East for master to give directly to pupil (a whack on the head) the sound, or the experience rather than a lecture or an indirect (notational) directive ... Paik doesn't tell somebody, he up and does it.'[18] In this way, the imagined projections of how a Zen master behaves became coupled with the reception of Paik's work, framing the critique of his performances not as artistic creation (in the manner of Cage) but rather as a direct embodiment, by virtue of his being Korean-born, of traditional Asian wisdom. Later, when asked if he were a Buddhist, Paik replied: 'No, I'm an artist ... Because I am a friend of John Cage, people tend to see me as a Zen monk ... I'm not a follower of Zen but I react to Zen the same way as I react to Johann Sebastian Bach.'[19]

Paik graduated from the University of Tokyo in 1956, wrote a dissertation on Arnold Schoenberg, and was closely associated with the Japanese intermedia avant-garde. He joined some twenty Japanese artists who participated in various Fluxus productions from its founding in 1961 through Fluxus organizer Maciunas' death in 1978. Besides Paik, whose family fled Korea with the outbreak of the Korean War, contemporary Japanese avant-garde artists dominated the American imagination of Zen. From their centres in Tokyo, where neo-Dada was ascendant from around 1960, and New York, where composers like Toshi Ichiyanagi, who had studied with Cage at the New School, were active in the downtown neo-Dada scene, young Japanese artists were cast as mediums of a non-Western, anti-rationalist aesthetic. They were seen as natural poets of quotidian existence, agents of Maciunas' theory of anti-art: 'Anti-art is life, is nature, is true reality – it is one and all. Rainfall is anti-art, a babble of a crowd is anti-art, a sneeze is anti-art, a flight of a butterfly, or movements of microbes are anti-art.'[20] Indeed, Maciunas' manifesto for Fluxus was a blatant call for the radical elimination of Western culture: '*Purge* the world of bourgeois sickness, "intellectual", professional & commercialized culture, PURGE the world of dead art, imitation, artificial art, abstract art, illusionistic art, mathematical art – PURGE THE WORLD OF 'EUROPANISM' [sic]!'[21] Maciunas exhibited Yoko Ono's *Instructions for Paintings* at his AG Gallery in 1961 and helped bring several composers associated with Tokyo's Group Ongaku to New York in the early 1960s, including Takehisa Kosugi, Mieko Shiomi, Yasunao Tone and Shigeko Kubota, who later became Paik's wife.

Like Maciunas, Kaprow used Japanese artists as radical embodiments of positive non-Western values. In 1966, he included Yayoi Kusama's environments and the Gutai group's actions in his landmark book *Assemblage, Environments and Happenings*. By incorporating Kusama and Gutai in his theory of avant-garde art, Kaprow, like Maciunas, could make his case for the end of formalist Western art. His proposal for a radical set of 'form-principles' that would render '*the line between art and life ... as fluid, and perhaps indistinct, as possible*,' included 'change', 'chance', 'accidents' and a notion of time that was 'variable and discontinuous'.[22] Significantly, Kaprow describes the new 'world-view' as 'primarily a philosophical quest and a finding of truths, rather than a purely aesthetic activity'. On George Brecht's 'sparse scores' of performance pieces and concept art, Kaprow writes: 'Certainly [he is] aware of the philosophical allusions to Zen Buddhism, of the subtle wit and childlike simplicity of the activities indicated.' These notations describe basic actions, such as Brecht's score that simply reads 'exit', or pose the re-enactment of daily life, such as Alison Knowles' *Identical Lunch* (1973), which calls for players to eat a daily lunch of a tuna fish sandwich. [...]

1 [footnote 6 in source] John Cage, 'Julliard Lecture' (1952), *A Year from Monday: New Lectures and Writings* (Middletown, Connecticut: Wesleyan University Press, 1967) 97.

2 [7] Original quote from Cage, 'Memoir' (1966), *John Cage*, ed. Richard Kostelanetz (London: Praeger, 1970) 77.

3 [8] Jasper Johns, 'The Fabric of Friendship', in Richard Francis, Mark Rosenthal, Anne Seymour, David Sylvester and David Vaughan, *Dancers on a Plane: Cage, Cunningham, Johns* (New York: Alfred A. Knopf/London: Anthony d'Offay Gallery, 1990) 138.

4 [9] Although Cage dates his attendance of Suzuki's lectures as 1945–47 or 1949–50, Suzuki only arrived in New York in summer 1950; gave his first lecture at Columbia in March 1951; and began his official teaching there in spring 1952. [...]

5 [10] Cage, quoted in George J. Leonard, *Into the Light of Things: The Art of the Commonplace from Wordsworth to John Cage* (Chicago: University of Chicago Press, 1994) 147. Original source not cited.

6 [11] Cage, in conversation with Richard Francis, June 27, 1989, in Francis, *Dancers on a Plane*, 31.

7 [12] Cage, 'Composition as Process' (1958), in *Silence* (Middletown, Connecticut: Wesleyan University Press, 1961) 22–3.

8 [13] Cage, 'Experimental Music: Doctrine' (1955), in *Silence*, 15.

9 [14] See Branden W. Joseph, *Random Order: Robert Rauschenberg and the Neo-Avant-Garde* (Cambridge, Massachusetts: The MIT Press, 2003). [...]

10 [15] See Vincent Katz, ed., *Black Mountain College: Experiment in Art* (Cambridge, Massachusetts: The MIT Press, 2002) 139. Participants in this prototypical work included Cage, Merce Cunningham, Charles Olson, David Tudor, M.C. Richards, and two unnamed others.

11 [16] Rauschenberg to Parsons, 18 October 1951, in Walter Hopps, *Robert Rauschenberg: The Early 1950s* (Houston: Menil Collection, Houston Fine Art Press, 1991) 230.

12 [17] Cage, 'On Robert Rauschenberg, Artist, and His Work', (1961), in *Silence*, 102–3. Cage prefaces this text, 'To whom It May Concern: The white paintings came first; my silent piece came later.'

13 [18] Irwin Kremen, 'On the Score of *4'33"*' (lecture, Central Park Summer-Stage, New York, 15 July 1994) on the program '4'33' and Other Sounds Not Intended: A Tribute to John Cage.' Copyright Irwin Kremen, 1994. E-mail to author, June 11, 2008.

14 [19] David. W. Patterson, 'Cage and Asia', in *The Cambridge Companion to John Cage* (Cambridge: Cambridge University Press, 2002) 55.

15 [20] Huang Po, *The Zen Teaching of Huang Po: On the Transmission of the Mind, Being the Teaching of the Zen Master Huang Po as recorded by the scholar P'ei Hsiu of the Tang Dynasty*, trans. John Blofeld (New York: Grove Press, 1958). An earlier translation was published in 1947.

16 [21] Cage, 'Composition as Process' (1958), in *Silence*, 22–3.

17 [22] Nam June Paik, 'To the "Symphony for 20 Rooms"', in *An Anthology*, ed. La Monte Young (New York: La Monte Young and Jackson Mac Low, 1963), n.p.

18 [23] Earle Brown, 'Planned Panichood', in *An Anthology*.

19 [24] Paik (1992), cited in Patricia Mellenkamp, 'The Old and the New: Nam June Paik', *Art Journal vol.* 54, no. 4 (Winter 1995) 44. The original text is from Paik, 'Interview 1992' by Otto Hahn, *Eine DATAbase*, eds. Klaus Bussmann and Florian Matzner (Stuttgart: Hatje Cantz, 1993).

20 [25] George Maciunas, 'Neo-Dada in Music, Theater, Poetry and Dance' (1962), reproduced in *In the Spirit of Fluxus*, ed. Elizabeth Armstrong and Joan Ruthfuss (Minneapolis: Walter Art Center, 1993) 157.

21 [26] Maciunas, 'Manifesto' (1963), *In the Spirit of Fluxus*, 25.

22 [28] Allan Kaprow, *Assemblage, Environments & Happenings* (New York: Abrams, 1966) 191. Italics are Kaprow's. The following quotations are drawn from this text. He published documentary photographs of both outdoor and stage 'theatre art' by nine Gutai artists, including Saburo Murakami, Kazuo Shiraga, and Atsuko Tanaka that date from 1955 to 1962.

Alexandra Munroe, extract from 'Buddhism and the Neo-Avant-Garde: Cage Zen, Beat Zen and Zen', in *Third Mind: American Artists Contemplate Asia, 1860–1989* (New York: Solomon R. Guggenheim Museum, 2009) 201–4 [some footnotes abbreviated].

Jacquelynn Baas
The Sound of the Mind//2005

[...] It is no surprise that Yoko Ono was attracted to the work of John Cage. The art historian Alexandra Munroe has foregrounded the importance to Ono and her fellow Fluxus artists of Cage's method of creating a 'score' for everything, including his artworks. According to Munroe:

> These terse instructions proposed mental and/or physical actions to be carried out by the reader/performer ... The early Fluxus scores were characterized by clarity and economy of language ... They could be performed in the mind as a thought, or

> as a physical performance before an invited audience ... Along with Brecht and the composer La Monte Young, Yoko Ono was among the first to experiment with the event score and its conceptual use of language as a form of art.[1]

An example of an event score is La Monte Young's 'draw a straight line and follow it' of 1960, which Nam June Paik performed to dramatic effect in 1962. A much earlier example is Ono's *Secret Piece*, which she dates to the summer of 1953:

> Decide on one note that you want to play. Play it with the following accompaniment:
> The woods from 5 a.m. to 8 a.m. in summer.[2]

These instructions are the verbal version of her original drawing of a score with the bass stave showing a sustained note, and a vacant treble stave with handwriting running along the top that reads: 'With the accompaniment of the birds singing at dawn'. One can imagine the wilful, twenty-year-old Sarah Lawrence poetry and composition major coming up with this score, which combines the focused intensity of Yves Klein's *Monotone-Silence Symphony* with the Zen openness of John Cage's *4'33"*.

The influence of Zen koans (paradoxical statements to which a 'solution' comes in a flash of insight) is evident throughout Ono's work. *Stone Piece (Tape Piece I)*, from 1963, instructs: 'Tape the sound of the stone ageing.'[3] *Map Piece* from 1964 says, 'Draw a map to get lost.'[4] Her *Snow Piece (Tape Piece III)* begins:

> Take a tape of the sound of the snow falling.
> This should be done in the evening.
> Do not listen to the tape.
> Cut it and use it as strings to tie gifts with.[5]

Snow Piece is a good example of the connection between Ono's work and haiku poetry, which relies on nature imagery. *Water Piece* (1964) is totally Zen in its imagery of moon and water and bucket:

> Steal a moon in the water with a bucket.
> Keep stealing until no moon is seen on the water.[6]

But not all of Ono's work is so serene. Her work tends toward the two ends of the emotional spectrum. It can be meditative and lyrical, as in *Snow Piece* or *Fly Piece*, but it can also be anguished, as in *Voice Piece for Soprano* from autumn 1961:

Scream:
1. against the wind
2. against the wall
3. against the sky[7]

Another example, from the previous winter, when Ono and La Monte Young presented a series of events in her New York loft, is *Painting to Be Stepped On*. This piece of canvas, as its title implies, was on the floor. Visitors were invited to step on it - that is, to do violence to it.

Step Piece derives much of its conceptual power from the fact that its creator is a woman. In this, it was a forerunner to Ono's impressive performance: *Cut Piece*, first performed in Kyoto in 1964. The instruction for the piece states simply: 'Cut.' In her book *Grapefruit*, she added the following gloss:

> It is usually performed by Yoko Ono coming on the stage and in a sitting position, placing a pair of scissors in front of her and asking the audience to come up on the stage, one by one, and cut a portion of her clothing (anywhere they like) and take it. The performer, however, does not have to be a woman.[8]

This apparently simple concept turns out, in performance, to be emotionally charged with violent and sexual content. Its most provocative element is contained in the last sentence of Ono's description: 'The performer, however, does not have to be a woman.' It is almost impossible to imagine a man performing this piece, which is the point.

It is instructive to compare the violence of *Cut Piece* with Nam June Paik's 1960 performance of *Étude for Pianoforte*. Paik ended the performance by cutting audience member John Cage's tie, as well as his shirt tail, with scissors. Ono reversed the situation, giving her audience the opportunity to cut her clothes. In response to their aggression she stoically maintained a meditative state that critiqued both societal expectations regarding feminine behaviour and art-world expectations that artists be self-revealing. *Cut Piece* is related to Duchamp's *Bride Stripped Bare by Her Bachelors, Even*, as both Ono and Duchamp's bride theoretically retain their emotional distance from the actions to which they are subjected. And, just as the experience of a performance of Cage's *4'33"* depends completely on its context, so Ono's experience in *Cut Piece* depended on her audience: she retained discreet remnants of her clothing in Japan and none in London, while in the United States she was left with something in between.

Ono showed *Painting to Be Stepped On* with twelve other 'instruction paintings' at George Maciunas' AG Gallery in June 1961. Although there were a few written instructions, she or Maciunas mostly gave visitors oral instructions to indicate that the thirteen unstretched, ink-covered canvases they saw were simply examples of paintings they themselves might undertake. The following year, in Tokyo, she took the radical step of exhibiting only the instructions. This, she believed at the time, 'would open up a whole new horizon for the visual arts. I was totally excited by the idea and its visual possibilities.'[9] The negative popular and critical response sent her, temporarily, into a mental institution. In retrospect, however, she remembers this as 'one of the most exciting moments of my life. It was great! It was fresh! It was a revolution! ... It was like a love affair.' But, like most passionate love affairs, 'somehow, it's too sad to do again.'[10] In exhibitions since then, Ono has resumed including an example along with each instruction.

Another of Ono's 'instruction paintings', *Smoke Painting*, is at once a meditation aid and a comment on the value of painting, as opposed to the value of what happens in the maker/viewer's mind:

> Light a canvas or any finished painting with a cigarette at any time
> for any length of time.
> See the smoke movement.
> The painting ends when the whole canvas or painting is gone.[11]

The instruction pointedly conflates the maker of the 'painting' and the viewer/reader. (Ono's instructions are, perhaps, best performed in the mind.) No matter who made the 'canvas or any finished painting' selected, the 'painter' of Ono's *Smoke Painting* is the one who 'finishes' it by burning the last bit. The 'end' of the painting thus refers at once to the completion of the instruction, the fate of the canvas, and its consumption as an occasion to 'see the smoke movement'. It is this complexity within the apparent simplicity of Ono's work that marks her as a 'fine artist', as Ad Reinhardt might have put it.

Whatever it may be for us, among the things *Smoke Painting* must have evoked for Yoko Ono was death by burning - something she may have learned more about from the fire-bombings of 1945 than she could process at the time. Her wish 'to assimilate art in life' is fundamentally a wish to make life assimilatable through art. Like Siddhartha, she wanted to put an end to suffering; like George Maciunas, she wanted to eliminate the role of the person who 'executes' art on behalf of others. She realized, however, that this utopian ambition might take a long time to achieve. In a 1965 letter proposing a show to Ivan Karp, then director of Leo Castelli's gallery, she wrote:

> I can just see a Bronxville housewife saying to her guests, 'do add a circle to my painting before you have a drink', or a guest saying, 'I was just admiring your painting by taking the previledge [sic] of adding another hole to it', etc. That is my

> dream, and something to come very much later, I suppose ... I hope many other instructions will come from people who take up this idea of painting. Soon there will be no need of artists, since people will start to write their own instructions or exchange them and paint.[12]

Karp's negative response at least showed an awareness of what she was up to:

> Thank you so much for your urgent missive. It is indeed laden with pungent metaphysics and adventurous aesthetics. It seems ... that the kind of show you have in mind fails to suit our temperament which is essentially restless, driven, aggressive, fiercely Western and concrete – not materialistic mind you – perish the thought – but terribly concrete ... you'll have to seek in other realms.[13]

In her lecture 'To the Wesleyan People', which she delivered the following year as something of a manifesto, Yoko Ono stated: 'The only sound that exists to me is the sound of the mind. My works are only to induce music of the mind in people.' She added: 'There is a wind that never dies.'[14] That wind is the moving mind, the mind that, according to John Cage, 'is part of the air',[15] the mind that is able to transcend 'the falsehood of consciousness' and fly.

1 [10] Alexandra Munroe et al., *Yes: Yoko Ono* (New York: Japan Society/Abrams, 2000) 18.

2 [11] Ono, *Grapefruit* (1964) n.p. (section 1, piece 2).

3 [12] Ibid. (section 1, piece 13).

4 [13] Ibid. (section 3, piece 17).

5 [14] Ibid. (piece 15).

6 [15] Ibid. (piece 30).

7 [16] Ibid. (piece 5).

8 [17] Ibid. ('Record of 13 Concert Piece Performances', piece 3).

9 [18] Ono, *Instruction Paintings*, no. 5.

10 [19] Ibid., 10.

11 [20] Ibid., 25.

12 [21] Ono, *Grapefruit*, n.p. (first item in the last section). Also Munroe et al., *Yes: Yoko Ono*, 286.

13 [22] Munroe et al., *Yes: Yoko Ono*, 287.

14 [23] From Yoko Ono, 'To the Wesleyan People' (1966), in ibid., 288.

15 [24] Joan Retallack, ed., *Musicage: Cage Muses on Words, Art, Music* (Hanover, New Hampshire: Wesleyan University Press, 1996) 75.

Alexandra Munroe, extract from 'Spirit of Yes: The Art and Life of Yoko Ono', in *Third Mind: American Artists Contemplate Asia, 1860–1989* (New York: Solomon R. Guggenheim Museum, 2009) 20–23.

Julia Robinson
The Sculpture of Indeterminacy: Alison Knowles' Beans and Variations//2004

Prelude: Proposition #1 – Make a Salad (1962)

As Alison Knowles stood with her assistants before an audience of more than a hundred people, preparing to perform her renowned 1962 score *Make a Salad* at the Baltimore Museum of Art in autumn 2003, there is an air of uncertainty as to how this now 'historical' piece would be understood. More than forty years since the inauguration of Fluxus and more than a decade since the death of John Cage, the original motivations and intentions behind such works have become somewhat opaque. The short, 'open' score (or 'proposition' as Knowles calls it) using everyday objects as instruments, can hardly make the same points it made to its first audience in 1962 at the Institute of Contemporary Arts in London, but perhaps now it makes different points. In the afterglow of the presentation Knowles made in Baltimore as part of the 'Work Ethic' exhibition, new questions emerged about the conceptual bases of early 1960s performance and about Knowles' role as a key figure in the 'labour-oriented' artistic practice that the exhibition defined. ['Work Ethic', curated by Helen Molesworth, Baltimore Museum of Art; Des Moines Art Center; Wexner Center for the Arts, 2003–5.]

The 2003 *Make a Salad* looked very different from earlier interpretations of the score, all of which occurred more than three decades ago. Before a vast audience (by 1962 standards) and on the grounds of a major visual arts institution as opposed to in a concert hall, the sense that this was a musical piece extending the boundaries of composition seemed to require particular emphasis. 'After two or three generations', Knowles has observed, this kind of piece 'no longer comes as a surprise.'[1] Although she knew she would not shock her audience as she stood before them with her fellow performers, their knives poised for a marathon of swift and rhythmic chopping, the sheer aesthetic pleasure of piles of carrots, radishes, lettuces and cucumbers loaded on the long table in front of the performers threatened to dilute the reading of the piece. Knowles sensed the value of bracketing her own music of chopping, pouring and tossing with conventional musical performances (selections from Mozart were chosen and a cellist and a violinist played their pieces before and after Knowles' performance). The juxtaposition of conventional musical pieces with one composed of everyday sounds dramatized the sense of both rupture and continuity within Knowles' composition. Without the Mozart these aspects may have been elided, the *Make a Salad* performance reduced to a gesture of mere iconoclasm. The audience was therefore given the opportunity to perceive the radical expansiveness of Knowles' practice, its role in extending musicality, through the subtle explicatory power of its presentation.

The brevity and openness of Knowles' textual 'proposition' allows for great freedom in the realization of the piece, and it includes the audience from the outset. Although it was Marcel Duchamp who first argued that the spectator completes the work, it was the sphere of performance and the radical scoring practices developed by John Cage that provided the impetus for Knowles and her peers to incorporate duration and experience into the very conception of the works they created. Disavowing convention and sacrificing structure, they made experience a kind of medium, as important as any other. The 'Work Ethic' exhibition rightly includes Knowles as a representative of Fluxus strategies, but what seems called for now is a closer examination of the ways in which Knowles has developed devices like the score and other Cagean and Fluxus models toward a sustained practice that demands its own unique terms.

Shaping Indeterminacy

The concept of indeterminacy stands as a source of the earliest affinity between Knowles and certain of her peers – particularly those closest to Cage – in the years leading up to the 1962 inauguration of Fluxus. While Cage had established (and taught) indeterminacy within the framework of his course 'Experimental Composition', those artists who adopted the concept took it in substantially different directions in their own projects. Indeterminacy created the preconditions for a work of art (or a performance) to be arranged by an artist without the artist knowing exactly how it would turn out. So rather than composing a score note by note, so to speak, the artists developed scores that operated as templates, open to expansion in the arena of realization. Elements of chance were incorporated into the temporal framework so that each performance of a single score might differ greatly, far beyond the expectations of the composer. The radicality of the concept of indeterminate composition lies in its mandate that the artist intentionally give up control of the work's outcome. Such a notion flies in the face of every idea of mastery bonded to the traditional work of art. In its complete disavowal of the unilateral decision-making process that would define a work of art in its entirety, indeterminacy split artists of the early 1960s between those who felt liberated by it and those who could not accept it.

For several artists momentarily associated with the Fluxus group who did not adopt Fluxus but instead made Happenings or shifted in altogether different directions – artists such as Allan Kaprow, Joseph Beuys and Wolf Vostell – the purely indeterminate work closest to the musical model of Cage was not desirable. The obvious divide between Fluxus and Happenings, which turns on this issue, is illustrated by the great difference between works by these latter artists and those of an artist like Knowles or her close colleague George Brecht (both of whom made the release of the work a kind of ur-principle of its formation). As two well-known modes of 1960s performance that have so often been discussed together, Fluxus and Happenings might be set apart through consideration of the level of the artist/composer's control over the work, from conception through to realization. This division emerges partly from the enduring proximity of Fluxus to music. Scores by Fluxus artists premiered at New Music festivals in Europe, inserted into the programmes of a vast, pre-existing sphere of radical musical production. In contrast, Happenings were defined almost exclusively in America (specifically out of the New York scene) and quickly abandoned music, save for transplating the score component of the Cagean model and transforming it into a set of increasingly programmatic instructions. For the few artists (like Knowles and Brecht) who pursued the bilateral operation of indeterminacy (as conceptual foundation) and the score (as structural foundation), the combination of openness and pre-established limitations proved enormously generative.

Score and Sole

Proposition #6

Shoes of Your Choice

A member of the audience is invited to come forward to a microphone if one is available and describe a pair of shoes, the ones he [sic] is wearing or another pair. He is encouraged to tell where he got them, the size, colour, why he likes them, etc.[2]

In the period that Knowles conceived and premiered *Make a Salad*, she produced another important score, *Shoes of Your Choice*, which was performed at the same concert in London at the ICA in autumn 1962. On that occasion Knowles walked out on the stage and announced the score to the audience. In a now memorable response, the British Pop artist Richard Hamilton rose to his feet, removed one shoe, and embarked upon a long and detailed description of it, one that involved intricate justifications for the particular heel height and witty explanations about the colour and the overall rationale for his 'choice'.

Shoes of Your Choice is a lucid illustration of indeterminate composition. It suggests the difference between Knowles' term, a 'proposition', and a conventional score, which would be composed from beginning to end. Like much of the art of the early 1960s, *Shoes of Your Choice* incorporates the everyday, the found object, into the frame of aesthetic consideration. But through its indeterminate nature, this score allows for an open work whose ultimate form and duration can never be known until each performance of it is complete. A dynamic of spontaneity helps define the found object (which also is or becomes a readymade). *Shoes of Your Choice* represents shoes as if for the first time, constructing them out of a kaleidoscopic constellation of perspectives. Unlike the consumer items that appear as painting or sculpture in Pop art, for example, the shoes Knowles represents do not parrot reified object relations. They are neither the simulacra of the shop window (echoed in art) nor the unilateral view of an object from the mind of the artist. Knowles' shoes take shape in unfolding time; they are performed into being, continually defined and redefined according to the idiosyncrasies of successive personal accounts. [...]

1 [footnote 2 in source] Alison Knowles, conversation with the author, February 2004.

2 [7] Alison Knowles, 'Shoes of Your Choice', reproduced in *by Alison Knowles*, Great Bear Pamphlet (New York: Something Else Press, 1965). In this pamphlet the work is dated as March 1963, with the première announced as Douglass College, New Brunswick. Knowles has explained that this was an error on the part of the publisher and editor, Dick Higgins, and that the piece was actually conceived and performed several months earlier (at the ICA in London, 21 October 1962).

Julia Robinson, extract from 'The Sculpture of Indeterminacy: Alison Knowles' Beans and Variations', *Art Journal*, vol. 63, no. 4 (Winter 2004) 97–100 [footnotes edited].

David Frankel
William Anastasi//2007

For perhaps four decades, William Anastasi has been a sort of New York art-world secret: a conceptual artist who in the early 1960s began to generate extremely original ideas that seemed to predict a range of later works by other artists but at the same time to have been only tangentially influential, for while those later works made it into the journals, textbooks and museums, Anastasi's own did to a far lesser degree. Yet artists and critics who saw his shows back then tend to remember them well. For others who came to New York later, but who have met Anastasi and talked with him about his work (the best, sometimes the only way to learn about it when it wasn't widely on view), his story has seemed a cautionary tale and his career an enigma: here was a man who seemed to have done all his time could have asked of an artist, and to have done it early, yet who had somehow failed to make for himself the name he deserved.

Anastasi has lately been getting some overdue recognition, of which this recent show [The Drawing Center, New York, 2007] was hopefully just a small part. Except for one sculpture and a couple of drawings, all of the works here re-created pieces that Anastasi first made in the early to mid 1960s. All started with a verbal prescription: in *Displaced Site*, 1966, for example, Anastasi wrote, 'Construct a corrugated cardboard box. Remove sufficient plaster from a wall to house half of the box horizontally. Fill box; insert.' Supplied with this linguistic recipe, anyone could make this work, including the different, older Anastasi of forty years later. In his present realization of it, the box of plaster rubble is three or four inches wide and high and is slotted into the hole made for it in the wall at about chest height. Other pieces – a work of two rectangular aluminium elements propped against the wall, a mural of carefully poured black paint, another piece involving the removal of plaster – were equally reproducible by others, as was *Sink*, the only object here with pre-existing longevity: the work consists of a solid steel plate on the floor, onto which, since 1963, Anastasi has regularly poured a film of water, replacing it when it evaporates. The pitted and corroded result certainly has auratic presence, but it is more that of a rock in a stream bed – aged, impersonal and tactile – than of any conventional sculptural skin.

The show evoked a number of New York artists of the 1960s: Sol LeWitt and Lawrence Weiner, in the idea of the verbal instruction; Robert Smithson, in the displacement and display of raw material (in this case plaster); Richard Serra, whose *Verb List* of 1967–68 harmonizes with Anastasi's basic sculptural and painterly actions of propping, relocating, pouring, and so on. Even as Anastasi shares interests with these others, though, the metaphor of the rock in the stream bed points in another direction that differentiates him and perhaps unifies these aesthetic impulses, at least in his handling of them, and that is toward a kind of artistic anonymity, a denial of signature, a relaxation of authorial control. Indeed, for the show's catalogue Anastasi selected a number of quotations referencing Eastern philosophies and religions such as Buddhism, of which the most terse and dramatic – 'The moment you open your mouth, you're wrong', from the fifth-century BCE Chinese philosopher Mo Tzu – seems quite strange for a conceptual artist pushing art toward linguistic precepts. And here one remembers an earlier New York generation, notably John Cage (with whom Anastasi used to play chess daily), and his interest in the *I Ching* – whose method of getting out of one's personality is to surrender oneself to chance. A rewritten history of conceptual art in which Anastasi featured more prominently might discuss a broader range of spiritual influences (in every sense of the word spiritual) than is currently associated with the form.

David Frankel, 'William Anastasi: The Drawing Center', *Artforum* (October 2007) 370.

William Anastasi
Interview with Thomas McEvilley//2005

William Anastasi In 1963 I compressed a tube of Titanium white in a vice at the top of a vertical canvas. The released paint rolled down the surface as gravity painted the picture. And then in 1964 I did a series in which I sandwiched open tubes of paint between Plexiglas sheets, then screwed the sheets together to squeeze the paint out.

Thomas McEvilley These predicted the throwing and pouring pieces, in that the paint finally assumes a random shape.

Anastasi Yes.

McEvilley The limestone frame also involves the theme of blocked vision. Like the wall removals, what you see when you look at it is not a window into another world but real material stuff actually present in this world. Since the limestone is a blank, opaque surface with no actual picture it relates to the idea of blindness, obstruction of vision, and so on, as in your blind drawings and paintings.

Anastasi Yes, I started those in 1962 or 1963.

McEvilley You were doing those dotted Constellations blind then, while listening to 'The Well-Tempered Clavier' [J.S. Bach].

Anastasi Yes, and during the whole period we've been discussing I continued to do blind drawings and paintings. I was doing the scribbles with black lead pencil and closed eyes by 1964.

McEvilley They were not exhibited until the 1980s?

Anastasi Virginia Dwan wanted to show the 96 'well-tempered' Constellations in the 1960s, but we never got around to it.

McEvilley But I have the impression that blind drawings and paintings really came to the forefront of your work in the 1980s.

Anastasi In the early 1970s I made the first large blind drawings. Then starting in 1977 I would go downtown on the subway a lot to play chess with John Cage. I would fill my pocket with a couple dozen sharpened pencils. Then on the subway I would put on firing range headphones to make it silent. It also makes people less likely to interrupt me. I would sit erect with my back away from the seat, with a pencil in each hand and a sheet of paper on a board on my lap. I would hold the pencils like darts and lightly touch the surface. The train ride is lurching enough so you need an external point to keep your balance; I would use the pencils for that and allow the swaying of my body as the train careened around curves to make the drawing. I bet I've done a thousand of those. I would ride from 137th street to 18th street and after the game back again.

McEvilley The results are extraordinary. It's interesting too that you got better at it, though some of the early ones are beautiful in a less knowing, more innocent way. This seems to go back to your paradoxical discovery, in 1962 or so, that you got better visual results with your eyes closed.

Anastasi You can see what a treasure randomness is. When you, for example, make random collocations of words through clipping or whatever, the results are always heartbreakingly beautiful.

McEvilley Yes, that's an amazing thing to contemplate, when we think of all our concern to control, and how it conventionalizes events. Others have done blind drawings – Robert Morris, I think, for example – but you seem to have made a special affirmation of them.

Anastasi I seldom do drawings with my eyes open anymore. The large blind drawings of course aren't done on the subway but in my studio. The subway drawings are timed by the ride; in the studio I set a time beforehand, usually between half an hour and four hours, and usually execute them non-stop. [...]

William Anastasi and Thomas McEvilley, extract from interview, in McEvilley, *The Triumph of Anti-Art* (Kingston, New York: McPherson & Company, 2005) 132–5.

Robert Rauschenberg
Interview with Dorothy Seckler//1965

Dorothy Seckler Coming back to the other thing you mentioned – that you had been very closely associated with John Cage and other musicians – I know many people have assumed that because of this association, accident – a philosophy, an outlook of accident – was important to your work, since it had apparently been in Cage's. And I gather that this was not your feeling, that you were once quoted as saying you didn't believe in accident any more than anything else. Was that a strongly developed attitude?

Robert Rauschenberg I was very interested in many of John's chance operations. Each one seemed quite unique to me. I liked the sense of experimentation that he was involved in. But painting is just a different medium and I never could figure out an interesting way to use any kind of programmed activity. And even though chance deals with the unexpected and the unplanned, it still has to be organized before it can exist. I think maybe chance works better in a situation like music because music exists over a period of time, and you don't maintain constantly that you can't refer back from one area to another area. One's familiarity or lack of familiarity with time is very different from, say, the size of a canvas, which is what I would compare it to. One can see that a canvas is six feet by eight feet, say, quite accurately. But you can spend two minutes and think it's five or thirty seconds and it's just a different bed for activities there. The only thing I could get with chance, and I was never able to use it, was that I would end up with something quite geometric, or the spirit that I was interested in indulging in was gone. I felt as though I was carrying out an idea rather than witnessing an unknown idea taking shape. If this is called accident I certainly used accident, and I certainly used the fact that wet paint will run, and lots of other things. It seems to me it's just a kind of friendly relationship with your materials, where you want them for what they are rather than for what you could make out of them. I did a twenty-foot print and John Cage was involved in that because he was the only person I knew in New York who had a car and who would be willing to do this. And I poured paint on one Sunday morning. I glued, it must have been fifty sheets of paper together; it was the largest paper I had, and stretched it out on the street. He had an A Model Ford then and he drove through the paint and onto the paper; the only direction he had was to try to stay on the paper. And he did a beautiful job of it. Now I consider that my print. It's just like working with lithography. You may not be a qualified printer but there again, like the driver of the car, someone who does know the press very well collaborates with you and they are part of the machinery, just as you are part of another necessary aspect that it takes to make anything. Would you call that accident?

Seckler Actually, I'm not sure I'd call anything accident. When paint drips, it's like an insurance company seeing a man cross the street and be hit by a car. To that particular individual, it's an accident. But to insurance companies who have tables showing how many people will be hit by a car that year, it's an expected event.

Rauschenberg Yes.

Seckler And in a sense though you don't know exactly where a drip will run, it may wiggle a little in the middle, you know that there's gravity and you know that paint will drip and so on.

Rauschenberg You know that it's not going to run up.

Seckler That's right. So there's a certain element in which some of the things that were called 'chance' weren't.

Rauschenberg Anyway, they weren't all done with ... I know maybe this is what you're getting at ... they weren't done with some kind of wild abandon where you just shut your eyes and throw things about.

Seckler Yes, well, I don't think anyone ever imagines that would be possible. Now one other thing that I thought might be a parallel ...

Rauschenberg I'm not saying that they're better for it. But that just never interested me.

Seckler ... was the use of intervals, because I understand in John Cage's work that he often emphasizes interval and waiting and silences a great deal. And I notice that you have also emphasized leaving open spaces in your paintings and areas in which there is less happening and those work very beautifully in relationship to the things that are happening very fast in other parts of the canvas; and I thought perhaps that there may have been a kind of sharing of feeling about this kind of thing, of the importance of interval and openness.

Rauschenberg Well, it's no secret that we admired each other's work very much, and still do. But I think that those are like some feeling of variety within a restricted area that is important if you're dealing with multiplicity and variation and inclusion as your content. Then any feeling of a complete feeling of consistence or sameness is a violation of that attitude. I had to try consciously to make work that would imply the kind of richness and complexity I saw around me, and I think those things just got into it. One of my painter friends says I'm awfully good at the edges. It was intended as a joke but I think this may be true. There's been a conscious attempt for me to not treat one area – whether I only have half an inch more before I hit the wall, or whether it's dead centre – with any kind of dramatic preference. I dealt with that several ways. One is with a kind of simple-minded, formal idea about composition, just putting something of no consequence dead centre so that when you look there, yes, there it is, but you see that this certainly doesn't matter any more than anything else; that's not what the centre is for. So that idea of a sort of relaxed symmetry is something I've been concerned with for years, because I think symmetry is a neutral shape, as opposed to a form of design.

Robert Rauschenberg and Dorothy Seckler, extract from interview (New York, 21 December 1965), Archives of American Art, Smithsonian Institution, Washington, D.C.

Robert Rauschenberg
Interview with Alain Sayag//1981

Alain Sayag Why don't you like perfect photography?

Robert Rauschenberg If by perfect photography one means a maximum of contrast, light and dark and high focus, then I don't necessarily want the perfect photograph. Just as in all other artforms, the object itself dictates your possibilities. Sometimes you make all the right decisions, sometimes you can only be either right or very wrong, and sometimes the wrong makes just as interesting a photograph as being right. But you're always working in collaboration with the amount of light you have, the scale of the objects, your own physicality – such as your size and the distance between you and the ideal photograph – and everything is moving. So I'm quite taken aback when I get something that appears to be technically a good photograph, because it's not necessarily my intention. One gets as much information as a witness of activity from a fleeting glance, like a quick look, sometimes in motion, as one does staring at the subject. Because even if you remain stationary your mind wanders, and it's that kind of activity that I'd like to get into the photograph – a confirmation of the fact that everything is moving. [...]

Sayag Your photographs are all full frame. Do you ever crop your images?

Rauschenberg I don't crop. Photography is like diamond cutting. If you miss you miss. There's no difference with painting. If you don't cut you have to accept the whole image. You wait until life is in the frame, then you have the permission to click. I like the adventure of waiting until the whole frame is full.

Sayag You don't miss very often, from looking at the contact sheets.

Rauschenberg It's because I wait; I wait until it's there again. Whatever is there is a truth, but a truth you have to believe in. What you see in front of you is a fact. You click when you believe it's the truth. The information is waiting to become in essence a concentration, concentrated so clearly that it can be projected back into real life, into your recognition. It could be any size.

Sayag You've said that time spent in the darkroom is a special kind of time that can't be measured. What makes it special?

Rauschenberg It's your final contact with an experience that you had outside the darkroom. It's sort of your contract with that experience. Sometimes I've taken photographs and just felt so excited that I could barely hold the camera steady, and the photo was boring. So it's the final contract, verification of the authenticity that began when you saw an image and decided to photograph.

Sayag When I look through the contact sheets there is not a lot of difference among them. Are your selections made only on the basis of size and quality and the final image?

Rauschenberg Right, but if there is inconsistency, then I re-evaluate the aesthetic of how important the technical is. Actually, with the new cameras, it's very difficult to make too many mistakes. The technology built into the camera insists that you do things right whether you want to or not. It would almost take a genius to bypass the electronics that are forced onto the camera and therefore the art. Perfection is static, and a flow continues the current. So perfection is not one of the goals because it's a dead end.

Sayag Does that mean that perfection is death, and instead you want to recreate at least a sensation?

Rauschenberg The eye that looks for perfection is the one that's anticipating a controlled retirement (no matter what the age). So with the photo. The photo can insist on reviewing moments that were unseen, or not know they were seen but passed in viewing. John Cage said (I don't know if they were his own remarks or Zen) his goal was not to get somewhere, he just wanted to enjoy the trip. That's the quality I want in all of my work, that a specific goal or accomplishment would be allied to the fact. I noticed a long time ago, when I went to a strange country, that I had the best time and the greatest experiences when I thought I was lost, because when you are lost you look so much harder.

Sayag What are the differences between the image you find and the image you make? Is there any difference in your mind?

Rauschenberg No, actually taking the photo accomplishes several things. One, it forces me to be in direct contact, intimately, unprotected, in an ambiguous outside world and therefore improve my sight. Also, it gives me a stockpile of both experiences and literal images to draw on for other works. So it's the experience of taking the photograph that keeps my mind open to unprogrammed images, uncontrolled, and then permits me to handle them rawly or allow them to be digested in a cacophony of other specifics.

Sayag For a long time you didn't include many of your own images in your work. Why?

Rauschenberg Until recently I've used my own photo imagery in paintings, lithographs and engravings only occasionally. I designed a dance set for Trisha Brown and her company that required several hundred unique photographs. For me to edit and select that many images required me to take around a thousand new photographs in a short period and I became addicted again. It's heightened my desire to look. The constant survey of changing light and shadows sharpens all the awareness necessary not only to make photographs but as 'fertilizer' to promote growth and change in any artistic project. Henri Cartier-Bresson said shyly that he only used his camera as an excuse to see the world. [...]

Robert Rauschenberg and Alain Sayag, extract from interview, in *Robert Rauschenberg: Photographs* (New York: Pantheon Books, 1981); reprinted in *Robert Rauschenberg: Works/Writings/Interviews*, ed. Sam Hunter (Barcelona: Ediciones Polígrafa, 2006) 151–2.

Jasia Reichardt
On Chance and Mark Boyle//1966

[...] Among the manifestations based on chance during the past ten years, including those of Georges Mathieu, Salvador Dalí, Piero Manzoni, Yves Klein and William Burroughs, the aleatory systems applied to interpretations of concrete poetry, musical composition and transformable works of art, one of the most interesting and moving solutions has been that reached by Mark Boyle. The essential attitude at the basis of his activities is the total acceptance of results which these provoke. In relation to the recent pictures which he calls presentations, this may not seem surprising – they are aesthetically pleasing (which is irrelevant), and they are original (which isn't, except to Boyle himself). The presentations are a relatively recent development, so it might be worthwhile initially to consider some of his earlier attempts at harnessing chance – i.e. the events which he has been organizing since 1963.

As the word '*Happening*' suggests a dramatic performance, Mark Boyle decided to call his total manifestations 'Events'. This presupposes a less deliberate way in which the unpredictable element is used, despite any preparation, rehearsal or expectations. Of these I have seen only five. Perhaps one that illustrates most accurately Boyle's approach was his item 'Any Play or No Play' – the final piece of a happening/event at Theatre Royal, Stratford East, London, in 1965. While the front curtain was down Boyle invited the audience from the stalls to come on to the stage through the side door. When the curtain went up five minutes later, the stage was full of miscellaneous people milling round, handling the various stage props and trying on the costumes scattered around in vast quantities. Members of the audience, finding themselves in the position of actors, felt that something was expected of them but without being sure what it might be. There were no directions. During the twenty minutes that followed nothing occurred that would suggest that the event was in any structured. The jukebox which was brought on to the stage in order to merge the proceedings with a party failed to work. The event could have been described as an essay in anticlimax – no one was happy about it except Mark Boyle, who accepted the outcome unreservedly as something that had occurred as it was meant to. If one provokes chance the result is what it is. The unexpected becomes the fulfilment of expectation. For Boyle the evening would have been more interesting had there been no props at all on the stage. This has also something to do with his attitude to boredom. To him no manifestation of life, whether provoked or not, is intrinsically boring. Boredom exists in the mind of the recipient, or consumer, spectator, and in his frustrated expectations, heightened by paying a sum of money at the door for which he wants to be recompensed in some way.

The events were the result of Boyle's search for an absolute and total work. Originally he attempted to achieve the same end through use of symbols in his assemblages. The archetypal work of this phase was his bed. This construction dealt with stages of life at which a human being ceases to be a self-conscious organism and becomes a part of the general forces of nature – birth, sex and death. All Boyle's poems and assemblages prior to the events were about these experiences expressed through use of deliberate symbolism. The bed – a complex construction which incorporated a hierarchy of objects representing various degrees of reality – was furthermore completely utilitarian and had been used by Boyle himself. The objects included: realistic painting, statues, wax casts of diseased faces, two television sets (one positive, one negative), mirror, window through the adjacent wall, and the bed itself. This and his other assemblages stressed the dichotomy between the aesthetic and the meaningful. The aesthetic quality which one might or might not find in his work is irrelevant to the concept and intent underlying these activities.

The presentations that Boyle started working on in 1965 deal with yet another type of exploration of chance. These consist of real street, beach and bomb site surfaces, permanently fixed with a plastic produced by Shell called 'Epikote', and shown vertically, i.e. hanging on the wall. The only deliberate act of transformation in this procedure is the placing of a horizontal surface vertically. The presentations are made as follows: with his house as the centre, Boyle has chosen a strip of London, approximately one mile wide and extending one mile north and one mile south of Shepherds Bush. This strip cut out of a map, scale fifteen inches to the mile, hangs on a wall in his studio. The selection of a site is made by throwing a dart at the map. When the site is located as exactly as possible, Boyle throws down a rod which represents a predetermined side of the picture, and thus the exact area is established. Plastic rubber is poured on to the surface to which any loose particles and fragments immediately adhere. The rubber is removed and later, in the studio, 'Epikote' is poured on to the underside of the rubber mould, which is eventually peeled off, leaving an exact replica of the site on the surface of the plastic.

Boyle aims at making as perfect a presentation of a given area as possible. Ideally there should be no difference whatever between a photograph of the site and one of the finished work. 'Epikote', which is tougher than concrete, is an ideal though expensive medium, and a five-gallon drum, which costs approximately £25, is just enough for a picture 7 x 7 ft, depending on the sort of material that is being presented (bricks, dust, leaves, sand, etc). This is the size Boyle would like to work in but at the moment finds too expensive.

The financial aspect also makes certain sites impracticable, as the equipment has still to be perfected. Apart from the site on the chosen four-square-mile strip of London, Boyle has also worked on a beach at Camber, Sussex, and has made a number of studies from it, which were included in his recent exhibition at Indica Gallery in London ['Presentation by Mark Boyle', 16 July–early August 1966].

Several points of great interest emerge from Mark Boyle's recent works with 'Epikote'. The viewer is presented with images which are intensely lyrical and aesthetic, although these qualities are as unintentional as any other effect which they create. The relationships of leaves, cigarette butts, bricks and shells are there by virtue of being isolated from their general environment. The process employed discards both art conditioning and anti-conditioning – it runs parallel to conscious attitudes of what art is or is not, should or should not manifest. If one finds the lack of such attitudes permissive and lacking in heroic declaration, then a whole sphere of creative activity as yet unexplored will be cut off from one's experience. Seeing Boyle's presentation in a gallery, one accepts them as an art experience – but what in fact happens is that the spectator is invited to look at something in a way to which he is not accustomed – to respond to and to examine nature in a critical way.

Jasia Reichardt, extract from 'On Chance and Mark Boyle', *Studio International* (October 1966) 164–5.

Robert Morris
Notes on Sculpture, Part 4//1969

[...] Certain art is now using as its beginning and as its means, stuff, substances in many states – from chunks to particles, to slime, to whatever – and prethought images are neither necessary nor possible. Alongside this approach is chance, contingency, indeterminacy – in short, the entire area of process. Ends and means are brought together in a way that never existed before in art. In a very qualified way, Abstract Expressionism brought the two together. But with the exception of a few artists, notably Pollock and Louis, the formal structure of Cubism functioned as an end toward which the activity invariably converged and in this sense was a separate end, image or form prior to the activity. Any activity, with perhaps the exception of unfocused play, projects some more-or-less specific end, and in this sense separates the process from the achievement. But images need not be identified with ends in art. Although priorities do exist in the work under discussion, they are not preconceived imagistic ones. The priorities have to do with acknowledging and even predicting perceptual conditions for the work's existence. Such conditions are neither forms nor ends nor part of the process. Yet they are priorities and can be intentions. The work illustrated here [Morris' *Threadwaste* and a Robert Smithson *Mirror Displacement*] involves itself with these considerations – that which is studio produced as well as that which deals with existing exterior zones of the world. The total separation of ends and means in the production of objects, as well as the concern to make manifest idealized mental images, throws extreme doubt on the claim that the Pragmatic attitude informs Minimal art of the 1960s. To begin with the concrete physicality of matter rather than images allows for a change in the entire profile of three-dimensional art: from particular forms to ways of ordering, to methods of production and, finally, to perceptual relevance.

So far all art has made manifest images, whether it arrived at them (as the art in question) or began with them. The open, lateral, random aspect of the present work does in fact provide a general sort of image. Even more than this, it recalls an aspect of Pollock's imagery by these characteristics. Elsewhere I have made mention of methodological ties to Pollock through emphasis in the work on gravity and a direct use of materials ['Anti Form' (1968)]. But to identify its resultant 'field' aspect very closely with Pollock's work is to focus on too narrow a formalistic reading. Similar claims were made when Minimal art was identified with the forms found in previous Constructivism.

One aspect of the work worth mentioning is the implied attack on the iconic character of how art has always existed. In a broad sense art has always been an object, static and final, even though structurally it may have been a depiction or existed as a fragment. What is being attacked, however, is something more than art as icon. Under attack is the rationalistic notion that art is a form of work that results in a finished product. Marcel Duchamp, of course, attacked the Marxist notion that labour was an index of value, but Readymades are traditionally iconic art objects. What art now has in its hands is mutable stuff which need not arrive at the point of being finalized with respect to either time or space. The notion that work is an irreversible process ending in a static icon-object no longer has much relevance.

The detachment of art's energy from the craft of tedious object production has further implications. This reclamation of process refocuses art as an energy driving to change perception. (From such a point of view the concern with 'quality' in art can only be another form of consumer research – a conservative concern involved with comparisons between static, similar objects within closed sets.) The attention given to both matter and its inseparableness from the process of change is not an emphasis on the phenomenon of means. What is revealed is that art itself is an activity of change, of disorientation and shift, of violent discontinuity and mutability, of the willingness for confusion even in the service of discovering new perceptual modes.

At present the culture is engaged in the hostile and deadly act of immediate acceptance of all new perceptual art moves, absorbing through institutionalized recognition every art act. The work discussed has not been excepted.

Robert Morris, extract from 'Notes on Sculpture, Part 4', *Artforum* (April 1969); reprinted in *Continuous Project Altered Daily: The Writings of Robert Morris* (Cambridge, Massachusetts: The MIT Press, 1993) 67–9 [footnotes not included].

Guy Brett
The Logic of the Web//2001

[Focusing on an aspect of art in Brazil from the beginning of the 1960s to the 1970s we find] a fascinating paradox: the fondness of Brazilian artists during this period for the formats of the box and the book. Why, when they were concerned with projecting art out into life-situations, were they so interested in these restricted and contained vehicles, with their associations of the library and the archive? One thinks of Hélio Oiticica's *Box Bolides*, Mira Schendel's flip-books and strange bindings, Lygia Clark's determination to record the stages of her development in the form of a manipulable book, Raymundo Colares' *Gibis*,[1] Anna Maria Maiolino's *Trajectórias*, Antonio Manuel's *Hot Urns*,[2] Artur Barrio's *Book of Meat* and his Notebooks, Cildo Meireles' ironic play on the box-form, Waltercio Caldas' *Perception Conductors*, and, of course, Lygia Pape's Boxes and Books. Perhaps they were attracted by very reason of the paradox involved, by the irony to be extracted from the gulf between the manageable, calm void of the page or container, easily within a hand's reach, and the uncontrollable reality all around, whether of 'nature' or 'city'. Interest in the book and the box accompanies closely these artists' attachment to the ordering rationale of geometric Constructivism. This attachment, as Paulo Venancio Filho has written of Raymundo Colares' works, could not be utopian but rather 'a ceaseless confrontation with our permanent chaos.'[3]

As if in subtle recognition of this dilemma, when she came to photograph pages from the *Book of Creation* (*Livro da Criação*, 1959), Pape took them out of the binding or box in which they normally reside, out of the neutral studio or gallery, and propped them in the streets of Rio. Working with the photographer Mauricio Cirne, she placed the 'cultivated earth' on a car hood, the 'keel' unnoticed on a rock as bodies dive into the sea, the 'fire unity' on the stall of a roadside drink-seller, beside the bottles of a strong Brazilian popular drink known as 'Paulista fire'. The idea was to 'take the book for a walk in the world'.[4] The contradiction was given a complete turn to demonstrate its fruitfulness.

In other words, and paradoxically, as much as 'containing chaos', the drive among the members of the avant-garde in Brazil during this period was to liberate the inherited paradigms of order with the influx of lived experience. The advanced thinkers, whatever discipline to which they originally belonged – visual arts, poetry, architecture, film – moved into an area of experimental fluidity, of polymorphous playfulness, where these categories were allowed to mingle and transform one another. It is as if artists' interest in the box/book were part of a polymathic interest in space as such, especially in the way space is directly experienced by the body-mind. In a sequence of experiments by poets at the turn of the 1960s, as Ferreira Gullar has pointed out, the *Book-poem* led to the *Spatial-poem*. An accentuation of the feel of the book between the hands led to a more sculptural participation – where, for example, the 'reader' would lift up a blue cube under which a word was written – which in turn led to a full bodily involvement.[5] Words plunged into the sea like a body (Regina Vater, Rubens Gerchman). Poetry discovered its interface with architecture. It is striking to what extent architectural space also exercised the thinking of many Brazilian artists of this period, Lygia Pape prominent among them. Architecture furthered the same interest in the enclosure of space vis-à-vis the limitless openness of the world or universe, the dialectic of inside and outside. The extraordinary dynamic of this Brazilian fusion is still to be appreciated internationally.[6]

The 'Rio' photos of Pape's *Book of Creation*, therefore, epitomize the two worlds of order and chaos in which her art moves. She confounds these worlds, conflating them, making bridges between them, setting them apart, in a process that can never be finished, and intuits a new kind of structural model. Writing in 1983, Mario Pedrosa hinted, somewhat cryptically but very interestingly, at the existence of such a model in Pape's work. She brings, he said, 'the touch of contemporaneity to the structure/state in which everything is again what it was not, and the post and the pre-images restore the cycle of creativity'.[7] Pape herself has described this structure as a 'web', understood from the point of view of the person – any person – who is both subject to it and weaves it. One of its incarnations is the city itself:

> In my comings and goings by car through the city (I drive a lot), I began to develop a new type of relationship to do with urban space, as though I were a kind of

spider, weaving webs. It is all this 'cross here', 'turn next corner' and so on, up and down viaducts, in and out of tunnels. Me and everybody else ... It is as though we were getting a bird's-eye view of the city: it was an immense web or maze. I called it 'Magnetized spaces' because it was something living. As though I was right inside there pulling on this thread that has no end.

The urban street-seller is one such example of the creation of magnetized spaces:

> He comes to his corner, opens up his little case and starts his sales pitch, suddenly creating a kind of magnetization. People flock around him, identifying with that irregular, sometimes brief, sometimes long-winded patter. And then, all of a sudden, he shuts his mouth, closes his case; the space dwindles into nothingness.[8]

The image of the web could have many meanings, just as it appears in Pape's work in many forms, from the physical to the 'virtual'. It could have a general meaning by giving visibility to a conceptual structure that is light, elastic, fragile but strong, that can preserve its geometry in awkward corners and precarious situations. It could have a more particular meaning as a metaphor for the flexibility needed, during the late 1960s and 1970s, as Brazil sank further into military dictatorship, to preserve the utopian drive of experimentation, while rethinking the role of the aesthetic in relation to harsh political and social realities. [...]

1 [footnote 14 in source] In Pape's recollection, Colares began making his *Gibis* [from 1968 onwards – artist's books named after the Portuguese word, *gibi*, for a comic book] after seeing her *Book of Creation*. Pape describes his 'reading' of her book as 'very rich and positive', as it resulted in the younger artist's very different sort of book. Lygia Pape, *Entrevista a Lúcia Carneiro e Ileana Pradilla*, (Rio de Janeiro: Lacerda Editores, 1999) 68.

2 [15] Originally, these were sealed boxes containing poems, photos, etc., and requiring violence to open them.

3 [16] Paulo Venancio Filho, 'Pintura e caos/Painting and Chaos', in *Raymundo Colares: Trajetórias* (Rio de Janeiro: Centro Cultural Light, 1997) 29; 31.

4 [17] Lygia Pape to Guy Brett, 13 July 1998.

5 [18] Ferreira Gullar, 'Lygia Clark's Trajectory', in *Lygia Clark* (Barcelona: Fundació Antoni Tàpies, 1998) 62.

6 [19] A vital part of this dynamic is undoubtedly the dialogue between the artists themselves, which has been so intricate and subtle that there is no need to get bogged down in ideas of linear evolutions of work or orders of precedence. To take one example, the use of the corner space. Lygia Pape's corner installation of linear threads, *Tteia no. 1* (1978), proposes a beautiful commentary on Cildo Meireles' transportable, mocked-up, domestic room-corners, *Virtual Space: Corners* (1967/68). Two artists' investigation of space see-saws between the

schematic and the organic, the day-to-day and the sublime.

7 [20] Mario Pedrosa, preface to *Lygia Pape* (Rio de Janeiro: Funarte, 1983) 1.

8 [21] Lygia Pape, in *Lygia Pape* (1983) 47. An English translation by Eric Charles Drysdale was inserted into this volume. For two photographs of such 'magnetized spaces', see *Lygia Pape: Gavea de tocaia* (São Paulo: Cosac & Naify, 2000) 50; 52–3.

Guy Brett, extract from 'The Logic of the Web', in *Forma Brazil* (New York: The Americas Society, 2001) n.p; revised version of text first published in *Lygia Pape: Gavea de tocaia* (São Paulo: Cosac & Naify, 2000) 305–15.

Cildo Meireles
Interview with Hans Ulrich Obrist//2000

Hans Ulrich Obrist Instructions have played a major role in your work since the 1960s; what place do you give to these instructions, these 'directions for use'?

Cildo Meireles Most often I construct my work from language. I try to distance myself from a pathological approach to the artwork (as something only the artist can produce). I prefer to imagine pieces that can be made by anyone at any time.

Obrist Anywhere?

Meireles Yes, by anyone, at any time, anywhere. I've coined an expresson to designate that type of work: '*fonomenos*'. It's a play on words: *fenomeno* (phenomenon) and *fonema* (phoneme). In English, it could be written '*phonomenon*', with a 'ph'. The first *phonomenon* I made were the *Insertions into Ideological Circuits* (*Inserções em Circuitos Ideológicos*, 1970). This work takes up the question of place, the concept of circuit. But even earlier, the *Virtual Spaces: Corners* (*Espaço Virtuais: Cantos*, 1967–1968), one of my very first works, was perfectly doable from instructions. At the time, I also made three studies focusing respectively on space, time, and space and time. The first study consisted of choosing a location, closing one's eyes and listening, and perceiving a pure sound environment determined exclusively by the auditory system.

Obrist A kind of subjective laboratory?

Meireles Absolutely. The second study, which had the beach as its setting, consisted of digging a hole in the sand and sitting inside it until the wind filled it. The third study required abstaining from drinking for 24 hours, then drinking the contents of a silver pitcher filled with cold water. I've only shown these studies once, as written instructions (typed on a sheet of paper) in Rio in 1969.

Obrist A year before the 'Information' exhibition at MoMA, New York, in 1970?

Meireles Yes. I even think that Kynaston McShine saw that piece. I didn't meet him at the time, but I know he came to Rio to prepare his exhibit.

Obrist In the texts relating to the *Virtual Spaces*, there's already the idea of a work emancipated from its author.

Meireles This idea was at the centre of all discussions at the time. The idea was to detach the work from its individual pathology. Only an artist with a truly extraordinary personal history can produce a personal, intimate work worthy of interest. Usually this is not the case and it is much more interesting to aspire to the illusion known as objectivity. I've been very interested in Werner Heisenberg's 'uncertainty principle', which in a way gives a scientific demonstration of the illusory nature of objectivity.

Obrist Yet throughout the twentieth century the fiction of the objectivity of science has endured. Francisco Varela, a brain specialist, wrote a text on that subject a few years ago. It consists of instructions for 'a laboratory of subjectivity', 'a portable laboratory'.

Meireles Yes, quite right. I'm not a specialist, but I think that's precisely the subject of the great controversy that opposed Einstein and Heisenberg. The theory of relativity rested, actually, on the idea of objectivity. In the end it prevailed and became the thought of the majority. For Heisenberg, on the contrary, we are always observing the disorder we cause while we are in the act of observing and by the very fact of observing. [...]

Obrist To return to the *Virtual Spaces*, you used the term virtual very early on. Today when it's used, people immediately think of virtual reality, whereas in your work, the idea is virtual as potential. How does this notion of instruction tie into your present large installations? Can the instructions be likened to musical scores? Do you conceive of the instructions as scores for your installations, devised so that, in a way, your works can be played again.

Meireles Virtual/virtuality designates etymologically that which is potentially present. It is in that sense that I used the term. There is a similarity between the instructions and musical notation. One day I'd like to make instructions so perfect that a piece could be accurately reproduced. *Através* [*Through*] (1983–1989) is a labyrinth made up of perfectly ordinary materials and objects found in shops and industrially manufactured. My friend Trudo Engels told me that in 15 years it would probably be difficult to find the same materials, and so what was originally a jumble of everyday objects would become a set of collector's items. It would be very expensive to follow the instructions then. Of course, this kind of work can be adapted. If you take the barrier for example, the idea in the work is to use it as a paradigmatic object – as a barrier, in fact. Obviously, if a Brazilian barrier is used in a piece that will be shown in Europe, it will not be perceived in the same way as it was in its original context. It is therefore indispensable to adapt the work to historical and geographical circumstances.

Obrist You recently mentioned the importance of the circus ... How is it linked to your work?

Meireles My work is centred on two main concepts: the first, of course, is the idea of *Pano de Roda*, linked to the decadence of the circus. The appearance of radio, film, and later television, virtually killed the circus, which had previously occupied an important place in Brazilian culture. When they could no longer honour their employees' contracts (jugglers, magicians, tightrope artists, etc.), circus owners would pay them by cutting out a piece of the big top. Gradually, as it was no longer possible to finance collective shows, each of the circus arts became individual again. Each artist travelled with a piece of canvas ... This process of transformation of the circus is called *Pano de Roda*.

Obrist Practical value became exchange value ...

Meireles I'm very fond of this idea because it once again gives a certain independence to the work and a central place to the notion of individuality.

Obrist There is no further question of objectivity then? What kind of economy is involved here?

Meireles The question isn't asked in theoretical terms. For economic reasons – a new area of survival – of artistic survival, was created. The other idea that I tried to develop was the idea of the ambiguity between the concrete nature of the materials and their symbolic value. For *Ku Kka Ka Kka* (1992–1999), I used flowers and shit, two materials that have a strong symbolic content, as do bones or money.

Obrist ... Yes, the 600,000 coins, 800 hosts and 2,000 bones that you used for *Missão/Missões (Como construir catedrais)* [*How to build cathedrals*] (1987), that was presented in 'Magiciens de la Terre' (Centre Georges Pompidou, Paris, 1989).

Meireles Yes, and the same goes for matchboxes. In Brazil, as everywhere, there's always a trademark that ends up being substituted, through metonymy, for the generic term. That's the case for the Olho 'Fiat Lux' brand matches that I used for *O Sermão da Montanha: Fiat Lux* [*The Sermon on the Mount: Fiat Lux*] (1973–1979).

Obrist The *Insertions into Ideological Circuits* are closely related to this set of problems, no?

Meireles Initially the project began as a text on the notion of 'Insertions'. This text has a completely autonomous existence. Then, as samples from the text, I made the coin, the banknote and the bottle of Coca-Cola. At the time I mostly showed the *Coca-Cola Project* (*Insertions into Ideological Circuits: Coca-Cola Project*, 1970). The *Coca-Cola Project* was about industry, capitalism; the *Cédula* [banknote] *Project* was about the state (*Insertions into Ideological Circuits: Cédula Project*, 1970). But at the time it was impossible to print a reproduction of a banknote; I would have had too many problems. Therefore I decided to use the Coca-Cola bottle as a metaphor for the banknote. This work has a lot of meaning for me. Of course, it expresses a definite political position.

Obrist Of political infiltration?

Meireles Yes, and I still think that's the way to take action, like the 'Insertions'. It's a good method that consists in finding a flaw in an existing system and using it to spread counter-information. [...]

Cildo Meireles and Hans Ulrich Obrist, extract from interview (Paris, 2000), in Hans Ulrich Obrist, *Interviews*, vol. 1(Milan: Charta, 2003) 580–84.

Vito Acconci
Following Piece//1969

The terms of the exhibition ['Street Works IV'] were: anytime during the month, do a piece using any street in New York City. My piece, then, was designed to use, potentially, all the time allotted, all the space available.

Each day, I pick out a different person, at random, in the street, any location: I follow that person as long as I can, until he/she goes off into a private place - home, office, etc.

A following episode might last two or three minutes (a person gets into a car, I can't grab a taxi in time, I can't follow); a following episode might last seven or eight hours (a person goes to a restaurant, a person continues his/her evening by going to a movie ...)

The next month, there's a follow-up to the *Following Piece*: each day, a letter is sent to a different person, somewhere in the United States – each letter describes the particular details of the following episode that occurred on that day, one month before. A month after that, there's a follow-up to the follow-up: each day a letter is sent to a different person, outside the country – each letter notates the letter sent on that day, one month before, each letter describes the following episode that occurred on that day, two months before.

Vito Acconci, text for *Following Piece*. Activity, 'Street Works IV', Architectural League of New York (1–31 October 1969).

Stanley Cavell
The World Viewed//1971

[...] Photographs are not *hand*-made; they are manufactured. And what is manufactured is an image of the world. The inescapable fact of mechanism or automatism in the making of these images is the feature [the art historian] Germain Bazin points to as '[satisfying], once and for all and in its very essence, our obsession with realism'.

It is essential to get to the right depth of this fact of automatism. It is, for example, misleading to say, as Bazin does, that 'photography has freed the plastic arts from their obsession with likeness', for this makes it seem (and it does often look) as if photography and painting were in competition, or that painting had wanted something that photography broke in and satisfied. So far as photography satisfied a wish, it satisfied a wish not confined to painters, but the human wish, intensifying in the West since the Reformation, to escape subjectivity and metaphysical isolation – a wish for the power to reach this world, having for so long tried, at last hopelessly, to manifest fidelity to another. And painting was not 'freed' – and not by photography – from its obsession with likeness. Painting, in Manet, was *forced* to forego likeness exactly because of its own obsession with reality, because the illusions it had learned to create did not provide the conviction in reality, the connection with reality, that it craved. One might even say that in withdrawing from likeness, painting freed photography to be invented.

And if what is meant is that photography freed painting from the idea that a painting had to be a picture (that is, *of* or *about* something else), that is also not true. Painting did not free itself, did not force itself to maintain itself apart, from *all* objective reference until long after the establishment of photography; and then not because it finally dawned on painters that paintings were not pictures, but because that was the way to maintain connection with (the history of) the art of painting, to maintain conviction in its powers to create paintings, meaningful objects in paint.

And are we sure that the final denial of objective reference amounts to a complete yielding of connection with reality – once, that is, we have given up the idea that 'connection with reality' is to be understood as 'provision of likeness'? We can be sure that the view of painting as dead without reality, and the view of painting as dead with it, are both in need of development in the views each takes of reality and of painting. We can say, painting and reality no longer *assure* one another.

It could be said further that what painting wanted, in wanting connection with reality, was a sense of *presentness* – not exactly a conviction of the world's presence to us, but of our presence to it. At some point the unhinging of our consciousness from the world interposed our subjectivity between us and our presentness to the world. Then our subjectivity became what is present to us, individuality became isolation. The route to conviction in reality was through the acknowledgment of that endless presence of self. What is called expressionism is one possibility of representing this acknowledgment. But it would, I think, be truer to think of expressionism as a representation of our *response* to this new fact of our condition – our terror of ourselves in isolation – rather than as a representation of the world from within the condition of isolation itself. It would, to that extent, not be a new mastery of fate by creating selfhood against no matter what odds; it would be the sealing of the self's fate by theatricalizing it. Apart from the wish for selfhood (hence the always simultaneous granting of otherness as well), I do not understand the value of art. Apart from this wish and its achievement, art is exhibition.

To speak of our subjectivity as the route back to our conviction in reality is to speak of romanticism. Perhaps romanticism can be understood as the natural struggle between the representation and the acknowledgment of our subjectivity (between the acting out and the facing off of ourselves, as psychoanalysts would more or less say). Hence Kant, and Hegel; hence Blake secreting the world he believes in; hence Wordsworth competing with the history of poetry by writing out himself, writing himself back into the world. A century later Heidegger is investigating Being by investigating *Dasein* (because it is in *Dasein* that Being shows up best, namely as questionable), and Wittgenstein investigates the world ('the possibilities of phenomena') by investigating what we say, what we are inclined to say, what our pictures of phenomena are, in order to wrest the world from our possession so that we may possess it again. Then the recent major painting which Fried describes as objects of *presentness* would be painting's latest effort to maintain its conviction in its own power to establish connection with reality – by permitting us presentness to ourselves, apart from which there is no hope for a world.

Photography overcame subjectivity in a way undreamed of by painting, a way that could not satisfy painting, one which does not so much defeat the act of painting as escape it altogether: by *automatism*, by removing the human agent from the task of reproduction.

One could accordingly say that photography was never in competition with painting. What happened was that at some point the quest for visual reality, or the 'memory of the present' (as Baudelaire put it), split apart. To maintain conviction in our connection with reality, to maintain our presentness, painting accepts the recession of the world. Photography maintains the presentness of the world by accepting our absence from it. The reality in a photograph is present to me while I am not present to it; and a world I know, and see, but to which I am nevertheless not present (through no fault of my subjectivity), is a world past.

Stanley Cavell, extract from *The World Viewed* (New York: Viking Press, 1971) 20–23.

John Miller
Double or Nothing: On the Art of Douglas Huebler//2006

In retrospect, Douglas Huebler seems to have framed the scope of his work (or at least the general reception of it) with two irreconcilable declarations, the first being conceptual art's most oft-quoted pronouncement, 'The world is full of objects, more or less interesting; I do not wish to add any more.' Despite its laconic tone, Huebler's remark, initially put forward in a 1969 artist's statement for a show at Seth Siegelaub's New York gallery [*January 5-31, 1969*], mercilessly lampoons the expectation that artists be prolific. It implies a cessation of production, not because the world is particularly wonderful, but simply because it meets a minimum standard: 'more or less interesting'. It hints at a certain ecology as well. To make more objects – particularly, boring art objects – would be redundant. Why bother?

As Huebler later complained, these words would come back to haunt him. During his lectures someone inevitably pointed out that he had gone on to add more things to our more or less interesting world. And, in fact, just two years after renouncing object making for good, Huebler seemed to double back, emphatically proclaiming his intention 'to photographically document ... the existence of everyone alive'. Although this proposition, from the prospectus for his *Variable Piece #70, (In Process) Global, 1971* (1971), clearly telegraphed its own inevitable failure, it still invoked a kind of frantic and imperious hyperproduction whose purpose, even so, was murky. Document to what end?

However confounding and diametrically opposed Huebler's two statements seem, together they amount to a binary proposition that redefines the role of the artist. What links them is the quandary of an individuated subject confronting 'the world' as an indifferent, globalized system. Rejecting production in the usual sense, that subject responds by systematically reproducing this uninflected world – or at least images of its inhabitants. This formulation is blasé and fatalistic. It is also discreetly utopian. The world itself is to remain as it is; the point is simply to recognize its completeness. Everything that need be known about it is known already.

Yet with these disarmingly provocative declarations – and the body of work that is keyed to them – Huebler, perhaps more vividly than any other artist, registers the drastic sense of ideological liberation and foreclosure swirling around photographic technology both then and now. What he grasped was the camera's force as an economic and social agent. He saw that its ability to produce an instant and objective image implies a process of continuous reproduction, that its ability to disseminate images widely, cheaply and immediately implies a degree zero of democratization bordering on complete devaluation.

These prospects are tied to a nascent post-industrial logic and ideology: the information economy. Huebler's work stands at the crux of that epochal shift. In a statement accompanying the 1969 group show 'Prospect '69' at the Kunsthalle Düsseldorf, he wrote of his working method: 'I use the camera as a "dumb" copying device that only serves to document whatever phenomena appear before it through the conditions set by a system.' Mike Kelley points out in his 1997 essay 'Shall We Kill Daddy?' that, here, Huebler seemed to contradict the gist of his own work, simply repeating the conceptualist mantra that photos are transparent. Clearly, none of the photos featured in his Location, Duration or Variable works are transparent. For example, on 17 March 1969, Huebler took a walk in Central Park. His goal was to shoot ten pictures in a ten-minute period: when he heard an 'individually distinguishable' birdcall, he would point his camera in that direction and shoot. The resulting photos, coupled with a short explanatory statement, became *Duration Piece #5, New York, 1969*. Obviously, the camera cannot capture what Huebler is after here; the birdcalls elude it. Ultimately, all ten pictures are rather opaque. They demonstrate little more than the camera's technological and existential facticity.

With this seeming contradiction in mind, it may be fruitful to reconsider Huebler's 'dumb' approach to the camera vis-à-vis philosopher and cultural critic Vilém Flusser's *Towards a Philosophy of Photography*. In this influential text (first published in 1983), Flusser accords the photograph the status of the first postmodern object and pessimistically links it to robotization of the social order. Ruling out the possibility of transparent copying – in a formulation that resonates with Huebler's 'conditions set by a system' – Flusser claims that 'the photographic universe' is a closed system that not only fails to represent phenomena, but also excludes them. He posits the camera as a programmable apparatus, one that, paradoxically, programmes the photographers (functionaries) who use it.

For Flusser, a programme is a set of possibilities, a 'combination game with clear and distinct elements', that serves to animate an apparatus; an apparatus, in turn, is any 'non-human agency ... organization or system that enables something to function', whether that thing is 'the camera, the computer ... the State or ... the market'. As he puts it, 'every photograph is a realization of one of the possibilities contained within the program of the camera. The number of such possibilities is large, but it is nevertheless finite: it is the sum of all those photographs that can be taken by a camera.'

As photographers discover new possibilities, the camera, in turn, incorporates these into its programme. In other words, the camera uses

AN AREA WAS ARBITRARILY SELECTED WITHIN WHICH A PERSON IN EACH CITY PHOTOGRAPHED PLACES THAT HE OR SHE FELT COULD BE CHARACTERIZED AS BEING **1 FRIGHTENING** 2 EROTIC 3 TRANSCENDENT 4 PASSIVE 5 FEVERED 6 MUFFLED

AN AREA WAS ARBITRARILY SELECTED WITHIN WHICH A PERSON IN EACH CITY PHOTOGRAPHED PLACES THAT HE OR SHE FELT COULD BE CHARACTERIZED AS BEING 1 FRIGHTENING **2 EROTIC** 3 TRANSCENDENT 4 PASSIVE 5 FEVERED 6 MUFFLED

AN AREA WAS ARBITRARILY SELECTED WITHIN WHICH A PERSON IN EACH CITY PHOTOGRAPHED PLACES THAT HE OR SHE FELT COULD BE CHARACTERIZED AS BEING 1 FRIGHTENING 2 EROTIC **3 TRANSCENDENT** 4 PASSIVE 5 FEVERED 6 MUFFLED

AN AREA WAS ARBITRARILY SELECTED WITHIN WHICH A PERSON IN EACH CITY PHOTOGRAPHED PLACES THAT HE OR SHE FELT COULD BE CHARACTERIZED AS BEING 1 FRIGHTENING 2 EROTIC 3 TRANSCENDENT **4 PASSIVE** 5 FEVERED 6 MUFFLED

AN AREA WAS ARBITRARILY SELECTED WITHIN WHICH A PERSON IN EACH CITY PHOTOGRAPHED PLACES THAT HE OR SHE FELT COULD BE CHARACTERIZED AS BEING 1 FRIGHTENING 2 EROTIC 3 TRANSCENDENT 4 PASSIVE **5 FEVERED** 6 MUFFLED

AN AREA WAS ARBITRARILY SELECTED WITHIN WHICH A PERSON IN EACH CITY PHOTOGRAPHED PLACES THAT HE OR SHE FELT COULD BE CHARACTERIZED AS BEING 1 FRIGHTENING 2 EROTIC 3 TRANSCENDENT 4 PASSIVE 5 FEVERED **6 MUFFLED**

Douglas Huebler, from *Location Piece #2, New York City–Seattle, Washington*, 1969 photographers as a feedback mechanism. Since their discoveries serve to expand the camera programme, they are, per Flusser, 'informative'. That is, they 'imprint a new, intentional form' on the programme. Conversely, a photo that reiterates a possibility that is already in the programme is redundant. What especially concerns Flusser in this respect is how images are made – their technical form, not the repetition of images per se.

Flusser also concerns himself with the large but finite sum total of all possible photographs. This yields the photographic universe, a Cartesian system in which every element corresponds to a point in the world, making the camera 'omniscient and omnipotent in the photographic universe'. Such matchings, of course, conjure up *Variable Piece #70*, Huebler's proposal to photograph everyone alive. The presumed one-to-one correspondence between (redundant) photographic images and the world population would map reality so closely that, as a map, it would be useless. In a 1969 interview with artist Patricia Norvell, Huebler observed: 'The map is only a chart, you know. It isn't really a real thing, and yet we begin to assume it is a real thing. Most people experience maps or clocks or charts and so forth as very real life-defining phenomena, or whatever.' (Likewise, Alexander Alberro characterized Huebler's *Rochester Trip, 1968*, which laid out the course of a road tip, as a representation 'pushed "to the point of imagining a map so rigorous and referential that it becomes coterminous with its object"'. Here, Alberro quotes Fredric Jameson, who himself had been influenced by the paradox of Jorge Luis Borges' life-size map.)

It is within such a pointless teleology that Huebler takes on the role of photographer-functionary, dutifully re-enacting the camera programme. The role is performative and mimetic, nothing less than mummery. Documentation is only the pretext for such a charade – Huebler does not and cannot fully enact all the elements in the camera's programme. His enactments are reduced to gestures.

The point of departure for Huebler's photo works is typically the experiment, couched as field research. Experimental protocols raise empirical expectations, and they also provide the pretext for following a set procedure. Thus it would be better to describe his activity as 'operating the camera' rather than 'shooting pictures'. In *Location Piece #5, Massachusetts–New Hampshire, 1969*, he photographed roadside snowbanks. In the statement that formed part of that work, he stipulated, 'Each photograph was made at an interval of every 5 miles; of every 5 yards; or of every 5 feet; or of a variable combination of all of those intervals.' *Duration Piece #2, Paris, 1970*, presents the viewer with eight snapshots said to illustrate the 'timeless serenity' of a statue seen behind some cement mixers. Here too he shot the photos at set intervals, then shuffled them out of sequence. The text for *Location Piece #2, New York City–Seattle, Washington, 1969*, tells readers that 'an area was arbitrarily selected within which a person in each city photographed places that he, or she, felt could be characterized as being (1) "frightening" (2) "erotic" (3) "transcendent" (4) "passive" (5) "fevered" and (6) "muffled"'. Despite the carefully enumerated adjectives, the operative word here turns out to be 'arbitrarily' – the resulting images are presented without any indication of which terms they are meant to represent. In *Variable Piece #135, Edinboro State College, Edinboro, Pennsylvania, 1974*, Huebler invited look-alikes – just ordinary people who happened to resemble one another – to submit five-by-seven-inch photos to a juried contest. Many other works play with doubling as well. In *Location Piece #17, Turin, Italy, 1973*, he even found a 'man who bears a strong resemblance to the artist ... at least more so than most everyone else in the world'.

Of course, such doubling raises the prospect of fooling the camera. Ultimately, the camera's claim on scientific objectivity can go no further than physiognomy. Although Huebler once asserted that 'art is a source of information', he consistently destabilizes the photo's documentary status by pointing to the kinds of information it cannot convey. As Margaret Sundell wrote in *Artforum* in 2002, Huebler applies 'a discourse developed for the collection of empirical data and the verification of objective truths to situations that are by turns aleatory, outlandish, or simply mundane ...'

All this, however, is not necessarily a misapplication of photography, especially if, as Flusser argues, 'the act of photography is that of "phenomenological doubt" to the extent that it attempts to approach phenomena from any number of viewpoints'. In other words, a looming array of possibilities leaves the documentary claims of any single photo tenuous and incomplete. Conversely, because cameras generate more information than the photographer intends, the multiplication of viewpoints only amplifies the fundamental doubt. Thus, as a means of reality testing, every photographic experiment is fated to collapse on its foundations. Huebler's phenomenological doubt is simply more overt and more discursive than that of conventional photographers. In noting 'a tension between surface blandness and infinite meaning' in Huebler's work, Kelley might just as well be describing the greater part of all photographic practice. But given photography's inherent equivocality, 'infinite meaning' may turn out to be nothing less than an abyss of meaning.

Before conceptual art, photography, even modernist photography, took painting, which is to say, pictorialism, as a model. Photographs were either 'mirrors' or 'windows', as photographer and curator John Szarkowski has said. In contrast, for conceptual artists, pictures – if used at all – became a means, not an end. As a discourse of so-called dematerialization, conceptualism favours documentation over object making, and the photo serves as its preferred vehicle. This destabilizes the conventional status of the picture and the image.

Photographic information can lie loosely, so to speak, on any number of surfaces, from Xeroxed flyers to archival prints. The support can be discarded and the photographic information regenerated at will. The material support is, essentially, immaterial. It is for this reason that Flusser says that the photograph is the first post-industrial object.

Against the background of today's burgeoning information and service economies, we can discern how Huebler's refractory 1969 and 1971 statements suggest something of photography's radically post-industrial nature. In a photo, the information – not the material support, not the technique, not the composition – is what counts. Moreover, the point is not to own information but to disseminate it. Even so, Huebler reminds us of such information's potentially dubious character and warns us not to mistake it for reality. As his work makes abundantly clear, information is not synonymous with meaning. The power of information lies in its abstraction, which, in turn, facilitates its exchangeability – but the inherently reductive nature of abstraction is its weakness as well as its strength. The political economy of the photo hinges on the play between the proliferation of meaning and its obviation.

Alberro, notably, applies Antonio Negri and Michael Hardt's notion of informatization to the emergence of conceptual art. As the two famously theorize in *Empire* (2000), the contemporary phase of advanced capitalism embeds an information infrastructure within production processes. Such an infrastructure is inherently interactive and gradually becomes immanent in production itself. Thus, Negri and Hardt maintain, 'Our economic and social reality is defined less by the material objects that are made and consumed than by co-produced services and relationships.' Yet, as Huebler intimates, the negative flip side of democratized, information-based co-production may be the onus of an informational phantasmagoria.

In his own model of conceptual art, Siegelaub distinguishes between 'primary information' (content: the signified) and 'secondary information' (the means of its presentation: the signifier). For example, in Huebler's *Duration Piece #5* (the birdcall piece), the primary information consists of the parameters within which the artist produced the work: shoot in the direction of an individually distinguishable birdcall; walk in that direction until the next call is heard; shoot as before, and so on. The specific images, which function merely as vehicles for the paradigmatic schema of the piece, are secondary information. The significance of both the photographic support and the secondary information is arbitrary. (Had Huebler executed *Duration Piece #5* just thirty seconds earlier or later than he did, his set of photos would have looked entirely different.) Not coincidentally, both primary information and photographic information lend themselves to easy and widespread dissemination. This is why, as Flusser avers, 'It is not the owner but the programmer of the information who is the powerful one.' Material accumulation, accordingly, becomes a secondary goal. In this sense, one might document every living person without necessarily adding more objects to the world.

The information of the camera programme differs significantly from the informational capacity of photographs. A photograph that disseminates information does not necessarily inform – in the sense of 'imprinting a new, intentional form on' – or develop the camera programme. The quest for new possibilities outside the camera programme lies, by definition, outside established applications, and while such discoveries continue to shape photography's practical uses (e.g. the Global Positioning System), it is not these discoveries that carry conventionally useful information on a day-to-day basis. It is their reiteration. Thus, what institutions typically want are redundant photos, regardless of whether a human functionary, a satellite, or an electron microscope shot them. Conceptual art thus embraces the redundant photograph's informational capacity. Conversely, pictorialist photography, read in Flusserian terms, may be said to constitute a flight from redundancy that is doomed to fail, since the images it produces, however 'original', will never be informative. Huebler, like other Conceptual artists – only more so – treats the photo as a readymade and the camera programme as a given, an approach that allows him to concentrate on the camera's social and political imbrication. To aspire to informativity is in fact to collude with the robotization of social relations, since informing the camera programme, after all, means expanding and strengthening it. Conceptual art rejects this aspiration. To the extent that it critiques framing and institutional frameworks, it is more concerned with the metaprogramme that encapsulates the camera (a nested complex of institutions) than with the camera programme per se. As such, Huebler's photos approach an 'art after philosophy', to use Joseph Kosuth's phrase, especially since they address not only their own a priori condition, but also that of the camera as a political and economic apparatus. (Ironically, Kosuth pointedly excluded Huebler from the realm of 'pure' conceptual art, relegating him to the status of 'stylistic' conceptualist.)

Negri and Hardt assert: 'The passage toward an informational economy necessarily involves a change in the quality and nature of labour' – a new type of labour, for which Huebler's oeuvre suggests the photographer's work serves as model. Again, here it is worthwhile to consider Flusser, who characterizes the photographer not as a worker but as someone who plays with the camera programme as a combination game. This inversion of work 'dialectizes' all the terms involved. A pure combination game most resembles gambling. Gambling departs from traditional work's focus on an exact outcome. Unpredictability is its essence. Significantly, Huebler uses chance and gamelike rules to generate most of his photos. In *Variable Piece #107, London, 1972*, to cite one example, the artist photographed eighteen mannequins on London's Regent Street. After each, he turned around and photographed the first passer-by of the same sex. This gesture caricatures the means by which conventional photos derive their authority: by resembling their subjects. Accordingly, Huebler revels in photography's exemplary arbitrariness – in the case of this piece, the unexpected likenesses and disparities between the idealized mannequins and quotidian pedestrians.

If Flusser likens shooting photos to throwing dice, this is disengaged play – the opposite of creative play, ordinarily associated with children – recalling Walter Benjamin's comparison of the gambler and the assembly-line worker. For his part, Huebler is more concerned with the rules than he is with playing. Or, more accurately, instead of playing with the camera, he plays with the rules. He brackets the work of the photographer-functionary by miming it, thus bringing its automated aspect to the fore. And here one may consider whether such automation, for all its darker implications, also harbours a liberatory potential. As Negri and Hardt argue, automation – or the robotization of productive relations – depends on an information infrastructure and therefore entails an increase of communication and interaction. They consider this spontaneous co-production a new form of commonality, which they equate with the historical commons, i.e. common property to which everyone has a right.

We might correlate this logic with that of Huebler's *Variable Piece #70*. Without knowing the total number of portraits it comprises, one can safely surmise that it falls far short of its stated goal of 'photographically document[ing], to the extent of [the artist's] capacity, the existence of everyone alive in order to produce the most authentic and inclusive representation of the human species that may be assembled in that manner.' By tying its prospective scope to a global demographic, the work quixotically aspires, for better or worse, to be an utterly democratic representation. It evinces the logic of an archive, albeit a fragmented one. As Webster's defines them, archives (in the plural) are both 'a place where public documents and records are kept' and 'the public records, documents, etc. kept in such a place'. Huebler's archive, in other words, would document, reflexively, the very public that archives ostensibly serve.

Allan Sekula's seminal 1983 essay 'Reading an Archive: Photography between Labour and Capital' argues the reverse: that what gives an archive its definition is its status as private property. He also argues that photography constructs an imaginary economy, representing not the real relations that govern people's lives but an imaginary relation to the real relations under which they live. As such, the archive's status as private property contrasts starkly with the imaginary aspect of its representative function. Proceeding from this logic, we might be tempted to conclude that any perceived liberatory dimension in

Huebler's oeuvre is itself a pipe dream. Flusser, for his part, stresses the anti-historical – and therefore, apolitical – nature of photographs, which 'replace events by states of things and translate them into scenes'. In Flusser's sweeping historical overview, the linearity of writing gave rise to historical consciousness, which the photograph then eroded, reinstantiating a kind of magical thought that confuses cause and effect (making it irrelevant whether, for example, the cock crows because the sun rises or the sun rises because the cock crows). Likewise, in his 1969 declaration, Huebler says he wants only 'to state the existence of things in terms of time and place'. Yet just as we may recall that Sekula insists that the unity of an archive – which is what *Variable Piece #70* purports to be – derives from ownership, so Bill Gates' monopolization of the Bettmann and United Press International archives (currently estimated at 27 million pictures) comes to mind. His company, Corbis Corporation, even went so far as to sequester these underground.

In dialectical opposition to the ever-expanding reach of monopoly capital, Negri and Hardt foresee that, through the process of post-industrialization, 'Private property, despite its juridical powers, cannot help becoming an ever more abstract and transcendental concept and thus ever more detached from reality.' Nonetheless, photography remains intimately bound up with the juridical powers that allow private property to persist as an operative reality, rather than an abstract and transcendent concept – especially through surveillance, an empiricist undercurrent running through *Variable Piece #70*. It is exactly these juridical regimes, moreover, that turn an otherwise abstract and transcendent concept into an operative reality. And yet, because this work also posits itself as a public archive, a commons – 'the incarnation, the production, and the liberation of the multitude', as Hardt and Negri would have it – it also militates against juridical power.

John Miller, 'Double or Nothing: On the Art of Douglas Huebler', *Artforum*, vol. 44, no. 8 (April 2006) 220-27.

Marcia Tucker
John Baldessari: Pursuing the Unpredictable//1981

[...] The most common method used by John Baldessari to keep himself and us 'off balance' is to incorporate accident and chance as source material for his work, in the tradition of John Cage. As early as 1966, he wanted to make work out of things that nobody else would think of making art of.[1] This impulse generated the first aluminium fragment pieces he made. Later, accident became a means of ensuring that the outcome of a piece would remain unknown until it was finished. A chance word or overheard phrase could trigger an entire body of work; in the case of *Floating: Color* (1972), the word 'defenestration' suggested the possibility of throwing something that was *not* an object out of the window. In his notes, Baldessari comments that

> using colour gave rise to a simple ordering system based on the colour wheel, which was useful here and in later pieces because it was sequential yet brief in number. I wanted a form that was static but not limitless. Also, the form provided a way to avoid relational colour choices, that is, colour combinations based on intuitive process.[2]

Baldessari's use of chance to avoid composition or aesthetic decisions had its prototype in an informal exhibition entitled 'Pier 18', held at The Museum of Modern Art, New York, in 1971. The projects were photography-oriented, and each participating artist was asked to meet two photographers at a deserted pier at a specific time and to present them with a project. Baldessari simply asked them to try to photograph a ball, which he repeatedly bounced on the pier, so that it would appear in the centre of the finished photograph. Consequently there was no opportunity to 'compose' or to try to make a handsome picture. Many other works grew out of this strategy, such as *Trying to Roll a Hoop in a Perfect Circle*; *Throwing 4 Balls in the Air to Get a Straight Line ...* ; and *Throwing 3 Balls in the Air to Get an Equilateral Triangle ...* (all from 1972–73). The hoop piece consists of 'the best sequence of 216 frames', while the throwing-balls pieces are 'the best of 36 tries' because there are 36 shots in a roll of 35-mm film. A later work, *Strobe Series/Futurist: Trying to Get a Straight Line with a Finger* (1975), is based on the same principle, wherein chance is an integral part of the activity itself. The results are thus limited by the arbitrary rules of the game, in other words, the number of tries will be limited to the number of available shots on a single roll of film. In some of the later works, particularly the

Blasted Allegories series, the images themselves have been obtained haphazardly by taking pictures of a television screen with an intervalometer. Such strategies were evolved, says Baldessari, because

> I'm concerned with the formal and aesthetic qualities to the point where I try to set up situations where I can't make any aesthetic decisions about it and that's very hard. I realize that as you go on you get better and better at making things look good, and you have to set up stumbling blocks so that you can escape your own good taste, and even that creeps in a lot.[3]

Far from being simply an aleatory artist, Baldessari further keeps us off balance by making an equal number of works based on concepts of choice and comparison, a diametrically opposed system to that of chance and accident. In the *Choosing* series (1971), for example, participants were asked to select, much in the manner of a game show, any three items (green beans, rhubarb, carrots, onions, beets, radishes, etc.) from a similar group. Baldessari would then choose one of the three by pointing to it, and a photograph would be taken. This single chosen item was then carried over to the next group, consisting of the selected item plus two new ones, and the entire process was repeated.

Many of Baldessari's videotapes are also based on the idea of making comparisons (and therefore, even unconsciously, choices), some of them minute and unlikely, as in *Examining 8d Nails* (from *The Way We Do Art Now ...*). In this video segment, painstaking attention is paid to which nail has more rust, or which appears 'cooler, more distant, less important' than the other two. The tape is funny because we tend not to compare common nails at all. On the other hand, *How Various People Spit Out Beans* forces comparison of an activity that has no reason for taking place at all *other than* for comparison, and it is the inappropriateness of the activity in relation to its function that makes it amusing. Both tapes highlight Baldessari's use of choosing and comparing, both on the part of the artist and the viewer, as strategies basic to both making art and to life in general.

An hour-long film called *Script* (1973–77) is Baldessari's most complex use of this strategy of choice. Ten very short, simple scripts for ten scenes are shown in printed form first. Seven couples, none of them professional actors, are given each of the scenes to act out in any way they wish. First, we see all ten scenes played consecutively by each of the seven couples, followed by each scene played, in turn, by all seven couples. Thus far, two sets of comparisons have been set up, the first consisting of choosing the favourite couple's version of each scene. Finally, when it seems that all possibilities for choice and comparison have been exhausted by repetition, Baldessari provides us with 'the top ten shots' ranked from one to ten. His choices are clearly not the ones the viewer might have made, further emphasizing the intensely personal nature of selection and judgement-making.

Another Baldessari strategy is to set up rules for making work which defy those in existence and considered basic to making art. For instance, he has stated that he became interested in doing sequential work because he never believed that 'any one thing was the final word. If one thing is happening here, what's happening there?' He says that he used to go around for days 'trying to look between things instead of at things', an idea which resulted indirectly in such pieces as *Car Color Series: all Cars Parked on the West Side of Main Street ...* (1976), where Baldessari photographed the centre of the door of a parked car, presenting the photographs, like a colour sample chart, in the same order in which all the cars were parked. Where a car wasn't parked, a blank space appears on the wall. 'It's a matter of focus', he says. 'If you believe your world is formed by what you look at, and you just don't look at the usual things, then your world will change.'[4] [...]

1 [footnote 35 in source] Marilyn Hagberg, 'Neglected, Under-Rated, Intellectual Baldessari', *San Diego Magazine* (January 1966) 66–8; 101.
2 [36] From the artist's notes for forthcoming catalogue [Van Abbemuseum, Eindhoven, 1981].
3 [37] Patricia Failing, 'John Baldessari: Taking Visual Notes', *The Oregonian (Northwest Magazine)* (5 February 1978) 11.
4 [38] Daniel McMullin, 'An Interview with John Baldessari', *Artists' News* (Topanga, Canada, October–November 1980) 9.

Marcia Tucker, extract from 'John Baldessari: Pursuing the Unpredictable' in *John Baldessari* (New York: New Museum of Contemporary Art, 1981) 18–21.

John Baldessari
Interview with Nancy Drew//1981

Nancy Drew Have you ever considered just being a writer?

John Baldessari All the time. I think sometimes that I'm somehow on this convolution of a journey ... The thing that seems to keep me from just being a writer is that I still need the non-verbal image.

Drew Do you think living in Los Angeles had anything to do with it – seeing so many signs and quick images, the information transmitted while you're driving?

Baldessari Yes, I think one is influenced by that kind of information. I stopped trying to be an artist as I understood it and just attempted to talk to people in a language they understood, such as hyperrealism, etc. But rather than paint realistically and aspire to the conditions of a photograph, why not just use the photograph or a text? I thought I would do all that on canvas so that the canvas would be an art signal. Also I remember asking myself, 'What if people like landscapes and stuff like that?' So I went around taking photographs, like in *Ballard Ambulance*. Rather than framing them, I just drove around, clicking out of the car window, not really looking ... using life like it really is. Seeing selectively means you screen out a lot of interesting things. A photographer spends so much time trying to take a picture according to the images in his mind. Probably one of the worst things to happen to photography is that cameras have viewfinders. [...]

John Baldessari and Nancy Drew, extract from interview, in *John Baldessari* (New York: The New Museum, 1981) 63.

Brian Eno
Interview with Hans Ulrich Obrist//2000

Hans Ulrich Obrist What particular musical experiments did you find influential at the time [the late 1960s and early 1970s]?

Brian Eno There was a particular piece of music that completely intrigued me and I spent a long, long time thinking about it and writing about it and trying to understand how it worked, because I felt it was the beginning of a new way of understanding art – actually, art and culture in general. The piece is by Cornelius Cardew and it is called *The Great Learning* (1969/1971). In fact, there is an essay about it in *A Year with Swollen Appendices*: it is an essay I wrote in 1975, so the writing style isn't that good, but I still really stick by the content of it. What I think I noticed there was that it was a way of composing that was really quite different from the way classical music is composed or from the way pop records were made. That way of composing is to suggest a set of rules and conditions, which are actually the piece of music, and then an individual performance is one possible outcome of those rules and conditions.

Obrist So it is a complex dynamic system that grows?

Eno That's right. Instead of building a house – which is the way classical symphonic composition saw itself: building a cathedral – instead of doing that it is like designing a seed. You plant it and it grows into something.

Obrist This time-based idea also makes me think of [the cybernetics theorist] Gordon Pask and the architect Cedric Price.

Eno You know, they both came to talk to us at Ipswich [School of Art, as part of the study course devised by the artist and theorist of cybernetics Roy Ascott]; those ideas really took root in me; the idea that an artist didn't finish a work but started it. You design the beginning of something, and the process of releasing the work is the process of planting it in the culture and seeing what happens to it.

Obrist Were there other main influences?

Eno There was one prior to *The Great Learning*: the Steve Reich tape pieces, which I thought were sensational because they were so economical. I loved the fact that you could get so much music out of such a tiny input. That piece called *It's Gonna Rain* (1965) is from a loop, which is less than two seconds long. I also liked the way that those things worked in that they were very simple forms, of which I have been doing a lot since, which is just setting in motion two processes and letting them overlap, letting them interact with each other in different ways without trying to control how they do it. So that happened. The other thing that happened towards the end of the 1970s was that I saw John Conway's *The Game of Life* (1970). John Conway is an English mathematician. He became interested in instruction theory and he invented this tiny little game. It starts with a grid. Each of these squares has only two conditions: it can either be dead or it can be alive. OK, we will say that is a live square. There are only three rules for this game. They tell you about what is going to happen in the next generation, about whether a square is going to come to life or whether it will continue being alive or whether it will die. Those rules have to do with proximity to neighbours, so a square with three living neighbours stays alive. A square with more than three living neighbours dies from overpopulation, and a square with less than three also dies from isolation. So there are only those three rules and you don't think much is going to happen. So, you tell a computer to do this and you press 'go' and it goes [*computer noise*]. This thing is the most beautiful thing you have ever seen. You go 'wow' and you change, you start it again and now you change the position of one square, just one, and it goes [*gesturing*], finished. It is the most unintuitive thing you have ever seen. The initial conditions are completely important in a way that you simply can't intuit. The rules are very simple: they are totally deterministic. Nothing exotic about them, you can easily understand them, but the interaction of those three simple rules produces a level of complexity that absolutely changes your life. Once you have seen that you believe everything about Darwinian evolution.

Obrist Is it also about unpredictability of outcome?

Eno Yes, and what is so fascinating is your complete inability to intuit what will happen. I always like to show this to people who think they have good intuitions. It just shows you that, even with three simple rules working, you simply can't predict the future. I think there is something about *Life* in there actually, John Conway's *Life*. I am giving a talk about that at the ICA [Institute of Contemporary Arts, London, March 2001], because I think it is the easiest way for artists to understand what is really exciting about science.

Obrist So it influenced your work in the sense that it was a model for doing rule-based music pieces?

Eno Exactly. Conway's game started me thinking about building rule-based systems. This led me into, on the one hand, things like *Music for Airports* (*Ambient Music 1: Music for Airports*, 1978) which is, yes, essentially, a rule-based piece of music, and on the other hand into working with computers. The interesting thing about working with computers is that they can handle a lot of rules at once. I had been working for a long time with a piece of software called Koan, which allows me to write a number of musical rules having to do with scale, harmonization, and pace, and I can write lots of probabilistic rules. I can say, 'Use this scale but only use this note an average of 40 per cent of the time and this one 80 per cent of the time', and so on. Each piece of music is a little machine, in a way, for producing. It is like each set of rules is a single kind of genome, and then each individual performance is one of that species. They are related, but they are not identical. Similarly, I have been working with a similar system where I make things that keep reconfiguring in different ways. The initial material can be quite small, but the number of reconfigurations is huge.

Obrist The unpredictability of the outcome, in the art context, is what makes the conceptual couple instructions/performances fascinating: this uncertainty gap between the imagination of how the piece should be or should look and the interpretation, the various interpretations that can be given following the instructions. For Fluxus artists, everything was about intention and misunderstanding. In Robert Filliou's words: 'It is either well done or badly done or it is not done at all, but there can't be hierarchy between these three.'

Eno One's position on these things depends on how much you think the work consists of the process of making it and how important it is for you to make something that sits separate from you and your explanations of it. For instance, I worked with Filliou and George Brecht thirty years ago. I worked with them on several things. Their process of working was totally intriguing. Very often, the result was almost irrelevant. But result is not the issue. The issue is the whole process, with the result included as a relic of it – really as a pointer back to it. I didn't want to make things only like that. I wanted to make things that had a separate existence in the world. When I talk about making seeds, I am very aware of the idea that you become aware of in pop. Pop music – the idea of planting something that is actually quite innocent, which flowers into something far beyond what any of its makers would have imagined, and which stimulates the active interpretation and participation of millions of people. That slightly changes how you fall on that spectrum of what kinds of instructions you are using.

Obrist Filliou's works were mostly made for 20 people, 20 testimonies ...

Eno That's the other thing. These twenty people were there with him, so that is a different feeling altogether. I like the idea of making things that exist quite happily without me being around them. In music, you talk about releasing records, and I always liked that expression because that is exactly what you do: you release it from yourself. You release it from you standing around and defending it and saying this or that about it. You set it free and it is just floating with everything else out there and then it takes whatever value is conferred upon it. I am very keen on this idea of conferral of value. The old idea with artists is that they take dead material and fill it with value, and I never liked that. From the age of fifteen I didn't like that. What I liked was the idea of making things that attract value to them. They can be quite small. You put something out into the world and either it disappears completely, which often happens, or it starts to accumulate resonance ... A record like *Music for Airports* was a very strange record to release in 1978, because it was completely minimal, but it was being put out into a pop context. It wasn't being put out as: here is a piece of arcane minimalist music. I put it out as a pop record.

Obrist Can you tell me more about the importance of titles in your work?

Eno Well, I stopped writing songs quite a long time ago, but I still love words, so the only lyrics I still have are titles. I have to use very few words to create a big picture. *Music for Airports* was successful at that because as soon as it came out everyone thought it was such a funny idea to call a record *Music for Airports.* It got tons of attention because of that title. I really like *Before and After Science* (1977) also. Titles are something I have put a lot of attention into. You only ever have to suggest to people that those ideas might be in there and they will find them.

Obrist Could you mention some of your unrealized projects?

Eno You mean deliberately unrealized projects?

Obrist Well, there are all kinds of unrealized projects, but I'm interested specifically in the projects that were too big to be realized, or too small, or too expensive, or censored, even self-censored, or just not realized yet – unbuilt roads.

Eno OK, one project which hasn't been realized, and I have thought about it for a long, long time, is to try to build music almost from the atomic level. I use generative and rule-based systems to organize sound, to organize already existing pieces of sound. But what I would like to do, really, is to use those same systems to actually make the sounds, to create the sound on the atomic level, as it were, in exactly the same way that I then configure the sound afterwards; to use the same set of principles all the way through. I haven't done it because it is technically quite difficult, but I want to do that. That is a very technical project that I've been thinking about for, well, 25 years or so, and I have made lots of notes and sketches for it and one day I think I will do it. Another unrealized, unbuilt road is my idea of 'quiet clubs', clubs you go to where nothing much happens.

Obrist What would that look like?

Eno I have had the idea to build a quiet club for a long time – not as a kind of art installation, but as a working club that people would go to and enjoy. It would support itself. I have done them as installations in museums. I have done demos of what they might be like, but that is not the same for me. I want to do it for real and see if it can survive. If I start thinking about unbuilt roads, I get depressed, really. There are so many of them. I've got a whole bloody road network of unbuilt roads. The other one that I am still working on is the idea of a text-generating machine. I've worked a lot with music software and it is very obvious that making music has become more and more easy. I work with a lot of people and I see the music appearing very, very quickly, but the lyrics are appearing incredibly slowly. The text does not happen. I start to think, 'Well, it should be very easy to start to build a software into which you can enter lots of bits of text that you are interested in, that you like, ideas you want to play with, and you should be able to enter rhyming schemes and stress metres, schemes for basically organizing the words.' Then it should be possible for the thing to start giving you arrangements of the things you put in. You might, very rarely, get finished lyrics from that, but what you would get would be very interesting beginnings. If you could take a line like 'desolation at epicentre' and put it in with phrases and words that kind of fit together in your mind ...

Obrist It's a bit like a computerized version of the generative constraints set by Georges Perec to write poems?

Eno But writing for songs is quite different from writing for poems. You have to consider rhythm, melody and stress very much more than you do in poetry. [...]

Brian Eno and Hans Ulrich Obrist, extract from interview (London, 2000), in Hans Ulrich Obrist, *Interviews*, vol. 1(Milan: Charta/Florence: Fondazione Pitti Immagine Discovery, 2003) 214–19.

Cerith Wyn Evans
Dreamachine (1984/98)//2002

[*Dreamachine* (1984/98) – a revolving cylinder producing a flickering light to induce a dream state in the viewer] was about forcing the hand of chance, making chance work for you; somehow manipulating chance in a more radical notion or even a more archaic notion than Cage's Zen-like notion. This is really much more wilful and much more in the realm of tuning in to the possibility of being able to control what happens – a much more proactive position. As concerns Brion Gysin and the 'Dreamachine', this goes back to links with a whole bunch of people I had met in London, some of whom were also collaborators with Derek Jarman. One of my great heroes was the musician and artist Genesis P. Orridge. At the Royal College, you could ask people to come in from the outside to give a tutorial, and I asked for Genesis. He came in and we ended up collaborating, with me supplying his band Psychic TV with visuals and them supplying a soundtrack for a film I made. Again, here is a story of a group of people who started off within a British Fluxus tradition and moved into the territory of being musicians and filmmakers, an interdisciplinary loose group. And through Genesis P. Orridge I was introduced to William Burroughs and Brion Gysin. There was a series of performances in London at the gay nightclub Heaven. Burroughs had come from New York and Gysin came from Paris; John Giorno came for a reading at the Wag Club, which was originally called the Whisky A-Go-Go in the 1960s. And I projected films on the walls while he read. I'd never met the man before, although I'd read some of his poetry and had seen Andy Warhol's *Sleep* (1963). I remember meeting this group of people at the time and going to an exhibition opening with Gysin, sharing a taxi with him. The following day, I was asked to show films at a festival in Turin, and we got talking, and Gysin said, 'What are you doing this evening?' and I said, 'Oh I'd better have an early night because I've got to catch a plane in the morning to go to Turin.' He then replied, 'Maybe I should come with you', and the idea of going on an adventure with Brion Gysin to Turin was very thrilling at the time, because I looked up to him so very much. We spoke about the 'Dreamachine', and made some together, as well as a film called *The Dream Machine* with Michael Kostiff, John Maybury and Derek Jarman (1982). About 15 years later, I decided to remake or 'reissue' the work. I was aware of the 'dreamachine' and the claims made for it, and I was very interested in constructing what Gysin describes as how each person who experiences it can have access to their own autonomous movies. And this was very interesting to me, because of the way in which it purportedly changes. He also says that it's 'the only work of art ever made to be looked at with your eyes closed', which I'm not sure is a true claim because of various works and experiments that have been made. The point he's making is that it is in some sense explicitly retinal, and so I think there is a relationship to Duchamp and particularly the Rotoreliefs – these kinds of machines. I've not read much work that goes into these kinds of comparisons or conjectures, but this playing of the conjecture between the authorship and the lineage, the parentage of these machines and their ways of working is, I think, a stimulating one. I then went on to design a more formal or specific version made in lacquered, laser-cut steel with various electronics. Originally, 'Dreamachines' were made with cut-out cardboard cylinders and recycled old record players, which would play at 78 rpm; you would then take a light bulb flex from the ceiling and hang it down the middle of the cylinder at a certain height. I felt it would be interesting to produce this – other people have too; there are many different versions of the 'Dreamachine' that exist. [...]

Cerith Wyn Evans, statement from interview with Hans Ulrich Obrist (Brussels, 2002), in Hans Ulrich Obrist, *Interviews*, vol. 1(Milan: Charta/Florence: Fondazione Pitti Imagine Discovery, 2003) 956–7.

Klara Kemp-Welch
Jirí Kovanda's Collisions//2009

On 3 September 1977, Jirí Kovanda walked around Prague and casually bumped into passers-by. These seemingly unintentional collisions were observed and photographed by his friend Pavel Tuc, standing a little way off. For those whom Kovanda 'contacted', the incident was soon brushed off as an insignificant chance occurrence, perhaps momentarily annoying. For the artist, however, such minor acts of aggression formed part of a systematic investigation of interpersonal relationships under what was known as 'normalization'. The 1970s saw an extended period of repression in Czechoslovakia, intended to secure political conformity and passivity. Forced emigrations and political purges across society had followed the Warsaw pact troops' invasion in August 1968. When dissident intellectuals signed Charter '77, in January 1977, they referred to the Helsinki Accord and to the United Nations' Conventions on Human Rights and expressed their regret that in Czechoslovakia these existed only on paper. The state's response was a media campaign, police harassment, and persecution of the Chartists, designed to force them to withdraw their signatures.[1] In such conditions, it was impossible for unofficial artists to make contact with an audience, beyond a close circle of acquaintances. Instead, the abnormal conditions of 'normalization' provided Kovanda with a highly charged framework for exploring what 'normal' relationships might be like. He called his collisions piece *'Contact'*, in inverted commas.

Kovanda's actions were orchestrated for participants who did not realize that they were participating, and would probably have had not desire to do so had they been informed. This denial of the random pedestrians' agency was significant for two reasons: firstly, because it reduced the chances of anyone realizing that the artist was carrying out an unauthorised public action; secondly, because it can be seen as a metaphor of broader social dispossession of agency. Kovanda engineered a situation regarded as accidental by the passers-by, and recorded without their knowledge. The passers-by whom Kovanda chose to 'contact' were not so much participants as targets or victims. But their faces do not register any response to these instances of environmental aggression, nor do they respond to the cameraman that observes them. On the contrary, the photo-documentation records the process of people going on their way as normal, ignoring the incident and the camera. The unwitting participants instinctively dismiss the possibility of a disguised motive, despite living in a political situation which might have afforded them good reason to be paranoid.

An archive containing almost one million photographs taken by secret police was recently 'discovered' amidst the Czech Ministry of the Interior's seventeen kilometres of box files. Tens of thousands were kept under surveillance by the *Statni bezpecnost*, who are estimated to have employed around 75,000 informers in the 1980s.

Reflecting later on how people had responded to the other action that he had carried out on 3 September 1977 (*xxx. On an escalator turning around, I look in to the eyes of the person standing behind me ...*) Kovanda recalled that they 'responded sheepishly ... they didn't want to have anything to do with it at any cost, be it in a positive or a negative sense'.[2] Moreover, Kovanda was himself ambivalent about whether or not he wanted to engage with people in a public space. These actions involved pushing himself to the limits of his timidity. He said that they 'arose in a state of tension or a sort of trance, because I'm a timid person ... they involved behaviour that was unnatural to me'.[3] Like the escalator piece, *'Contact'* was designed, in the first instance, as an opportunity for the artist to work on himself. Small repeated transgressions of interpersonal boundaries served as exercises intended to develop his own self-knowledge. He insisted that the problem of contact was 'more of a personal matter for each individual and not a social matter'.[4]

Kovanda's commitment to the personal (to personal dialogue, to a personal relationship to reality, to a personal mythology) is symptomatic of the general discrediting of ideas of the 'social'. After all, the 'personal' had remained a category under siege since its official abolition within socialist ideology. Thus, if Kovanda's collisions interrupted, for a moment, the totalising experience of Czech normalization, then it was just when Kovanda claimed to be least interested in society that he showed himself to be acting most clearly in response to his political experience.

Buddhist practices were gaining currency among unofficial artists in Prague in this period, filtered through publications such as D.T. Suzuki's *Essays in Zen Buddhism*. The opening of Suzuki's anthology reads: 'Zen in its essence is the art of seeing into the nature of one's own being, and it points the way from bondage to freedom'.[5] In the late-socialist context, the practice of Zen, however watered down, offered a way to approach the world internally and to regain a level of control on a micro-level that remained indiscernible from outside. Over on the other side of the Berlin Wall, Roland Barthes had also been reading Suzuki in the summer of 1977.

In his lectures on *The Neutral* at the Collège de France that year, Barthes drew on Zen and Tao wisdom to propose ways to 'baffle' or 'outplay' the (capitalist) paradigm. One of the paths he advocated consisted 'in not being systematic ... a series of temporary retreats not even cyclically organized. But this nonorganization, the lack of foreseeable rhythm that would, that indeed will ensue, will deliver an incomprehensible, "scandalous" image of the subject to the world surrounding him'.[6] Kovanda's actions were certainly scandalous. On January 23, 1978, he vanished from his actions. The caption of the photograph documenting his flight reads: *xxx I arranged to meet a few friends ... we were standing in a small group on the square, talking ... suddenly, I started running; I raced across the square and disappeared into Melantrich Street ...* His escape from contact marked a further twist in Kovanda's *détournement* of the technique of the chance encounter. This time, the victims were his friends.

1 Vladimir V. Kusin, *From Dubcek to Charter 77. A Study of 'Normalisation' in Czechoslovakia 1968–1978* (Edinburgh: Q Press, 1978) 381.

2 Barbora Klímová, *Replaced 2006* (Brno: Moravská Galerie Brno 2006) 32.

3 Jirí Kovanda, 'Conversation 1: I always felt that I didn't need a studio. Hans-Ulrich Obrist talks with Jirí Kovanda', in *Vít Havránek, ed. Jiri Kovanda. 2005–1976 Actions and Installations* (Zurich: Tranzit, 2006) 107.

4 Ibid.

5 Daisetz Teitaro Suzuki, *Essays in Zen Buddhism* (New York: Grove Press, 1949) 13.

6 Roland Barthes, *The Neutral. Lecture Course at the Collège de France (1977–1978)*, trans. Rosalind E. Krauss and Denis Hollier, text established by Thomas Clerc under the direction of Eric Marty (New York: Columbia University Press, 2005) 148.

Klara Kemp-Welch, 'Jirí Kovanda's Collisions', 2009; previously unpublished.

THESE MOMENTARY OPENINGS, THE POCKETS BETWEEN, THEIR TRANSITORY SPACES, IGNORED SEAMS AND FORGOTTEN VISTAS, PROMISE A SITE FROM WHICH THE EITHER/OR OF UTOPIAN AND APOCALYPTIC THINKING, OR THE POLITICAL/FORMALIST OPPOSITION CAN BE DISMANTLED

REPETITIONS, RETRACINGS, RELAPSES

Jacques Lacan
Écrits//1966

[...] The most serious reality, and even the sole serious reality for man, if one considers its role in sustaining the metonymy of his desire, can only be retained in metaphor.

What am I trying to get at, if not to convince you that what the unconscious brings back to our attention is the law by which enunciation can never be reduced to what is enunciated in any discourse?

Let us not say that I choose my terms in it, regardless of what I have to say – although it is not pointless to recall here that the discourse of science, in so far as it commends itself by its objectivity, neutrality and dreariness, even of the Sulpician variety, is just as dishonest and ill-intentioned as any other rhetoric.

What must be said is that the I of this choice is born somewhere other than in the place where the discourse is enunciated – namely, in the person who listens to it.

Doesn't this provide the status of rhetorical effects, in showing that they extend to all signification? Let people object that they stop at mathematical discourse – I will agree all the more in that I place the highest value on that discourse precisely because it signifies nothing.

The only absolute statement was made by the competent authority – namely, that no roll of the dice in the signifier will ever abolish chance. This is so because chance exists only within a linguistic determination, no matter how we consider it, whether in combination with automatism or encounter. [...]

Jacques Lacan, extract from *Écrits* (Paris: Éditions du Seuil, 1966); trans. Bruce Fink (New York: W.W. Norton, 2002) 758.

Jacques Lacan
The Unconscious and Repetition//1973

[...] What is repeated, in fact, is always something that occurs – the expression tells us quite a lot about its relation to the *tuché – as if by chance*.[1] This is something that we analysts never allow ourselves to be taken in by, on principle.

At least, we always point out that we must not be taken in when the subject tells us that something happened to him that day that prevented him from realizing his wish to come to the session. Things must not be taken at the level at which the subject puts them – in as much as what we are dealing with is precisely this obstacle, this hitch, that we find at every moment. It is this mode of apprehension above all that governs the new deciphering that we have given of the subject's relations to that which makes his condition.

The function of the *tuché*, of the real as encounter – the encounter in so far as it may be missed, in so far as it is essentially the missed encounter – first presented itself in the history of psychoanalysis in a form that was in itself already enough to arouse our attention, that of the trauma.

Is it not remarkable that, at the origin of the analytic experience, the real should have presented itself in the form of that which is *unassimilable* in it – in the form of the trauma, determining all that follows, and imposing on it an apparently accidental origin? We are now at the heart of what may enable us to understand the radical character of the conflictual notion introduced by the opposition of the pleasure principle and the reality principle – which is why we cannot conceive the reality principle as having, by virtue of its ascendency, the last word.

In effect, the trauma is conceived as having necessarily been marked by the subjectifying homeostasis that orientates the whole functioning defined by the pleasure principle. Our experience then presents us with a problem, which derives from the fact that, at the very heart of the primary processes, we see preserved the insistence of the trauma in making us aware of its existence. The trauma reappears, in effect, frequently unveiled. How can the dream, the bearer of the subject's desire, produce that which makes the trauma emerge repeatedly – if not its very face, at least the screen that shows us that it is still there behind? [...]

1 [Lacan proposed the term *tuché* to signify an aspect of repetition that interrupts (through an encounter, or misencounter, with the real – ranging from a minor chance disturbance to trauma) another aspect of repetition, *automaton*, that is symbolic, arising from rules that a set of signifiers adhere to.]

Jacques Lacan, extract from *Les quatre concepts fondamentaux de la psychanalyse* (Paris: Éditions du Seuil, 1973); trans. Alan Sheridan, *The Four Fundamental Concepts of Psychoanalysis* (New York: W.W. Norton, 1977) 54–5.

Brad Spence
The Case of Bas Jan Ader//1999

In considering the work of artist Bas Jan Ader, there is an almost irresistible temptation to lapse into speculative narratives of the sensational and popular variety. This is perfectly understandable, since his story climaxes with the artist lost at sea in a risky performance – leaving behind only a modest number of works that seem laden with foreboding clues. Even aside from dramatic questions of the artist's ultimate fate, responses to his work are rife with personal projections and detective-style sleuthing as to his psychological state and artistic intent. Such a frenzy in the interpretive process suggests that a measure of self-consciousness is warranted in any narrative voice-over to Ader's tragic plight.

While it would be premature to describe the case of Bas Jan Ader as a mystery of grand and deliberate design, intended simultaneously to interrogate and exploit our tendencies to construct retroactive, narrative meaning, the artist's work *was* persistently engaged with these issues. With a certain obsessive consistency, Ader would repeatedly thrust himself into the centre of an irreconcilable dichotomy: the contradictory position of being both the subject and object of a story – director and actor in his own production. In the short films, photographs, slides and performances which comprise his remarkably short career as an active artist (1970–1975), Ader casts himself – a handsome, mute, vulnerable presence – as the protagonist in scenes that are simultaneously melodramatic, funny and strangely opaque.

To begin a discussion of Ader's work in terms of scripting, performance and artistic personae is to employ a vocabulary that is entirely comfortable in the late 1990s. Presently, the *self* as a discursive construction of competing roles has been extensively theorized as well as thoroughly canonized in the work of artists such as Cindy Sherman. It is noteworthy that Ader studied art in Southern California in the late 1960s when a minimalist-conceptualist practice was attempting to eliminate the contaminating 'cult of personality' from art making, in favour of a more objective, scientifc approach. While Ader adopted much of conceptualism's orthodoxy, particularly its evidentiary treatment of the art object, he often chose subjects – e.g. flowers, sunsets, tears – which engaged the sort of vulgar sentimentality that was antithetical to the prevailing empirical ethos.

The circumstances of Ader's disappearance are follows: On 9 July 1975, he departed from Cape Cod, Massachusetts in a 12 foot, 6-inch sailing boat. His destination was Falmouth, England, on a solo voyage he projected to take 67 days – a record for the smallest vessel to cross the Atlantic. Three weeks in to

Ader's voyage, radio contact was broken, and there were no further signs of him until the empty hull of his craft was discovered off the coast of Ireland the following April. His body was never found.

Ader's trans-Atlantic feat was conceived as the second part of a trilogy titled *In Search of the Miraculous* (1975). The first part was held at the Claire Copley Gallery in Los Angeles, where a small choir with piano accompaniment sang sea shanties. The third was planned for a museum in his native Netherlands. Initially, Ader's disappearance met with nearly unanimous scepticism. Even those close to the artist interpreted the event as a fabricated stunt perfectly in keeping with his sly, cryptic approach to art and life. Known for his enigmatic presence (e.g. he perpetually wore navy blue seafaring garments) Ader had a demeanour which has been described as one part prankster and another brooding, melancholy European – he emigrated alone to Southern California in 1963 at age 22. Certain apparent clues, such as the copy of *The Strange Last Voyage of Donald Crowhurst* found in his faculty locker, seemed to point to a hoax or dubious intent. The discovered text gives a non-fictional account of a sailor's attempt to fake a non-stop, solo voyage around the globe and his eventual loss of sanity and life to the sea. Only after several years was it finally accepted that, whatever the circumstances, the artist was in fact gone.

Much of Ader's work centred on the simple act of falling. *Fall I (Los Angeles)* (1970), documented in black and white, conceptual-style photographs, finds the artist sitting in a chair atop the roof of his California bungalow. In the sequence that follows, he inexplicably loses his poise, awkwardly rolls down the roof and plummets into the bushes below. Similar pieces find the artist biking into a canal: *Fall II (Amsterdam)* (1970); and loosing his grip on a tree branch: *Broken Fall (Organic)* (1971). By removing these perilous moments of action from any motivating context, Ader invites two almost mutually exclusive possibilities for interpretation. The first focused on the irreducible physicality of his performance; the artist, in experiencing the corporeal threat of a particular situation, offers his body as the finite producer and bearer of meaning. That is, in the modernist-materialist tradition of 'it is what it is', the body becomes the ultimate interpretive measure. Although Ader was unusually guarded in speaking about his work, he pointedly denied this perspective as his sole intent: 'I do not make body sculpture, body art or body works. When I fell off the roof of my house or into a canal, it was because gravity made itself master over me.' Thus Ader opens his work to a second group of more literary possibilities: metaphor, allegory, irony and the corresponding narratives of the self. His *falls* make themselves available as symbols ranging from subjective failure and dissolution to that of a theological order.

Ader repeatedly enacts the Cartesian contradictions between the experience of bodily pain and the intersubjective production of consciousness. In his essay

'On the Essence of Laughter' (1855), the poet Baudelaire discussed the comedic convention of falling in terms of this experience of fragmentation: 'The man who trips would be the last to laugh at his own fall, unless he happens to be a philosopher, one who had acquired by habit, a power of rapid self-division, and thus of assisting as a disinterested spectator at the phenomenon of his own ego.' Thus for Baudelaire, falling can engender a sense of doubling. A person who has tripped and is falling is losing the self-possession of consciousness and becoming an object. To laugh during a fall is not merely to imagine yourself as another spectator, that is in another subjective state, but to recognize the smug folly of consciousness in facing its own material constitution.

In some sense, falling, as a forced union of mind and matter, could be seen as a rehearsal for the more immutable event of dying. This analogy is palpable in Ader's short film *Nightfall* (1971). Shot in his garage-studio, the camera records the artist painstakingly hoisting a large brick over his head. His figure is harshly lit by two tangles of light bulbs. He suddenly loses control of the brick, crushing one strand of lights. As he again lifts the brick, allowing tension and dread to accrue, the climax seems inevitable – the brick will (and does) fall and terminate the camera's remaining illumination. Here the film abruptly ends with the irrevocable logic of consciousness extinguished. This simple cause and effect sequence performs a narrative that is startlingly incongruous with its conclusion. The brick is witnessed demolishing the lights, but that seems to be an insufficient explanation for the void of meaning it leaves in the wake of the film's ending – the blunt finality of another's death, by implication, creates a similar scramble to find language for a disturbing rupture.

All artists, of course, eventually yield the interpretive legacy of their work to their audience. Ader, however, from early on, seems preoccupied with this eventuality and makes work as if he were already absent. Conscious that popular conceptions of the tragic artist frequently dominate the public's reception of art, he willingly casts himself in the role of the troubled genius. The following notebook entry provides a clue to his degree of self-consciousness: 'Write an article regarding Van Gogh's genius and pre-eminence as modernist through the price of the cutting off of an ear (public always recognized implicitly his real achievement as an artist was this act.)'

In a very early series of photographs, eventually abandoned, Ader decidedly assumes the position of 'the artist'. One image, titled *The Artist as Consumer of Extreme Comfort* (*c.* 1968), shows Ader reclining by a fire, sipping wine and reading a book. Another, *The Artist Contemplating Forces of Nature* (1967), finds him smugly smoking a cigar in a wicker chair that is balanced on his rooftop (he will later begin his first fall from this vantage). This early ironic posturing clearly illustrates Ader's interest in fulfilling romantic expectations for 'the artist' in the manner of a character actor.

In his later work, a degree of irony is still palpable through the use of kitschy, sentimental imagery, even as the act becomes increasingly difficult to discern as such. The series of films and photographs *I'm too Sad to Tell You* (1970-71), document Ader crying for the camera. This trope of Hollywood melodrama, the teary close-up, becomes a rather convincing display of emotion. Here again, he isolates the action from any narrative context, which the Hollywood counterpart depends upon for effect. In one version of this piece, Ader reproduced a tearful still as a postcard – writing the title on the verso and sending copies to art-world denizens. Thus 'the artist's' personal misery is converted into a consumable souvenir. Language's failure to convey experience – 'my sadness cannot be told in words' – is quickly supplanted by its ability to tell narratives. Ader purposefully lends this scene of despair to a storyline of the romantic, miserable artist, however trivialized in the translation. [...]

The fact that Ader's body was never recovered continues to allow manifold speculative scenarios of suicide, new lives or brazen recklessness. His story's ambiguous dénouement finds an ominous parallel in a 1972 performance *The Boy Who Fell Over Niagara Falls*. For the duration of this exhibition, Ader would, twice daily, sit in the gallery and read aloud a short story from that quintessential source for abridged, popularized narratives, *Reader's Digest*. The piece tells of a boat excursion that inadvertently carries the captain and a seven-year-old passenger over the Niagara Falls. This true story is simultaneously tragic and miraculous, as the captain perishes and the boy survives. In the narrative form as it is methodically conveyed by the artist, the characters drift toward consequences that, with the emphasis of repetition, seem fated; and like Ader's own artistic plight, ends with poignant ambiguity.

Brad Spence, extract from 'The Case of Bas Jan Ader' (Vancouver, 1999) n.p. Previously published online only on the website dedicated to the artist (www.basjanader.com)

Gerhard Richter
Statement//1985

Letting a thing come, rather than creating it – no assertions, constructions, formulations, inventions, ideologies – in order to gain access to all that is genuine, richer, more alive: to what is beyond my understanding.

At twenty: Tolstoy's *War and Peace*. It doesn't matter how rightly I remember, the only thing that stayed with me, that struck me at the time, was Kutuzov's way of not intervening, of planning nothing, but watching to see how things worked out, choosing the right moment to put his weight behind a development that was beginning of its own accord. Passivity was that general's genius. (The Photo Pictures: taking what is there, because one's own experiences only make things worse. The Colour Charts: the hope that this way a painting will emerge that is more than I could ever invent. At the same time, no truck with chance painting, painting blind, drug painting.) The Abstract Pictures: more and more clearly, a method of not having and planning the 'motif' but evolving it, letting it come. (About six years ago, that endless series of lacquer studies, all of which I destroyed: letting the lacquers merge, observing the countless rich pictures that emerged – and disappointment at a kind of naturalism that was completely unusable, arty-crafty, kitschy.) Now the constant involvement of chance (but still never automatism), which destroys my constructions and inventions and creates new situations. (As ever, Polke, I am glad to say, is doing something comparable.)

Using chance is like painting Nature – but which chance event, out of all the countless possibilities?

Gerhard Richter, statement from journal (28 February 1985), in Gerhard Richter, *The Daily Practice of Painting: Writings and Interviews 1962–1993*, trans. David Britt, ed. Hans Ulrich Obrist (London: Thames & Hudson, 1993) 119–20.

Gerhard Richter
Interview with Benjamin H.D. Buchloh//1986

Benjamin Buchloh What part does chance play in your painting?

Gerhard Richter An essential one, as it always has. There have been times when this has worried me a great deal, and I've seen this reliance on chance as a shortcoming on my part.

Buchloh Is this chance different from chance in Pollock? Or from Surrealist automatism?

Richter Yes, it certainly is different. Above all, it's never blind chance: it's a chance that is always planned, but also always surprising. And I need it in order to carry on, in order to eradicate my mistakes, to destroy what I've worked out wrong, to introduce something different and disruptive. I'm often astonished to find how much better chance is than I am.

Buchloh So this is the level on which openness is still thinkable and credible in real terms? Chance?

Richter It introduces objectivity, so perhaps it's no longer chance at all. But in the way it destroys and is simultaneously constructive, it creates something that of course I would have been glad to do and work out for myself.

Buchloh But you don't take that personally any more? You don't regard it as a failure on your part? You see it as a generalized factor?

Richter No, I now see it as a generalized factor, something entirely positive. Jacques Monod's *Chance and Necessity*, and all sorts of other facts and reflections that have evolved on the subject, all confirm me in that.

Buchloh Would the same principle apply to the structure of the work itself, its apparent repeatability, the apparent arbitrariness and openness of every individual painting? Is there a structural analogy to the structure of chance, in the fact that the work itself – like the separate work clusters – has no closed quality left but appears totally open?

Richter Possibly; and, if we disregard the closed quality that every picture has to have – if it is not to be a random detail of something else, or just plain unfinished – then non-closure may perhaps be a positive quality, because it relates more closely to our reality.

Buchloh Then it might be said that the compositional structure, in its openness, is the other dimension of a still-credible, substantive utopian factor?

Richter That may be so. Especially because so many paintings nowadays look so stupid precisely because they lay claim to being closed works. That's the deception.

Buchloh Yes, and I find this open dimension in very few artists. It's the radicalism that leads the artist to run the risk of ending up with a work that looks unfinished, infinitely reproducible and internally repetitive.

Richter The only paradoxical thing is that I always set out with the intention of getting a closed picture, with a proper, composed motif – and then go to great lengths to destroy that intention, bit by bit, almost against my will. Until the picture is finished and has nothing left but openness.

Buchloh The fiction of an openness, a total openness, just as the use of chance is not real but a fiction of chance.

Richter I can only hope that I haven't lost my naïvety, and that I shall go on making all the same effort – which is actually quite superfluous.

Buchloh What about colour – I mean, can the involvement of chance be extended to colour relationships, the colour scheme? Up to now, we have only talked about the compositional order, but I'd say that the same principle defines the relations between colours.

Richter Not to the same extent. It sometimes happens that I mix the paint for a particular painting and then put it onto another – and this has hardly ever turned out to be a mistake. But this is really an unconscious strategy that I can use to outwit myself.

Buchloh In the permutational colour paintings, you worked on a logical, consistent, random basis. There it was the form that was laid down in advance, and here in the abstracts it's largely the colour. And in contrast to the systematic manner of the Colour Charts, the permutations in the Abstract Pictures emerge naturally.

Richter Yes, chance is natural too, and it's an element that modifies.

Buchloh This freedom of colour, or this apparent arbitrariness of colour, as found in your Abstract Pictures, never appears in Neo-Expressionism, where the colour is always still regulated by aesthetic preconceptions, representational functions and harmonic compositions.

Richter Yes, that's right.

Gerhard Richter and Benjamin H.D. Buchloh, extract from interview (1986), in Gerhard Richter, *The Daily Practice of Painting: Writings and Interviews 1962–1993*, trans. David Britt, ed. Hans Ulrich Obrist (London: Thames & Hudson, 1993) 159–61.

Benjamin H.D. Buchloh
The Diagram and the Colour Chip: Gerhard Richter's *4900 Colours*//2008

[...] It is necessary for us to differentiate between those seemingly similar, yet ultimately rather different approaches to the relationships of colour, grid composition and chance distribution that Richter has deployed throughout the various phases in his oeuvre when painting colour grids: from his first colour chart paintings of 1966 through to *1024 Colours* of 1971, to the new project of *4900 Colours*, 2007.[1] One could argue, for example, that the colour charts were still enacting a Warholian celebration of the platitudinous condition of readymade experience. In the wake of the increasing industrialization of desire, colour had simultaneously to mimic and differentiate itself from the design objects of consumer culture as much as from the registers of mere fashion cycles, while recognizing them at the same time as the ultimate masters of chroma's fate. At the same time, or rather, as a consequence of these developments, modernist conceptions of self-referential or self-sufficient colour had come increasingly under pressure and had entered a condition of crisis (manifestly opposed by Ad Reinhardt, for example, or at times almost programmatically performed in Barnett Newman's work with the primaries).

Written in 1972, Leo Steinberg's diagnosis of these problems – albeit historically incomplete – looked back at the decade of the 1960s. It still appears to be devastatingly accurate, both in its description of early 1960s American painting and in its analysis of the waning of a primarily Greenbergian formalist criticism that had accompanied it (and it is worth quoting at some length):

> In the criticism of the relevant paintings there is rarely a hint of expressive purpose, or recognition that pictures function in human experience. The painter's industry is a closed loop. The search for the holistic design is simply self-justified and self-perpetuating. Whether this search is still the exalted Kantian process of self-criticism seems questionable; the claim strikes me rather as a remote intellectual analogy. And other analogies suggest themselves, less intellectual but closer to home. It is probably no chance coincidence that the descriptive terms which have dominated American formalist criticism these past fifty years run parallel to the contemporaneous evolution of the Detroit automobile.[2]

Colour Chances

Richter's new series *4900 Colours* has repositioned itself at quite a distance from any affirmative or ambiguous ironies of early 1960s pop culture. Every aspect of *4900 Colours* (facture, surface, distribution, composition) is now fully subjected to the order of the diagrammatic: abstraction becomes a purely quantitative regime and functions as a schema of data collection and registration. And the series' transposition of a commercially produced chromatic order of everyday life inevitably associates it with an *episteme* of control, if not with one of confinement and spatial restriction. Once again, Steinberg's criticism of the period, especially his famous definition of the flatbed picture – written in the same decade as Richter's permutational colour paintings of the early 1970s were made – contains the crucial descriptive elements that could be transferred from the author's discussion (of Rauschenberg's and Johns' work) to that of Richter's paintings:

> The flatbed picture plane makes its symbolic allusion to hard surfaces such as table tops, studio floors, charts, bulletin boards, any receptor surface on which objects are scattered, on which data is entered, on which information may be received, printed, impressed – whether coherently or in confusion. The pictures of the last fifteen to twenty years insist on a radically new orientation in which the painted surface is no longer the analogue of a visual experience of nature, but of operational processes.[3]

Steinberg had already suggested at that moment that the new 'operational processes' of painting could either be organized, as he states, 'coherently' or 'in confusion'. The simultaneous deployment of this duality, as we are arguing, has distinguished Richter's work since the mid 1960s from that of most of his American peers (with the possible exception of Sol LeWitt), since Richter's procedures were always engaged in the parallel pursuit of these opposite approaches, of the 'coherent' or the 'confused', either simultaneously or in alternating sequences.

The most obvious, if not the most important change in *4900 Colours*, is of course the fact that rather than leaving the selection of colours and their constellations to chance operations performed by the artist (i.e. numbering the colours and drawing the numbers out of a hat), the selection and compositional distribution of colours is now executed according to the instructions of a computer programme. Analogously to expanding the technological order of painting's composition, Richter has also decided to dislodge the very process of manufacturing the painting from the hand to the mechanical devices of the spray gun handled by a technical collaborator. (The colour chips making up the paintings are individually spray-painted lacquer squares. Once solidified, they are inserted like elements of a mosaic into the prefixed structural arrangement. Each element consists of 25 coloured squares glued or taped onto the supporting Aludibond panel.) These decisions form the base for the permutability of the 4,900 colour chips and panels, since they were conceived from the start as a structure of permutation that could vary its own quantitative arrangements in 11 different presentational constellations.[4]

How many times in the twentieth century have those types of decisions – which shifted painting from the artisanal to the lower levels of industrial production – been accompanied by triumphant declamations of the superceding of paintings' artisanal past? However, these triumphant declarations, first pronounced by László Moholy-Nagy in 1926 and again as recently as the 1960s by Donald Judd, are now replaced by Richter with a rather detached, not to say resigned, acceptance of the inevitable regimes of technological production.

Yet it is crucial to recognize that even within Richter's most rigorous grid formations, which appear in full compliance with the administrative order and quantifying powers of the diagram, the artist mobilizes a counterforce, the most violent opposition to that matrix of statistical spatial mapping: aleatory chromatic constellations. Richter grasps the inevitable aesthetic necessity of inserting a fundamental contradiction within the essentially positivist project of diagrammatic abstraction. [...]

1 [footnote 4 in source] For an excellent discussion of Richter's work with the colour charts, and of the problematic complex of colour in art of the 1960s and 1970s in general, see Briony Fer's essay 'Colour Manual' in Ann Temkin's important catalogue and exhibition *Colour Chart: Reinventing Colour, 1950 to Today* (New York: The Museum of Modern Art, 2008) 28–38.

2 [5] Leo Steinberg, 'Other Criteria' in *Other Criteria: Confrontations with Twentieth Century Art* (New York: Oxford University Press, 1972) 79.

3 [6] Leo Steinberg, 'Reflections on the State of Criticism' (1972); reprinted in Branden W. Joseph, ed., *Robert Rauschenberg* (Cambridge, Massachusetts: The MIT Press, 2002) 28.

4 [7] The current installation at the Serpentine Gallery, London [2008] is *Version II*, consisting of 49 plates containing 100 colour squares each, amounting to *4900 Colours*. Previous installations such as the one at the Museum Ludwig in Cologne in August 2007 (*Version XI*), consisted, for example, of a single mural-sized plate, 680 by 680 centimetres and containing all 4,900 colour chips.

Benjamin H.D. Buchloh, extract from 'The Diagram and the Colour Chip: Richter's *4900 Colours*', in *Gerhard Richter: 4900 Colours* (London: Serpentine Gallery, 2008) 65–7.

Sophie Calle
Suite vénitienne//1980

For months I followed strangers on the street. For the pleasure of following them, not because they particularly interested me. I photographed them without their knowledge, took note of their movements, then finally lost sight of them and forgot them.

At the end of January 1980, on the streets of Paris, I followed a man whom I lost sight of a few minutes later in the crowd. That very evening, quite by chance, he was introduced to me at an opening. During the course of our conversation, he told me he was planning an imminent trip to Venice. [...]

Sophie Calle, Prologue [describing the artwork first realized in 1980], in Sophie Calle, *Suite vénitienne* / Jean Baudrillard, *Please follow me* (Paris: Éditions de l'Étoile, 1983); trans. Dany Barash and Danny Hatfield (Seattle: Bay Press, 1988) 2.

Luc Sante
Sophie Calle's Uncertainty Principle//1993

Like a sculptor of a past century, Sophie Calle in her art manipulates and reconfigures a commodity central to the economy of her time. This commodity does not happen to be bronze or marble, however, but information, the elusive stuff that circulates incessantly between consciousness, document, and cyberspace. It is a maddeningly imprecise and unquantifiable commodity, hovering somewhere on the border between objective and subjective, public and private, hot and cold. It is farmed in huge quantities, fought over, stolen, adulterated and negotiated by credit bureaus, intelligence agencies, polling organizations, market-research firms, and yet its value resides in minute specifics and fugitive shades of meaning. Its pursuit thus resembls experimental science – vast quantities of print-outs are generated for every nit that can be seized upon and exploited – as well as art: it is at every point along its process so immaterial, so woozily figurative or abstract, that its commodity status seems like a bit of *legerdemain*, and its manufacture and trade a kind of parody.

Calle is not the first artist to work this medium, of course. The Surrealists probably were the pioneers, notably in their fascination with opinion polls. The aphorist and suicide Jacques Rigaut put his own spin on the matter: he carried on his person a tiny pair of scissors with which he used to remove surreptitiously a button from the garment of every person he met; this he insisted was a form of art collecting. The novelist Philippe Soupault once staged a version of a highway robbery: he stopped a bus on the Avenue de l'Opéra late at night by extending a chain across its path; then entered it and ordered all the passengers to tell him their birth dates (the combination of violence and trivia present in this act does not seem very far from Calle's concerns). Trivia devoid of violence, data accumulated for their own sake, the relentless documentation of the most apparently boring processes – these are traits associated with various phases of conceptual art, which pursued the sublime through several disciplines, one of them being busywork. The Surrealist and conceptual approaches to the management of information as a medium in itself could be said to represent in their very different ways the mingled fascination and horror inspired by the looming triumph of bureaucracy. The Surrealists responded with bemusement and savagery, the conceptualists with Zen, which is not identical to complacency.

The work of Sophie Calle appears at various times to display all of these qualities, at others only some. Her first work, *The Sleepers*, resembles straightforward conceptual bookkeeping but with an added layer of sexual risk, at least by implication. Risk, as well as stealth, deception and intrusion, dominates her most notorious works, *Suite vénitienne*, *The Shadow*, *The Hotel* and *L'Homme au carnet*. The commanding metaphor here is espionage, with more than a suggestion of sadomasochism. *Anatoli* is a portrait, sharing with her earlier works the fact of having been assembled not in spite of but through adverse conditions, in this case the lack of a common language. In its plainness it throws into relief this common thread, which we might name 'the blind men and the elephant'. Not surprisingly, her next piece is *The Blind*. This work, which connects as well to the earlier and more prosaic *The Bronx*, employs hearsay in pursuit of the ineffable, in effect constructing an artwork only alluded to and not represented by the objects on the gallery wall, a pursuit taken up in *Ghosts*, *Blind Colour* and *Last Seen*.

There seems to be a rough split in Calle's career to date: her earlier works are, broadly speaking, concerned with narrative, and the later ones with image. In both, the principal tool is language, with the visual component filling an illustrative role. In this way, her work suggests the forensic process during a police investigation: she assembles clues, descriptions, guesses, allusions, and pieces them together into an approximate rendering. In the earlier works, this rendering takes the form of a dossier; in the later ones it resembles an identikit sketch. *Cash Machine* might be a sort of pun on this idea, with its disembodied, almost ectoplastic surveillance-camera portraits. *Autobiographical Stories* and *The Tombs* extend the principle of the visual substitute or approximation in another direction, toward the iconic. The objects that stand in for epochal incidents in the artist's life and the laconic gravestones that reduce entire existences to a mere familial title possess a weight of their own; the referent is almost beside the point. If one were to hear or read a description of Calle's work and try to reconstruct it on that basis without actually seeing it, it is possible that one might imagine its theme to be the poverty of language or of image, the insufficiency of second-hand experience. Instead, her work continually stresses the beauty of imprecision, the poetry of gaps and lapses.

She is, in other words, a kind of impressionist. Uncertainty dapples her pictures the way the sun's rays spatter the leaves and splash the grassy swards in the Bois de wherever. But that's not all there is to it. Uncertainty is an inevitability when it comes to information; information is uncertain in the same way that humans are mortal. But information nevertheless strives for certainty, or rather its purveyors do, whether quixotically or disingenuously. The police tipster, the industrial spy, the political clairvoyant, the highly placed source – all are in the business of pretending infallibility. And their commerce, once a small-time traffic, is in the process of becoming ever more institutionalized, increasingly central to the global economy as it moves from nocturnal alleys to glass-walled offices. Tremendous financial decisions are made on the basis of lore – consumer profiles, focus-group questionnaires, extrapolations of trend curves – that are about as reliable as the divination of bird entrails. This metaphor is not idly chosen: the commerce of information is descended in part from that of the augurers who advised military leaders in antiquity. It has merely been dressed up with technology and soft science for the benefit of contemporary rationalists.

Calle's work is to a certain degree a parody of this trade, and so could be said to be a parody of a parody, a simulacrum of a sham. But to the extent that her portraits – the address-book man, Anatoli, the occupants of the hotel rooms, herself even – are distortions, they are no more so than a Cubist head, say, would be as compared with a photographic likeness. Even when the deck appears stacked – the address-book scheme, viewed from one angle as a tin-pot Citizen Kane, might prompt questions about her motives – enough air is admitted in the form of indeterminacy to prevent any agent including Calle from having full control of the drift. Uncertainty, in short, is the footprint of truth. It is the only aspect of any piece of information that can always be relied upon, and, of course, it is the aspect that diminishes information's value as a commodity. It is nearly always inconvenient; it is unproductive and inefficient; it is often dangerous. And that is why it is so beautiful, as Calle repeatedly demonstrates in her work.

Luc Sante, 'Sophie Calle's Uncertainty Principle', *Parkett*, no. 36 (1993) 74–8.

Fischli & Weiss
Interview with Jörg Heiser//2006

Jörg Heiser There seem to be four steps inherent in your approach. The first is to collect, amass, using coincidence and memory rather than a systematic approach. The second is to introduce a particular order, a hierarchy – especially if that means ignoring or inverting an existing one. The third concerns time: stretching and compressing it – from 80 hours to the blink of an eye. The fourth, I'd say, is to twist and turn and sometimes subvert the methods I just mentioned, with a penchant for the deadpan, for slapstick. Would you agree with that description?

Peter Fischli Yes, that's right. But we might give these four steps different names: the first two steps of archiving and ordering are more like provisional storage. We do these things and then they're there. When they've been in the studio long enough maybe later we will begin to evaluate them, establish a hierarchy. And as far as the final step's concerned, it's about getting all of this into an artistic form. And that does involve reinterpretations. In the case of the 'Fotografias' it was a relatively simple reversal; these pictures are normally very large and colourful; we removed their colour and their size, made them very small, black and white. It's not slapstick, perhaps, but it does involve tricks, artistic methods.

Heiser By 'slapstick' I mean calculatedly amusing collisions, muddles: doing something crazy in a very sober way, or something very sober in a very crazy way. The idea of working against an initial impulse with a sense of enjoying the absurd.

David Weiss Well, with the airports there's nothing to tell you where they are, for example. That's the simplest one, a cheap trick. It leaves the viewer slightly at a loss, so it's just some place or other. And the same happens with the 'Fotografias', when you take what are actually very different images and relate them via the format and the black and white.

Heiser Do you work together on every step?

Fischli When we're photographing flowers or paintings, each of us goes off on his own and then we meet up after two or three days and look together at each other's results.

Heiser Is it a competition – who can get the best pictures?

Fischli It's competitive in a positive sense. Each of us brings back hunting trophies and we show them to each other. [...]

Heiser From the 'question pots' (*Kleiner Fragentopf, Grosser Fragentopf*, Big Question Pot, Little Question Pot, 1984), on the insides of which weighty and not so weighty questions are asked, through to *Kleine Fragen, Große Fragen* (Small Questions, Big Questions, 2003), comprising slide projections of questions, there seems to be a therapeutic idea at work – questioning yourselves, anxiously. New Age, self-help. Imagine someone trying to find their feet in this cultural milieu.

Weiss In very vague terms we did imagine someone asking himself slightly paranoid questions that revolve very much around himself. That is part of the legacy of psychoanalysis: broody self-questioning. Questioning first appeared in *Rat & Bear*, who made these drawings for themselves, *Ordnung und Reinlichkeit* (Order and Cleanliness, 1981). And then came the pair of opposites 'small questions and big questions': for example, small question – 'Has the last bus gone?' – as compared to big question – 'Where is the galaxy going?' The answer to the former question may, of course, be far more important than the latter, which one can take more time over.

Heiser It's like Woody Allen or Larry David rendering therapeutic self-questioning absurd by shifting the scale.

Weiss Precisely. But it is also a matter of going through life with the question of what is important and what is unimportant. We are constantly making judgements on this. And when things go slightly awry, it is sometimes amusing, sometimes sobering.

Fischli Boris Groys has a theory that there are two different types of question. One is: 'What is the diameter of the Earth?' and you immediately begin thinking, 'Oh yes, we learned that in school'. The second question is: 'Why is the Earth not a cube?' and you immediately begin wondering about the person who asked the question. Many of our questions go more in the latter direction.

Weiss For example, the 'question pots' contain the question 'Was I a good child?' That is a question of the introspective type.

Fischli And in the little book, it's handwritten notes – faked, of course – a look into the profane notes of a strange person. We're not especially interested in getting answers to these questions. We're more interested in creating an appropriate place to store them, be it in a pot – you only have to take one step back and you can no longer see them – or as a slide projection: they appear slowly and quickly fade away again.

Heiser Nocturnal visions, someone who can't get to sleep.

Fischli Right. And correspondingly, these questions are not carved in stone.

*The series of staged photographs 'Stiller Nachmittag' (*Quiet Afternoon, *1984–5), or 'Equilibrium' series, employs everyday objects in the most absurd, gravity-defying constellations rivalling Chinese circus acts: for example, an empty wine bottle site on top of an apple that sits on top of an eggcup, while a plate balances on the cork of the bottle, held in place by a counter-balance of a fish slice and a ladle, the latter holding an onion in a net (*Natürliche Grazie, *Natural Grace*).

Der Lauf der Dinge *(*The Way Things Go, *1987) takes the issue of tinkering with gravity one step further, setting it in motion. The result is a 30-minute sequence* *of enduring triumph: car tyres, candles, plastic bottles, fire crackers, suspicious liquids, planks and balloons are all lined up like dominoes (only occasionally bamboozled by way of a well-hidden cut). The sheer amount of Sisyphean work that must have gone into this is astounding, as is the ease with which the result sets itself at the head of a comical tradition of wacky, complex machineries fulfilling simple tasks in a convoluted, yet suspenseful way (though Fischli/Weiss remove even the simple task – the domino effect just ends in fog). It's a tradition that leads from the cartoons the American engineer Rube Goldberg thought up in the early twentieth century (his British counterpart was W. Heath Robinson with his cartoons of wacky machines run by balding bespectacled types in overalls), through Gyro Gearloose, to Kermit demonstrating the 'What Happens Next machine' to his eager* Sesame Street *audience.*

Heiser In the 'Equilibrium' series and in *The Way Things Go*, slapstick features not only in methodical terms but also directly – the physical comedy of objects. How did the one lead to the other?

Weiss First there were the 'Equilibriums'. We were sitting in a bar somewhere and playing around with the things on the table, and we thought to ourselves, this energy of never-ending collapse – because our construction stood for a moment and then collapsed before we built it up again – should be harnessed and channelled in a particular direction. That was also the original idea for *The Way Things Go*, in the Tate Modern exhibition; when you see the 'Making of', it becomes clear that the creative process was not funny at all. I've always found that astonishing anyway – the way people always laugh when the next thing falls over. Because for us it was more like a circus act, trained objects. And the ones that didn't do it were badly trained or badly positioned. It required considerable patience.

Fischli Strangely, for us, while we were making the piece, it was funnier when it failed, when it didn't work. When it worked, that was more about satisfaction. And that the film created the impression that the things move on their own, without human help, that they become spirited, living beings.

Heiser These stories of failure and collapse and then not failing after all – that's also the heroic theme of slapstick: the hero who accidentally breaks something, but in so doing brings about a stroke of good fortune and knocks over the villain etc. In *The Way Things Go* you laugh because something that cannot really work actually does work. It's a kind of triumph.

Fischli And there's an element of comedy in your identifying this heroic theme in the pathetic falling-over of objects. I see it too, and I think you're right, but if that is the case, then it has an element of comedy in itself.

Weiss A professor in Germany once asked us whether we were thinking about the French Revolution when we were making that film.

Heiser Why?

Weiss Because of the upheavals that lead to further upheavals. And in China a student asked me if we had been thinking of reincarnation and the transmigration of souls ...

Heiser The title *The Way Things Go* suggests the historical, a concatenation of fateful events.

Fischli I don't really like it, that title.

Heiser Why?

Fischli Well, it's somehow ...

Heiser ... a bit Wim Wenders?

Fischli Yes, and it's not my favourite title, because it's too close to what we see – 'Suddenly this Overview' is a better title, for a series of small clay sculptures.

Heiser 'Suddenly this Overview' refutes itself, whereas *The Way Things Go* reaffirms.

Fischli Yes, it's a little bit unsophisticated.

Jörg Heiser, Peter Fischli and David Weiss, extract from interview, 'The Odd Couple', *frieze*, no. 102 (October 2006) 202–5. www.frieze.com

Claire Bishop
Fischli & Weiss: *Equilibres – Quiet Afternoon* (1984–85)//2008

One of my favourite pieces of writing on Fischli/Weiss is by Peter Schjeldahl, because he openly refuses to make grand claims for their work. In fact, he does the exact opposite: 'As professional artists, these guys are pretty jejune. Their ideas are hybrids or retreads of precedents they don't advance or otherwise alter significantly.'[1] It's true: Fischli/Weiss don't strive to be the first or best or most spectacular. They even seem to harness mediocrity. As a result, all attempts to stake them a place in art history appear painfully strained, since every aspect of their work actively resists aggrandisement. *Stiller Nachmittag* (*Quiet Afternoon*, 1984/5) is completely typical in this respect. It comprises a series of twenty-seven photographs of sculptures made using everyday objects precariously arranged into understated, pointless and often unmemorably complex configurations. The titles veer from daft narrative to deadpan allegory, neologisms, untitleds and the utterly inexplicable. None of the compositions bear any significant relation to any of the others in the series, which is so disparate that it fails to produce a coherent whole. There could be forty pictures or only five; it wouldn't make that much difference.

Such slack randomness has an immediately deflationary effect on art-historical analysis. If anything, *Quiet Afternoon* is a send-up of traditional sculpture and the language with which we read it. Composition, matter, dynamism, weight, pictoriality: all these terms fall flat in the face of ropey materials and bathetic titling. It's hard to discuss a work as sculpture when the object of your study is a quizzical courgette tentatively gracing a stumpy carrot supported by a slim cheese grater. What follows, then, is a replacement for such potentially excruciating legitimations. It's a short compendium of art references that come to mind when perusing *Quiet Afternoon*. What comes to the fore is the recurrent theme of gravity: a split second of provisional balance before the objects come clattering to the floor. Perhaps those afternoons weren't so quiet after all.

Am Abgrund (On the Brink)/*Das Experiment* (The Experiment)/*Die Verfeinerung* (Refinement)

> Raised up, but visually unstable, these table sculptures could be smaller in scale, skeletal, and so present faster, dynamic compositions. Elegant drawings in space, they lead the eyes like swift dancers, seemingly ready to step gracefully free of the table's boundaries.[2]

Schlummerschlinge (Slumber Loop)/*Ohne Titel* (Untitled)/*Die Verschwörung* (The Conspiracy)

> Sometimes a direct manipulation of a given material without the use of any tool is made. In these cases considerations of gravity become as important as those of space. The focus on matter and gravity as means results in forms that were not projected in advance. Considerations of ordering are necessarily casual and imprecise and unemphasized. Random piling, loose stacking, hanging, give passing form to the material.[3]

Ohne Titel (Untitled)/*Ehre Mut und Zuversicht* (Honour Courage Confidence)/*Die Barrikade* (Barricade)/*Die Gesetzlosen* (Outlaws)/*Ohne Titel* (Untitled)

> For these sculptures are resolutely vertical, their internal dynamic securing their independence of any external 'ground', be it floor or wall. And the extremely simple principle of their verticality is the heaviness of lead and its earnest response to the downward pull of gravity; for in that pull there operates the resistance that is the principle of the prop – stability achieved through the conflict and balance of forces.[4]

Der Kreislauf (Melancholy, Longing, Strategy, Tactics, Fulfilment. A Cycle)/*Masturbine*/*Flirt, Liebe usw.* (Flirtation, Love etc.)/*Die Gefahren der Nacht* (Night's Danger)

> These objects, which lend themselves to a minimum of mechanical functioning, are based on phantasms and representations susceptible to being provoked by the realization of unconscious acts. Acts of realization from which one can hardly explain the pleasure drawn, or which render account of the erroneous theories elaborated by censorship and repression. In all the cases analysed, these acts correspond to fantasies and desires clearly characterized as erotic.[5]

Frau Birne bringt ihrem Mann vor der Oper das frischgebügelte Hemd. Der Bub raucht (Mrs Pear Bringing her Husband a Freshly Ironed Shirt for the Opera. The Boy Smokes)/*Natürliche Grazie* (Natural Grace)/*Hase* (Hare)/*Zorn Gottes* (God's Wrath)/*Die Seilschaft* (Roped Mountaineers)

> To quote Roland Barthes, he never tired of using 'different forms to represent the same thing. Does he want to paint a nose? His multitude of synonyms proposes a branch, a pear, a pumpkin, corn, flowers, fish.' Interest is centred neither in the fish nor in the nose alone, but in teasing the very concept of reciprocity [...]

By exploiting duplicity and reversibility, the artist makes of the canvas at once a grotesque portrait and a still life. However abstract, linear perspective accepted space as the gravitational link between man and reality. For Arcimboldo, the only centre of gravity was his own mind, in which eccentricity reigned supreme.[6]

Ohne Titel (Untitled)/*Die gefeierte Rübe* (Triumphant Carrot)/*Stiller Nachmittag* (Quiet Afternoon)/*Der dunkle Trieb* (Dark Impulse)

Typically involving feats of balancing, the actions that comprise *One Minute Sculptures* often suggest a bizarre type of object-assisted yoga. In the video *One Minute Sculptures* (November 1997), Wurm attempts, among other things, to do a headstand with a chair on his back; to stand on a pair of plastic polka-dot balls; to lie on his side along the length of a narrow wooden stud; and to balance a yellow bucket on his head.[7]

Das Provisorium (Provisional Arrangement)/*Reagans Modell von der bewaffneten Raumfahrt* (Reagan's Model for Armed Space-Travel)/*Die Gewerkschaft* (Trade Union)/*Die missbrauchte Zeit* (Time Abused)

The earliest performance things that were filmed were things like you sit in the studio and what do you do. Well, it turned out that I was pacing around the studio a lot ... That was an activity that I did so I filmed that, just this pacing. So I was doing really simple things like that ...[8]

1 Peter Schjeldahl, 'Child's Play', *Artforum*, vol. XXXIV, no. 10 (Summer 1996) 126.

2 Julius Bryant, *Anthony Caro: A Life in Sculpture* (London: Merrell, 2004) 13.

3 Robert Morris, 'Anti Form' *Artforum*, vol. 6 (April 1968); reprinted in *Continuous Project Altered Daily: The Writings of Robert Morris* (Cambridge, Massachusetts: The MIT Press, 1993) 46.

4 Rosalind Krauss, 'Richard Serra/Sculpture' (1986); reprinted in *Richard Serra*, ed. Hal Foster (October Files series) (Cambridge, Massachusetts: The MIT Press, 2000) 108.

5 Salvador Dalí, 'Objets surréalistes', *Le Surréalisme au service de la révolution*, no. 3 (Paris, 1931).

6 Giancarlo Maiorino, *The Portrait of Eccentricity: Arcimboldo and the Mannerist Grotesque* (Pennsylvania: Pennsylvania State University Press, 1991) 34.

7 Ralph Rugoff, 'Liquid Humour', in *Erwin Wurm, I Love my Time, I Don't Like my Time*, ed. Berin Golonu (Ostfildern Ruit: Hatje Cantz, 2004) 19.

8 Bruce Nauman, in *Bruce Nauman* (Minneapolis: Walker Art Center, 1994) 73.

Claire Bishop, 'VIII' [on Fischli & Weiss: *Equilibres – Quiet Afternoon* (1984–85)], in *Fischli/Weiss. Flowers & Questions: A Retrospective*, ed. Bice Curiger (Zürich: Kunsthaus Zürich, 2008) 97–100.

Russell Ferguson
The Variety of Din//2003

[...] John Cage's most famous work, the so-called 'silent' piece, *4' 33"*, of 1952, is not really about silence at all. Rather it is about an enhanced listening – an active listening that opens up the listener to sounds that are normally ignored. David Toop has written about a recorded version he has of *4' 33"*: 'The idea seems ridiculous yet, for the first time, I listened to the surface noise of a bad vinyl pressing from Italy with interest rather than irritation.'[1] This anecdote makes clear the connection between *4' 33"* and Christian Marclay's *Record Without a Cover* (1985), a vinyl record that was distributed, just as the title indicates, without any kind of protective cover, and thus accumulates a series of scratches that in the end constitute an integral part of the audible elements of the record. In both cases, precisely what the listener will actually hear is largely determined by chance.

In Marclay's case, the embrace of sounds of all kinds can take him far from silence, and at one of his performances listeners are perhaps less likely to think of John Cage than of those Futurists who championed 'The Art of Noises': 'the crashing down of metal shop blinds, slamming doors, the hubbub of crowds, the variety of din, from stations, railways, iron foundries, spinning mills, printing works, electric power stations and underground railways.'[2] His music demands an engaged listener, one willing to accept the challenge posed by the barrage of sound that constitutes one of his performances. And the barrage is not merely audible; it is tactile too. He leaves behind him a trail of shattered records littering the floor.

Marclay recognizes that, if music's primary incarnation is as an object, rather than as an activity or a service, then music enters the world of exchange value. As he has said, 'The invention of recording technology has transformed sound into tangible objects and thus commodities (i.e. records, magnetic tapes, CDs). The contradiction between the transitory nature of sound and those material objects continues to fascinate me.'[3]

It is not coincidental that it was through violence – broken and melted records – that the transition between object and sound was made. Destruction of the commodity is a common thread throughout Marclay's work, beginning with the countless records scratched and smashed in performance.[4] *Footsteps* (1989) challenged taboos by calling for its audience to walk all over a floor tiled with pristine records. Even works that are not themselves broken, like his drumsticks made of glass, often seem to imply destruction. It is the potlatch of destruction that makes the commodity visible. In the name of the aleatory, the spontaneous, and the excessive, the capacity of the recording to deliver endless, unchanging reproduction is disrupted.

Instead of the perfection of repetition, which is the Platonic essence of commodification, Marclay invokes the pleasure of the fragmentary. Snatches of familiar melodies and glimpses of half-forgotten record covers appear and disappear in his work. As the novelist Thomas Bernhard has his character Reger say: 'Our greatest pleasure, surely, is in fragments, just as we derive the most pleasure from life if we regard it as a fragment, whereas the whole and the complete and perfect are basically abhorrent to us.'[5] The fragment resists the smoothness of perfection and insists on its own rough edges.

Throughout Marclay's work we can trace an attraction not just to the fragmented object, but to complete erasure. Even in his early Imaginary Records series, this theme is already evident. Works such as *Ghost* (1988) or *Smoke Rings* (1999) make that clear, as does *Remember* (1991), the ripped cover that is almost literally not there. Other Imaginary Records go beyond erasure to death itself. One group of them addresses directly the theme of the memento mori, including *Skull* (1989), *Mort* (1992), *Blind Faith* (1997), *Bubbles* (1997), and *Blue Candle* (1997) (the last recycled from Gerhard Richter via Sonic Youth).

Erasure is perhaps most powerfully present, if one can say that, in *Tape Fall* (1989). *Tape Fall* consists of a reel-to-reel tape recorder mounted near the ceiling. A tape plays the sound of trickling water. There is, however, no pick-up reel, so that after the tape has passed over the heads and given up the sound, it flows downwards into an ever-growing mound on the floor. The piece must be constantly replenished with new reels of tape.

On one level *Tape Fall* pays homage to a Fluxus tradition of ephemerality expressed through the sound of dripping water, including George Brecht's *Drip Music* (1959–62) and Mieko Shiomi's *Water Music* (1964, and its 'record variation' of 1965).[6] But it also speaks more broadly to the irrevocable passing of time, and counters the idea of ephemerality even as it incarnates it, by leaving visible the physical evidence of sound's passage. *Tape Fall* is a rare and profoundly contradictory object. It is a monumental sculpture that memorializes nothing more than the passage of time, and destroys its own materials in the process of creating itself. [...]

1 [footnote 19 in source] David Toop, *Ocean of Sound* (London: Serpent's Tail, 1995) 140–41.

2 [20] Luigi Russolo, 'The Art of Noises' (1913) in Umbro Apollonio, ed., *Futurist Manifestos* (London: Thames and Hudson, 1973) 74–75.

3 [21] Christian Marclay in *The Alpert Award in the Arts*. See also Theodor Adorno, 'The Form of the Phonograph Record' (1934); trans. Thomas Y. Levin, *October*, no. 55 (Winter 1990), 74–88.

4 [22] Marclay remembers that the first sculpture to make an impact on him was Jean Tinguely's

Eureka (1964), which he saw in Zurich when he was nine years old. Tinguely's work, of course, almost always plays with the possibility of its own potential collapse.

5 [23] Thomas Bernhard, *Old Masters* (1985); trans. Ewald Osers (Chicago: University of Chicago Press, 1992) 18.

6 [24] The 'Water Flows and Flux' section of Douglas Kahn's *Noise Water Meat: A History of Sound in the Arts* (Cambridge, Massachusetts: The MIT Press, 1999) 242–88, gives a thorough account of the dripping water motif. Kahn notes that at the first performance of John Cage's *4' 33"* in Woodstock, New York, it began to rain during the second movement.

Russell Ferguson, extract from 'The Variety of Din', in *Christian Marclay* (Los Angeles: UCLA/Hammer Museum, 2003) 42–3.

Fei Dawei
Two-Minute Cycle: Huang Yong Ping's Chinese Period//2005

On 1 December 1987, Huang Yong Ping placed a classical Chinese art history book and a Western art history book into a washing machine and washed them for two minutes. These two long-standing histories were transformed into a pile of unreadable pulp within two minutes. One of the most significant Chinese artists on the post-1990s international contemporary art scene, Huang was born in Xiamen, China, in 1954. He went abroad in May 1989 to participate in the exhibition 'Magiciens de la terre' at the Centre Georges Pompidou and has resided in Paris ever since.

Huang's work can be divided into two distinct phases, clearly marked by the reality of his overseas immigration. What distinguishes these two phases and how are they interrelated? Is it that, as Western critics maintain, his earlier works were simply limited experiments within an authoritarian system, but his later works truly blossomed? Or is that, as some within China assert, his previous works are free and subversive, whereas his later works are simply sell-outs to the Western art system?

Before going abroad in 1989, Huang was already well established and enjoyed a great reputation within the Chinese avant-garde art movement. As he stated in an interview in 2000, 'My entire creative methodology – the direction of my path – was primarily formed in China, and I have not fundamentally changed. Of course, the world is constantly changing, but ... one always adheres to a certain perspective, and at the age of thirty-five, my world view had already been formed, so it was very difficult to change.'[1]

The period prior to Huang's going abroad obviously played an important role in his later development. The Western world, however, is familiar only with his work from the period after he immigrated. What is this worldview that Huang has said is so difficult to change later in life, and how was it formed in China? By exploring these questions, we may gain a better understanding of the continuities within Huang's practice.

The Emergence of an Avant-garde

At the end of the 1970s, after having been isolated for more than thirty years, China began to open up to the rest of the world. With the relaxation of censorship and the exchange of new ideas, the Chinese art world gained access for the first time to information about contemporary Western art. Five years later the first avant-garde art movement in its history (later called the 85 Movement) exploded onto the Chinese cultural scene. Countless spontaneous exhibitions and small avant-garde discussion groups, accompanied by intense debates and pioneering publications, mushroomed throughout the country. People were suddenly in the midst of a new 'cultural revolution'. At that point, Chinese culture moved into a period of intense change. This movement lasted for four years and completely undermined the dominant position of Socialist Realist art.

This revolution raised some fundamental questions: How should Socialist Realism's reign be overturned? What approaches or strategies should be employed to replace the old culture with the new? Is cultural change a change in form or a conceptual change? How does one realize conceptual change? How does contemporary Chinese art find a dialectical juncture between its traditional culture and Western culture? How can art transcend language limitations? Huang's works are the manifestation of his unique thoughts on these questions.

Huang's artistic ideas, formed in the 1980s, were derived primarily from his studies of contemporary Western philosophers (Ludwig Wittgenstein, Michel Foucault, Martin Heidegger, Roland Barthes, and others) as well as from ancient Chinese Chan (Zen) and Taoist philosophies. The abundance of translated Western philosophy in the 1980s had, without doubt, a huge impact on Huang's creative work. His early works often use the method of subverting logical thinking to reveal the internal contradictions of art as a cultural phenomenon. The work he produced in the nine-year period from 1980 to 1989 – in its prodigious quantity and in the scope and scale of the issues involved – was like an exploratory fleet getting ready to pull up anchor and set sail.

The Death of Painting

There are two coexisting components of the modernization process in Chinese art: the importation of Western contemporary art and its subsequent use in achieving self-transformation of native artistic forms. This type of importation cannot be a direct transplantation of current Western art; instead, it should be based on the internal logic of art history. When there was a huge influx into China of information about Western art during the 1980s, the changes that resulted from how Chinese artists chose to absorb Western influences gave the history of avant-garde contemporary art in China the beginnings of an internal logic. This transformation more or less followed the progression of modernist art in the West, from realism to Abstract Expressionism (via Expressionism) to complete an internal revolution in painting, which later gave way to multimedia-based, conceptual and installation art. The changes in Chinese art from the beginning to the end of the 1980s reflected this series of transformations. Its early period was influenced mainly by Western Expressionism and Abstract Expressionism, and its later period focused on the exploration of media other than painting.

In the early 1980s Huang's work was also limited to the realm of painting; this was his most prolific period of painting. From the beginning, his work was not an expression of passion; rather, it was a process of questioning issues in painting through experimentation with various languages. To free himself from a fixed aesthetic model of painting, he started experimenting with changes in stylistic language and gradually moved to changes in tools and materials. His study of methodologies and conceptual issues became pronounced. By the mid 1980s artefacts started to appear on his paintings' surfaces, and aesthetic issues were gradually replaced by conceptual ones. But Huang soon realized that an internal revolution in painting was far from sufficient to establish real relationships between art and life and to realize the subversion of art history through avant-garde methods. In a note written in 1987, he stated: 'Only now am I really able to understand the state of mind that made Duchamp say, "The traditional idea of the painter, with his brush, his palette, his turpentine, is one which had already disappeared from my life." This is a revolutionary and irreversible change for me.'[2]

All of Huang's works produced after 1986 took the form of installations of modified prefabricated objects and performance art. This shift away from painting towards installation and performance art became an increasingly important trend in the Chinese avant-garde as a whole between 1985 and 1989. Huang developed the most radical methods and the most comprehensive theory for this transformation.

Extinguishing the Self

Huang's assassination of painting wasn't merely an exchange of raw materials, however; it was also a transformation of artistic ideas. What he wanted to subvert was not painting but rather an artistic attitude. The attitude in question was the emphasis on self-expression that was prevalent in the avant-garde movement of the time. Before the 1980s, notions of 'individual' and 'self' did not have a place in Chinese art. After the opening and Western-influenced reform, self-realization and the liberation of individuality erupted like an unstoppable torrent. In the avant-garde movement, self-expression became a very appealing slogan that could be widely promulgated. Expressionist and Abstract Expressionist art that directly articulated individual feelings became the dominant fashion. Huang believed that in order to subvert painting, one must first subvert these 'soaking' emotional outpourings, in effect drying up the 'moisture' from art and banishing self-expression.

In 1985 Huang invented a mechanism of random choice, using the results from a roulette wheel and a toss of dice to decide the form of a painting at its inception. His *Four Paintings Created according to Random Instructions* (1985) was produced precisely through this random-choice mechanism. For Huang, this mechanism possesses a variety of meanings: to cut off the inevitable relationship between self and artwork, to negate the creator's originality, to abnegate the tradition of painting and its corresponding aesthetic appreciation, to remove the self from creative expression, and to let 'nature' take its course to form the work of art. This work – although presented in the form of paintings – is at its core no longer painting, but the deconstruction of the painting method.

After 1986, in order to further disrupt the traditional relationship between the artist and the work, Huang utilized an even greater number of creative methods: tossing coins, throwing dice, spinning roulette wheels and drawing lots, as well as employing lottery and divination systems. Right after his *Four Paintings*, he went on to create the *Large Turntable with Four Wheels* (1987) and the *Roulette Wheel with Six Criteria* (1988), in which he further developed the random painting mechanism. These variously sized wheels or turntables were simultaneously closed and open systems, which not only made the artwork independent of the artist but also made the process of creating art less likely to be influenced by the artist's eyes or brain. In the frenetic, self-aggrandizing avant-garde movement, Huang's methods undeniably established an alternative approach to conceptualizing the self. This type of self is not one that is over and above nature, but rather coexists with nature, aligned with nature's evolutionary process.

The decision as to whether to emphasize or negate self-expression also involves the issue of cultural differences between East and West. In the Western mentality, artistic creation is equivalent to God's creation of the world. The creator and the created are diametrically opposed and unequal. Self-expression in modern art is actually a continuation of this relationship. Chinese philosophy, in contrast, is based on the belief that the human (author) is not the ruler of the universe: he coexists with nature equally. The universe was not created out of nothing but rather is an eternal process of mutual permeation. Classical Chinese aesthetic theories stress that 'speech does not exhaust meaning', and Chan Buddhist philosophy goes even further, proposing that one cannot 'understand the mind and see nature' without 'renouncing words'. Through the use of 'chance painting' to relinquish self-expression, Huang proved that he recognized the importance of borrowing from Chinese tradition, and this recognition was developed one step further after he immigrated to France.

For Huang, the relinquishment of the self also means – at the same time – rejecting other peoples' expectations of you, rejecting following the latest trends, rejecting participation in avant-garde competitions, and forsaking status as an individual artist. At the 1987 Chinese avant-garde artists' symposium 'Huangshan (Yellow Mountain) Conference', artists from all over China brought slides of what they considered to be their most iconoclastic works to share with one another. One of the underlying motivations for these artists to participate in the conference was to see who was the most avant-garde. To everyone's astonishment, however, Huang, as the representative of Xiamen Dada, presented four slides of classical Western art. He proceeded to explain that when he was leaving he had inadvertently grabbed the wrong slides and therefore could present only these mistaken pictures. Fortunately, he continued, it was of no consequence that he had grabbed the wrong slides, because it was unimportant whether they were avant-garde or not. It was not important whether they were his own work or otherwise, or if they were by Chinese artists or not. The only thing that mattered was that there were slides to project. Huang's strategy was to establish another approach to 'self', presenting a self that is in tune with nature and is modest but also replete with militancy because of its modesty.

Two Minutes

During the twentieth century, while accepting the influence of Western culture, China persistently sought its own path. Which parts of Western culture should China accept, and which parts of Chinese culture should she reject? In the process of accepting contemporary Western culture, how does one 'separate the wheat from the chaff'? For more than a century now, this has been an incessant debate among Chinese intellectuals and theorists.

The History of Chinese Painting and the History of Modern Western Art Washed in the Washing Machine for Two Minutes is a work of art from 1987.

Huang used two art history books – Wang Bomin's *History of Chinese Painting* and Herbert Read's *A Concise History of Modern Painting* – as the raw material for this work (the latter being one of the few introductory modern Western art books to be translated into Chinese, and one that at the time had an enormous influence in avant-garde art circles). He put the two books through a two-minute wash cycle in his washing machine at home and afterward placed the pulplike remains atop a wooden box. Using this instantaneous method, his work provided a Chan answer to a significant cultural question: the mutual influence between the two cultures does not follow any method, logic, concept, or ethics, but is achieved in an uninterrupted instant. It is not about replacing one tradition with another, but rather about two cultures chaotically overlapping after their original structures have been pulverized. Based on what Huang himself has said, since the basic concept of cultural history has continually been 'sullied', it must therefore continually be washed and dried. The purpose of washing and drying is not to make this concept purer, however, but rather to make it 'dirtier'. Only when there is no pure culture can 'dirty' culture become more vivacious and wide-ranging. [...]

Divergent Thinking

In the 1980s Huang's body of work demonstrated different, and even unrelated, directions. In order to destroy the structure he was in the process of forming, and to diversify his style, he developed two important methods: the use of roulette wheels and the conversion of words and expressions.

The main function of the Roulette series, which Huang began in 1985, was to make the creative process unpredictable and uncontrollable. He decided that the creative process should come not from the artist himself, but rather from the random operation of the tools used. He assigned the 'responsibility' for artistic formation entirely to his tools and claimed that the work had become 'independent' while he hid behind the roulette wheels and no longer revealed himself. With the introduction of these 'tools', the unity of both language and methodology was smashed into little pieces. From Huang's perspective, this step undoubtedly formed some sort of objective basis for the 'liberation' of art. It also opened the door to discovering new possibilities for creation. In order to advance the objectivity of this approach one step further, he incorporated methods from the *I Ching (Book of Changes)* into his roulette wheels after arriving in France, so that their operation could be even more independent.

To unpack art's innate conceptual structure, besides taking objective approaches, Huang also developed a set of more 'subjective' methods through the free association of words and expressions. There is no better embodiment of the operation of this methodology than the notes he wrote on this subject between 1989 and 1991. Within this complex conceptual map, every word and expression branched into an unequal number of other words and expressions, all intertwined with one another. Washing machine – Laundromat – rinsing – tumble dry – changing colours – cycles – muddy – clean – brainwash ... relying on this blithe free association, Huang wove a conceptual network like a spider's web, jumping from one concept to another. He avoided the logical relationship among rationally arranged concepts, moving forward in an ambiguous random logic, which caused his thinking to slide from one concept to another, extending outward limitlessly. He used characteristics of the Chinese language, sliding between homonyms and synonyms, continually capturing new intentions and submerging them into an ultimately unpredictable process. This pattern of divergent thinking gave him the ability to incessantly alter the vantage point from which he observed issues and to discover new angles from which he could continue developing his creative approach. This set of methods proved to be very useful in his later works.

Huang's art was created during the unique historical era of 1980s China. Like other avant-garde artists of that time, he was devoted to pioneering a new genre of art that would shatter conventional artistic modes. But unlike most of his contemporaries, who were targeting the art censorship system in China, Huang's critique targeted the mainstream avant-garde artistic trends of the time, and this enabled him to transcend historical and geographical limitations to take up more universal issues. In the Chinese avant-garde art movement, Huang was the first to recognize that revolutions in form first require a conceptual revolution as their base. His works offered a set of comprehensive personal theoretical foundations for this era's artistic transformation. [...]

1 Huang Yong Ping, interviewed by Qiu Zhijie, October 8, 2000, *Jinri Xianfeng* (Avant-garde today), no. 10 (January 2001).

2 Huang Yong Ping, *Notebook 01* (1980–89); quotation from Marcel Duchamp is from Pierre Cabanne, *Dialogues with Marcel Duchamp*, trans. Ron Padgett (New York: Da Capo, 1987).

Fei Dawei, extract from 'Two-Minute Cycle: Huang Yong Ping's Chinese Period', trans. Tzu-Wen Cheng, *House of Oracles: A Huang Yong Ping Retrospective* (Minneapolis: Walker Art Center, 2005).

Paul Auster
Statement//1992

In the strictest sense of the word, I consider myself a realist. What I'm after, I suppose, is to write fiction as strange as the world I live in. When I talk about coincidence, I'm not referring to a desire to manipulate – mechanical plot devices, the urge to tie everything up, the happy endings in which everyone turns out to be related to everyone else – but the presence of the unpredictable, the powers of contingency. We brush up against these mysteries all the time. Meeting three people named George on the same day. Or checking into a hotel and being given a room with the same number as your address at home. Seven or eight years ago, my wife and I were invited to a dinner party in New York, and there was an exceedingly charming man at the table – very urbane, full of intelligence and humour, a dazzling talker who had all the guests captivated with his stories. My wife had grown up in a small town in Minnesota, and at one point she actually said to herself, 'This is why I moved to New York, to meet people like this.' Later on in the evening, we all started talking about our childhoods and where we had grown up. As it turned out, the man who had so enthralled her, the man who had struck her as the very embodiment of New York sophistication, came from the same little town in Minnesota that she did. The same town! It was astonishing – like something straight out of an O. Henry story.[1]

These are coincidences, and it's impossible to know what to make of them. You think of a long-lost friend, someone you haven't seen in ten years, and two hours later you run into him on the street. Things like that happen to me all the time. Just two or three years ago, a woman who had been reading my books wrote to me to say that she was going to be in New York and would like to meet me. We had been corresponding for some time, and I welcomed the chance to talk to her in person. Unfortunately, there was a conflict. I already had an appointment with someone else for that day, and I couldn't make it. I was supposed to meet my friend at three or four o'clock in a delicatessen in midtown Manhattan. So I went to the restaurant – which was rather empty at that hour, since it was neither lunchtime nor dinnertime – and not fifteen minutes after I sat down, a woman with an absolutely startled expression on her face walked up to me and asked if I was Paul Auster. It turned out to be the same woman from Iowa who had written me those letters, the same woman I hadn't been able to meet with because I was going to this restaurant. And so I wound up meeting her anyway – in the very place where I hadn't been able to meet her!

Chance? Destiny? Or simple mathematics, an example of probability theory at work? It doesn't matter what you call it. Life is full of such events. As a writer of novels, I feel my job is to keep myself open to these collisions, to watch out for all these mysterious goings-on in the world.

1 O. Henry is a pseudonym of the American short story writer William Sydney Porter, known for his surprise endings.

Paul Auster, statement from interview with Larry McCaffery and Sinda Gregory, in *Contemporary Literature*, vol. 33, no. 1 (Spring 1992) 24.

Gabriel Pérez Barreiro
Jorge Macchi: The Anatomy of Melancholy//2008

Parallel Lives

In two [of Jorge Macchi's] works called *Parallel Lives*, two accidents occur simultaneously and impossibly. In one, an open box of matches reveals an identical pattern of matches in two compartments, something that could certainly happen in the realm of theoretical statistics, but we would never expect to see. In another, two panes of glass are broken in exactly the same pattern. The relationship of chance and accident is a constant in Macchi's work. On one hand, it is possible to read this in metaphysical terms, as a proof that the universe contains and foresees every possible act, and so finding two identically broken panes of glass is ultimately only a question either of time, luck, or patience. This is the universe so elegantly described in Borges' *La Biblioteca de Babel*. However, Macchi's choice of title, *Parallel Lives*, immediately introduces a personal and emotional note beyond the intellectual conceit. The search for the perfect match is one of the clichés of everyone's sentimental life, the tantalizing belief that the perfect soulmate exists if only we knew where. At the same time, the image we are presented with in both cases is an accident, something that disrupts the expected order of things. The broken glass immediately leads us straight into another emotional cliché: the dramatic landscape of the traumatic breakup. Once again, contradictory and emotionally charged contents are placed in conflict with one another, in both cases through objects that have barely been touched by the artist.

The works in the *Parallel Lives* series, perhaps more than any other, show how different Macchi's logic is from a Hegelian or Platonic model in which the purer the object, the closer it is to an abstract archetype. In Macchi's case, the simpler and cleaner the object, the more references it contains, and the more personal and sentimental those relationships are. The strategy of oblique and concentrated looking could be included in the list of media for Macchi's work, as could a refined and dark sense of humour. The matchbox and broken glass are almost dumb in their lack of pretension and elaboration, yet they are also far from the intentionally clumsy or adolescent work of many of his contemporaries on the international contemporary art scene. The essentially adult nature of his work, its resigned and wistful air, are all the more remarkable for being made by an artist who was in his early thirties when some of his most significant and delicate work was produced.

Incidental Music

When Macchi left Buenos Aires in 1996 looking for new horizons, his first stop was the Duende Initiative in Rotterdam, in what would become several years of moving from one European residency programme to another. This move can be understood as both a push away from the limits of the Buenos Aires scene, and a pull toward a desire to test himself in a new context. The sense of dislocation, vulnerability, and creative misunderstanding that always happens in a new location was to become the central factor in his work over the following years.

One of the first works produced on this residency, *Accident in Rotterdam*, was a breakthrough towards a more conceptual practice and away from the more sculptural or object-based works produced in Buenos Aires. In *Accident in Rotterdam*, two toy cars collide on the intersection created by the shadow cast by a window on the studio floor. Once more, the references range from literature (Edgar Allan Poe) to the anxiety of a recent break-up, and an overwhelming sense of bad luck as accident and chance meet again in an unlikely place. This work, perhaps more than any other, suggests that there is a parallel world to ours, and if we only look hard enough we can find it. Here we have a shift from Macchi as producer of anxious objects to Macchi as the seer of a mysterious world that lies just under the surface of banality. This ability to find the meaningful in the everyday has very little to do with a formal language and everything to do with refining a sensibility and an eye for the remarkable within the commonplace.

While on residence in London, Macchi's eye was caught by the bizarre, violent and apparently meaningless stories that appear in the British popular press. These were stories of random tragic accidents that evade any rational explanation, but that register the most important moments in certain people's lives. In his 1998 exhibition at the University of Essex, Macchi took one of these small stories on the inside pages – the story of a drunken babysitter who fell asleep on top of the baby she was supposed to be watching – and magnified it to the size of the large front window of the gallery. The huge scale of this story, its amplification out of its literally marginal position in the newspaper into a public display forced a moment of coming to terms with the ridiculous and tragic nature of this story, and with the transgressive feeling that this story didn't belong anywhere in the world, or even worse, that it was somehow funny. Once again, only by focusing the eye on something that seems insignificant does its cosmic significance and ability to destabilize expectations come to life.

Macchi calls this type of news 'incidental music', referencing the movie soundtracks that contribute to creating a mood but need to always be in the background. His 1997 installation *Incidental Music* was a breakthrough in articulating this shift from background to foreground, and also represents his first use of music as an essential element in the work. *Incidental Music* consists of three large sheets of paper onto which are collaged a large selection of these stories of random accidents and acts of violence from the popular press. The stories are laid out in straight lines to form a musical staff. The small gaps created on the lines where one story ends and the other begins are the basis for a musical composition that plays through headphones suspended from the ceiling. As the viewer listens to the tranquil Satie-like composition through the headphones, a perceptual cycle is created between the formal beauty of the work and the bloody and random nature of the stories. The music itself is also caught in the tension between intention and accident, as the notes are generated by a decision that has nothing to do with the laws of composition, yet we want to find a purpose and system to the music as badly as we want to find a reason to explain why these stories exist and a way to justify or rationalize them.

Macchi's use of music again marks a fundamental difference from the modernist trope of music as the perfect and purest artform. By generating music from sensationalist stories of violence, from tenuous strands of human hair, or by dissolving notes with drops that could be rain or tears (*La Tempestá*), Macchi takes music almost as a cultural readymade, a magnet for personal and collective stereotypes and attributions. In the 2006 work *Time Machine*, the endings of 1940s Hollywood movies are looped to create a horror movie soundtrack from the heroic culminations of the original films. [...]

Gabriel Pérez Barreiro, extract from 'Jorge Macchi: The Anatomy of Melancholy' in *Jorge Macchi* (Porto Allegre: Fundação Bienal do Mercosul, 2008) n.p.

Cornelia Parker
Interview with Lisa Tickner//2003

Lisa Tickner *Cold Dark Matter: An Exploded View* (1991) began with a garden shed, filled with the kinds of lumber that accumulates in sheds: gardening tools, a wheelbarrow, prams, walking sticks, old toys, sporting equipment, household objects exiled from the house – a mix of the outdoor and the washed-up – together with a volume of Proust's *Remembrance of Things Past* and an obscure memoir entitled *The Artist's Dilemma*. The shed was photographed at Chisenhale Gallery, London, in the space where it would subsequently be reassembled, and then taken away to be blown up by the British Army School of Ammunition. The fragments were collected by a platoon of soldiers and returned to the gallery, where this 'embarrassment of dubious riches' was suspended around a 200 watt light bulb like 'a constellation of burnt-out stars, stray planets and dead asteroids'.[1] The process of violent destruction and loving recreation, of chaos and contingency redeemed by order and necessity, is visibly present in the end result: a purposeful suspension of fragments, like a flashback or memory trace, projects an extraordinary play of shadows on the gallery walls and floor, such that the interplay of chance and necessity becomes one of the things that the work is about.

Cornelia Parker It was about a lot of things. The work points out into the world, or inwards into your psyche, and I like to do both. The explosion might be looking at the universe, at the Big Bang, but it might also be looking into an inner psychological state. *Cold Dark Matter* is a scientific term for the material within the universe that we can't see and can't quantify, but it also means something psychological, something upsetting (as in 'what's the matter?'). So, cold dark matter is in the universe, but it's also in the mind.

Tickner It's an almost absurd literalization of the 'exploded view' that you find so often in old encyclopaedias, but it isn't explanatory, it's destructive, though it goes on to make something new and very beautiful out of the fragments.

Parker I've always been fascinated by old encyclopaedias, with their exploded diagrams and confident explanations of how things work (electricity, weather, volcanoes, machinery, the cosmos), primates trudging up the evolutionary slope, the Statue of Liberty set for scale against Everest, that kind of thing.

Tickner The text is always patiently expository and the illustrations inadvertently surrealist.

Parker With mysterious and ambiguous titles. Different associations converge. But the shed also represented the home. The project had to do with living in Leytonstone [in East London] when houses were being knocked down to build the M11 link road, which made me think about transience and ephemerality. I really wanted them to blow up a house, but I felt that was going too far.

Tickner [In the original 1991 installation] at Chisenhale Gallery, the fragments still had the smell of the explosion on them. At the end of the exhibition they were taken down and, with nothing but the institutional record to identify them as 'art', stored in cardboard boxes under a stairway until taken in – given refuge and a permanent status as art – by the Tate collection.

Parker What I love about it is that it's getting older. In a hundred years' time it will be a 112 year-old explosion. The Tate curators have talked to me about conservation and whether or not it's got woodworm. I love the idea that an explosion might have woodworm. [...]

1 [footnote 10 in source] Adrian Searle in *Cornelia Parker: Cold Dark Matter: An Exploded View* (London: Chisenhale Gallery, 1991) n.p.

Lisa Tickner and Cornelia Parker, extract from 'A Strange Alchemy: Cornelia Parker', *Art History*, vol. 26, no. 3 (June 2003) 375–7.

Sarat Maharaj
Monkeydoodle: Annotating the Anti-Essay 'After History'//1997

What does it look like, that fog-wrapped spot where art history/theory and visual art practice collide? How to describe the fallout? It seemed unlikely that it could be mapped by words and concepts only. We would have to use them against themselves by passing over into the visual, into the business of making, even constructing an object. What started off as a regular art history essay soon enough passed into its queer opposite – an anti-essay.

In Marcel Duchamp's *Large Glass/Green Box* there is a mysterious fog-ridden zone where word and image, verbal and visual elements coalesce. He spoke of a 'retail fog', that is to say, not a wholesale one, not quite the thick, pea-soup killer that blanketed London in pre-pollution times.

At Goldsmiths' College, London, art history/visual art students set about probing this foggy spot. The probe is called *Monkeydoodle*. It consists essentially of two stages. The first involves making a contemporary version of Daniel Spoerri's *Anecdoted Topography of Chance*. The idea is to get under the skin of an artist who embodied in visual/textual terms some of the issues of historical writing we grapple with today – long before the armoured tanks of theory overran the subject with abstract concepts. The illustrations here are of contemporary Topos – some constructed as objects, some handmade, others computer based.

In a second step, the anti-essay is conceived around body fluids – orgasm, excrement, blood, lymph. This is realized in print, published in *Art & Design* (1995 and 1996), and on the Internet as *Monkeydoodle Archive*.

Monkeydoodle plans to set up as a public group. The idea is to use notions of randomness, noise, chance and accident in an account of the political present through anecdoted histories of refugees, asylum seekers and exiles in London today. The *Monkeydoodle* project ranges over the following issues:

1 'After History', what remains? As the History machine judders to a halt, hapless, bogged down, dialectical wheels in a spin – what form might historical thinking and writing assume? Away from linear coherence and grand narrative, how do we take on board chance, accident, sticky singularities, the aleatory, difference? Such a gear shift, in Perry Anderson's words, amounts to a 'randomization of history'. *Monkeydoodle* does not shy away from trying it on for size.

2 After the historical job is done, what 'remains' of the art object? How is the difference of the visual to be acknowledged and articulated? Duchamp speculated on a visible grammar – Adorno on a wordless syntax – prompted by misgivings about the limits of the conceptual and what is forsaken in its wake. For Adorno, the conceptual steam-roller reduces and flattens out difference and otherness – identifying and labelling experience on its own image. Like some juggernaut cruncher, it chews up and spews out everything in its path as concept, idea, sign. The concern is not only with what slips through the conceptual net but with the 'difference' that has to be teased through and beyond it – the 'remainder of the visual'. He rues the fact that we cannot escape the 'frozen wastes of conceptual abstraction' by actually

pasting and sticking in the brute particulars of objects and things into the philosophical text – however seductive still lifes or landscapes might make the notion. *Monkeydoodle* tries its luck with the idea: starting off as abstractive explanation and exposition, writing turns into making – into constructing itself with objects and things. From the straight, sober essay we pass over into the bent, queer business of the anti-essay.

3 *Monkeydoodle* is a way of looking and thinking that apes the straight essay only to muck up its system by letting loose the baboonery of a counterforce.

4 Does the conceptual originate in mimicry – a simian, arboreal state it shook off and grew ashamed of as it evolved into a hard-nosed mode at the top of the cognitive pack?

5 It goes against the grain of the anti-essay to theorize it. We are dealing less with principles than with rough-and-ready thumb rules. The anti-essay has to dredge these from the depths of its own practice. They are rules for the nonce – applicable perhaps only in the single instance, having to be thrashed out and coined afresh each time. These annotations do not so much add up to a systematic account of the anti-essay as they graph its drifts and meanders, sounding out its blanks and gaps.

6 In Kazuo Ishiguro's *Remains of the Day* (1989), the butler, Stevens – in service to Mr Faraday, the American master of Dartington Hall – takes meticulous stock of household order. The inventory is doggedly shadowed by what has yet to be accomplished. All the time, he is taking the measure of what is left over.

7 Daniel Spoerri glued down the scraps and remains of a meal onto the dinner table that he hung up on the wall. He called these snare-pictures (1960–64) – fixing down a jumble of plates and bowls, cutlery, crockery, and chinaware, trapping them where they stood, ensnaring the world.

8 Marcel Duchamp tripped up the visitor with *Trebuchet* (1917) – a coat hanger nailed down to the floorboards, against which thinking stubs its toes. A barbed ready-made, a conceptual ambush. Arturo Schwartz's gloss on the piece is a line from *Ulysses*: 'It would have served her just right too if she had tripped over something accidentally on purpose with her high crooked French heels on her to make her look tall and got a fine tumble.' The anti-essay teeters on stilettos, not quite sensible footwear, spiked between brute object, art image and concept.

9 In 1958 John Cage wrote 'Indeterminacy: New Aspect of Form in Instrumental and Electronic Music.' It consisted of a chain of anecdotes growing in its final form to ninety stories.

10 Daniel Spoerri's *Anecdoted Topography of Chance* (1962–95; nicknamed the Topo) mapped out the everyday domestic clutter on a table – odd bits of grub, comestibles, knick-knacks, everyday articles such as a screw, button, nail, alarm clock, paperclip, ashtray, electric plug, toilet paper, coins, condoms, etc., through to cigarette burn, wine stain, sugar granules and spilled salt. Each item was inventoried and anecdoted by Spoerri (DS) helped by Robert Filliou (RF) in 1962. When Emmett Williams (EW) translated the work into English with his annotations in 1966, Spoerri put in further entries, which he repeated with Dieter Roth's (DR) annotated German translation in 1968. In 1995 all the versions involving the three authors were put together. Each article on the table is the occasion for recounting the circumstances surrounding its purchase or possession. The tale about any one triggers further stories, incidental remarks and counterversions in each subsequent edition, which are signaled visually by typographic changes. The anecdotes fan out into an ever-widening tissue. The following – entry 5 on spilled salt (cross-referenced in entries 1, 1A, 2 and 12) – shows the structure:

> **5**. Grains of salt spilled(a) (as everybody does) by KICHKA while she salted her soft-boiled egg [1, 1A, 2, 12]
> **a**. 'The mother of a very dear friend of mine who had invited me to dinner for the first time said to me before we went to the table: "I have read all your books, very lovely, but I didn't understand a word." I felt sorry for her because of her son, and a few minutes later, at the table, she upset the salt and I felt sorry for her because of superstition. Everybody knows(b) that upsetting the salt bring bad luck,(c) and that writers are the salt of the earth.' (DS 1962) **b**. I less than most. In a sort biographical sketch published on the occasion of the Festival der Neuen Kunst in Aachen, West Germany, July 20, 1964 (the twentieth anniversary of the plot to kill ADOLF HITLER), I pointed out: 'Although I am married and have three children I live alone in the crumbling chateau in the heart of France's sugar beet country. Before we married POLLY wrote me from Washington: "We need each other like meat needs salt." Since I don't like salt, I misunderstood, as I always do with proverbs, even those literal ones scavenged and pasted and labelled and framed into works of art by my two closest friends, DANIEL SPOERRI and ROBERT FILLOU.' [See 31, c] (EW 1966) **c**. I recall that JUDAS, in DA VINCI'S 'Last Supper', has just upset the salt. (EW 1966)

11 The entries and emendations bunch up, branch out – entry 32 illustrates this. The structure is arboreal.

12 Behind the Topo's tree structure, however, lurks the systemic code with its iron grip: entries unreel with an inexorable cumulative force, a logical order of linear descent. But they also remain a congeries of facts, a nonlinear, higgledy-piggledy spread, a milky way of data. As anecdotes pile on, they amplify and counterpoint, collide with and jam one another. Versions vie with counterversions. The build-up to a single, macro-narrative is thwarted. *Trebuchet* (1917). To use Duchamp's words, we are witness to 'a liquid elemental scattering without direction.'

13 System-anti-system. Spoerri juxtaposed the *Topography of Chance* with the *Topography of Order* to highlight the difference. [...]

Sarat Maharaj, extract from 'Monkeydoodle: Annotating the Anti-Essay "After History"', *Art Journal*, vol. 56, no. 1 (Spring 1997) 65–71 [footnotes not included].

Gabriel Orozco
On Recent Films//1998

What I'm after is the liquidity of things, how one thing leads you on to the next. These films [*From Green Glass to Federal Express*; *From Container to Don't Walk*; *From Cap in Car to Atlas*; *From Dog Shit to Irma Vep*; *From Flat Tire to Airplane*, all 1997] take place in very ordinary urban settings. I'm not concerned with spectacular events or frantic rhythms. The works are about concentration, intention and paths of thought: the flow of totality in our perception, the fragmentation of the 'river of phenomena', which takes place all the time.

I avoid all postproduction because I want to keep the clumsiness, insecurity and ambiguity of the actual shooting. It's really the awareness involved in the shooting itself that is important to me, not what one can do with images afterwards. The tension between my intentions and reality itself is what drives the films. I devote a day to creating a kind of 'story'. Walking down, say, Sixth Avenue, I'll suddenly see something that intrigues me – a plastic bag, a green umbrella, an aeroplane tracing a line in the sky. That's how I get started.

One can't really see the films as entries in a diary, because they're not at all private. I'm very conscious of the fact that they'll be viewed by somebody else. I think about the viewer all along. The presence of the viewer makes me want to be more precise. But more important, the fact that the thoughts of the spectator are with me as I shoot the film short-circuits all ideas of privacy. There's nothing private about the process of creation.

The metaphoric links between things are not something I plan but something that just happens. The kind of connection that intrigues me is contiguity. I move from one thing to another, and in the film they'll be situated next to each other or happen right after one another, although there may be ten or twenty minutes between them in reality.

The connections themselves are real, not metaphoric. Borges wrote somewhere that all these things that are next to each other, we call the universe. It's this 'being next to each other' that appeals to me. In the films things are related, but through proximity rather than narrative. Therefore you can begin in one place and wind up in another that doesn't seem related to the starting point. For example, the tape I like the most, *From Dog Shit to Irma Vep*, traces a series of connections between two things: a piece of dog shit I saw in the street at 10:45 a.m. and this beautiful Chinese actress whose face I found on a poster at 4:45 p.m. Between these two events there's an entire day of walking, now condensed into forty minutes of recording on a tape.

There could be some kind of resemblance between what I'm doing and John Cage's recordings, but Cage's work has so much to do with chance, whereas I'm really focusing on concentration and intention. The same goes for the automatic writing of Surrealism. That's all about losing control, whereas the flow of images in my work is extremely controlled. I trace certain intentions with the camera, and then suddenly the tension between my intentions and reality becomes too great and the whole thing breaks down.

I wake up in the morning. The light has to be okay. I have breakfast and then start walking down some street until something catches my attention. That's when the movie starts. When I begin recording something, I don't know how long it's going to last, maybe thirty seconds, maybe five minutes, so I improvise, watching and walking at the same time. I always hope to be able to stop filming at the right moment, not before something great happens or after my finger and future viewers get *calambres* [cramps/spasms] of boredom.

Sometimes I focus and just wait. I like the sounds in the video to connect in the same way as the images. I'm actually amazed by how 'normal' my video sounds, just like real life – collapsing sounds and noises that overlap and connect without logic. I move the camera, I walk with it, I take stills, I use the zoom a lot and play with scale and distance. Sometimes I intervene in reality, like at this bar in Amsterdam, where I turned all the beer coasters upside down on a table and then taped them. Sometimes I follow a dog and sometimes I follow a backpack.

These are the things I normally look at when walking down the street. They wouldn't be interesting in photographs, but perhaps they are in a movie. After a day of walking I have twenty to forty minutes' worth of tape. I like to sit at a bar and have a beer while going through it. It's nice to see all the fragments of a day condensed. The narrative is like a series of punctums – focal points of attention. There's no postproduction – it's all left as it is: a day of awareness. I think that if I were to edit these films and try to make sense out of them, the final result would still be the same: '*Las partes son el todo, el todo son las partes*' [The parts are the whole, the whole are the parts].

Gabriel Orozco, 'Gabriel Orozco Talks About His Recent Films', *Artforum* (New York, June 1998) 115.

Gabriel Orozco
Interview with Guillermo Santamarina//2004

Guillermo Santamarina Why the flags without coats-of-arms?

Gabriel Orozco I made flags in a sudden burst. Many years ago I did some Palestinian ones, in which I started to play with the colours of the flag and to divide it geometrically, making variations on the geometry of the Palestinian flag.

Santamarina And above all Palestine ...

Orozco Yes, in fact it has to do with the idea of a country in a state of extreme vulnerability. Vulnerability as a concept of nation, as community. Mexico is in a state of vulnerability, so I put the hole in the flag. Instead of the national coat-of-arms it has a hole, you look through the hole and what might there be? Well there might be a plant or a tree behind, a landscape, some person's face or a white wall.

Santamarina Do you inevitably ascribe meaning to that circumstance of vulnerability?

Orozco Vulnerability is normally considered a defect, particularly in the sort of large-scale political art that functions to affirm nationality. Obviously, to doubt who you are and allow yourself to be influenced by others implies a certain vulnerability and that is considered negative. The first work in which I assimilate this vulnerability as an act of strength is *Piedra que cede* (*Yielding Stone*, 1992). That stone is vulnerable, it always will be, the knocks it has received have become part of it and give it its form. But that's what makes it indestructible. Instead of making it from bronze or steel, which would theoretically be invulnerable, I made it from a soft material which makes it vulnerable, and that vulnerability gives it a constant form and a permanent state of change which makes it indestructible.

Santamarina You've created a number of works which have a degree of social reference, as national symbols that are being violated.

Orozco Yes, because this is what vulnerability means. The idea of the container or vessel is important in my work. The shoe box is an empty space that holds things. I am interested in the idea of making myself – as an artist and an individual – above all a receptacle.

Santamarina But the holes are not so much inevitable as a natural circumstance.

Orozco Because you need the holes to create movement. When the Greek Atomist philosophers considered atoms as the smallest unit, they also considered the void, because to conceive of the idea of contact between atoms – which is what the different elements in the world are made of – one needs to conceive of the void in which the atom moves. For the atom to move from a to b you need the void. The country, the individual, is a space, a zone, also constituted from the void, and in which there are displacements and movements. The ideas of the void, of the container and of vulnerability have been important in all my work. I also work a lot with the idea of the accident. We think of an accident as an unfortunate instant, we think that we are in reality living in a state of constant stability and that an accident interrupts that stability. But one could see it in reverse: that we live in a constant state of accident and that stability is the moment of exception. One could think of the universe as an accumulation of accidents which happen moment after moment, and that what we are seeing is a series of numerous accidents, and that in fact it is the moments of apparent stability which are exceptions. [...]

Gabriel Orozco and Guillermo Santamarina, extract from interview, in *Gabriel Orozco* (Madrid: Museo Nacional Centro de Arte Reina Sofía, 2005) 142–3.

Michael Archer
On Ceal Floyer//1998

[...] *Butterfly Effect* (1998), consists of a single shot taken across a road in a fairly dilapidated light industrial area. A factory or warehouse wall on the far side of the road sets a limit to the space of the shot. No people or cars appear on the screen at any time. The only moving thing is a white butterfly that comes into view and flutters across the screen from right to left before disappearing out of shot. There is nothing else except the delicate, jerkily haphazard journey of the butterfly, and once this short sequence is over it repeats. Although the camera is fixed the knowledge that the tape continually loops back to the beginning produces disorientation with respect to the flow of time. One reading of the title would take it to imply that the flight of the butterfly is sufficient to trigger a causal chain the ultimate effect of which might be terrifyingly large. More immediately it is, in common with the straightforward descriptive nature of Floyer's titles, a direct reference to the effect of the butterfly's appearance, passage and disappearance.

Blind (1997), another video work to be displayed on a monitor, is similarly simple in structure, yet dense and complex in its implications. It is a long take from a fixed camera position of a white blind drawn down over a window. Because (one assumes) the window is slightly open the blind moves gently, sometimes getting sucked back against the frame so that its outline can be seen through the translucent fabric. For much of the time the screen appears to be effectively blank, and it is only when the blind moves against the window frame that it is possible to see that it is a blind at all. In that moment of contact what is revealed on the screen shifts from being an abstract field to a graspable representation. Where before the viewer was blind to the object they were seeing, its revelation as an object accomplishes a further concealment. What the blind obscures – the view through that particular window of the world outside – the mind attempts to see in or on its surface. Not blank, it is a monochrome, moved in its effort to represent the world beyond the window by the forces of that world. Recounting the Greek legend of the painting competition between Zeuxis and Parrhasios, Lacan reminds us that the latter won because, while Zeuxis managed to fool the birds with his cleverly depicted grapes, Parrhasios' *trompe l'oeil* curtain was able to deceive humans: 'If one wishes to deceive a man, what one presents to him is the painting of a veil, that is to say, something that incites him to ask what is behind it.' [...]

Michael Archer, extract from essay, in *Ceal Floyer* (Berlin: Kunstlerhaus Bethanien, 1998) n.p.

Bruce Nauman

On *Mapping the Studio I (Fat Chance John Cage)* (2001)//2002

What triggered this piece were the mice. We had a big influx of field mice that summer, in the house and in the studio. They were so plentiful that even the cat was getting bored with them. I was sitting around the studio being frustrated because I didn't have any new ideas, and I decided that you just have to work with what you've got. What I had was this cat and the mice, and I happened to have a video camera in the studio that had infra-red capability. So I set it up and turned it on at night and let it run when I wasn't there, just to see what I'd get.

I have all this stuff lying around in my studio, left-overs from different projects and unfinished projects and notes. And I thought to myself, Why not make a map of the studio and its left-overs? Then I thought it might be interesting to let the animals, the cat and the mice, make the map of the studio. So I set the camera up in different locations around the studio where the mice tended to travel just to see what they would do among the remnants of the work. The camera was eventually set up in a sequence of seven positions that I felt pretty much mapped the space.

I had only one camera, and I could only shoot one hour per night. So it's a compilation. There's 42 hours altogether, made over 42 nights of shooting in the course of four months. Before I went to bed I'd turn the camera on, and then in the morning I'd go out and see what had happened. The piece ended up being about six hours. (That is, each of the seven simultaneous video projections – representing each of the camera positions – runs six hours.) It just felt like it needed to be long so that you wouldn't necessarily sit down and watch the whole thing but could come and go, as with some of those Warhol films. I wanted that feeling that the piece was just there, almost like an object, just there, ongoing, being itself. I wanted the piece to have a real-time quality. I like the idea of knowing it is going on whether you are there or not.

'Fat Chance', which I think is just an interesting saying, refers to a response for an invitation to be involved in an exhibition. Some time ago Anthony d'Offay was going to do a show of John Cage's scores, which are often very beautiful. He also wanted to show work by artists who were interested in or influenced by Cage. So he asked if I would send him something that related. Cage was an important influence for me, especially his writings. So I sent d'Offay a fax that said FAT CHANCE JOHN CAGE. D'Offay thought it was a refusal to participate. I thought it was the work.

I was interested in the relationship between cat and mice, but more in a psychological way. Their relationship exists somewhere between a joke and reality. They've been cartoon characters for so long that we think of them as light-hearted performers, but there is this obvious predator-prey tension between them. I wanted to create a situation that was slightly unclear as to how you should react. The overall effect is ... ambiguous, maybe a little anxious. Then you can hear the dogs barking once in a while and the coyotes howling now and again. So there is also an element of what's going inside and what going outside, which I like.

What I've felt in watching is almost a meditation. Because the projection image is fairly large, if you try and concentrate on or pay attention to a particular spot in the image you'll miss something. So you really have to not concentrate and allow your peripheral vision to work. You tend to get more if you just scan without seeking. You have to become passive, I think.

Because I wasn't shooting every night, every hour the camera moves a tiny bit. The image changes a little bit every hour regardless of any action that's taking place. I was working in the studio during the day all that time, and I would unconsciously move things around. Maybe organize a few things – what you do in a studio when you're supposedly not making art. So the areas that I was shooting tended to get cleaner or have fewer objects in them over the six hours. I thought that was kind of interesting.

It ends pretty much how it starts. It begins with a title and a few credits, and then basically it just starts, and then it ends. The image goes blank. No crescendo, no fade, no 'The End'. It just stops, like a long slice of time, just time in the studio.

Bruce Nauman, 'Bruce Nauman Talks about Mapping the Studio', *Artforum* (March 2002) 120–21.

Lynne Cooke
Bruce Nauman: *Mapping the Studio I (Fat Chance John Cage)* (2001)//2002

Art is a means of acquiring an investigative attitude.
– Bruce Nauman

Mice invaded Bruce Nauman's studio two summers ago. In response, he bought an inexpensive video camera and an infra-red lamp to track their nocturnal activity. In late August, he began recording, having established seven camera positions that mapped junctions of wall and floor around the perimeter of the studio, a prefabricated building on his ranch near Galisteo, New Mexico. Continuing to shoot intermittently over the next three months, he amassed some forty-five hours of footage. During the following year, he edited this material, compressing it onto DVDs whose duration, five hours forty-five minutes, happens fortuitously to equal that of the daily opening hours of Dia [Center for the Arts, New York], where the work has its debut. Consequently, a full 'screening' takes place every day; no looping is involved.

For this presentation of *Mapping the Studio I (Fat Chance John Cage)* (2001), Nauman has overlaid his studio onto the gallery.[1] Using the distance between pilasters on the building's east and west walls as a fixed dimension for the seven projections, he arranged them around the room to mimic the original camera placement. The murky tonalities are integral to infrared tape. The jittery unfolding is caused by technical limitations; large quantities of information cannot be seamlessly assimilated and can only be incrementally absorbed, stored and then released. Each projection is accompanied by its own stereo soundtrack, which consists mostly of ambient noise: trees rustling in a gale, in heavy rainstorm, the occasional barking of a dog, a train passing in the distance, a cat's plaintive meow ... Pinned to the entrance wall of the gallery, a log charts the key visual and aural events within each projection, serving as a temporal corollary to the spatial map within. Standard office stools that roll and swivel offer long-term viewers the opportunity to rest as they wait and watch for who knows what.

The studio reveals evidence of daily activity, as well as accumulated residues of past work. Storage crates, moulds for cast pieces, tools and sundry off-cuts cohabit with a pair of Nauman's signature heads, a partially obscured reclining figure, plus drawings and sketches for various projects, some finished, others abandoned. Depending on the work carried out during the day, this paraphernalia shifts around or even disappears: the ladder, for example, is removed midway through the cycle; the bobcat mould is propped upright against a wall; and the screen door shuts, presumably as the weather cooled. A couple of chairs, stacks of video cassettes and several monitors create a kind of oasis near the centre of the room - the site for reviewing the previous night's footage. Occasionally, a blurred figure can be glimpsed crossing the camera's sightline, as the artist exits the room after having inserted a new cassette into the camera. Odd moths and other insects interrupt the static mise-en-scene, their brief trajectories limning eerie staccato gestures. But the real stars are Toonsis – the tail-less cat – more bored than excited by the invasion of potential prey, and the effervescent mice that have appropriated the studio as their stage. They scamper, saunter and roam, sometimes freezing momentarily, their eyes glowing incandescent as they glance unwittingly into the camera before resuming their self-appointed tasks.

Mapping the Studio I reprises key themes and preoccupations Nauman has mined and honed over a career spanning more than thirty years – with the telling difference that the extended periods now devoted to looking and thinking were once consigned to enacting myriad forms of repetitive activity. In the late 1960s when a recent graduate with scant means, Nauman explored a trio of interwoven subjects: the studio, the daily practice of making art, and the role of the artist. He adumbrated the latter, for example, in a memorable neon sign, alongside more commercial counterparts affixed to the exterior of his building. Its cool spiral letters traced the claim, at once ironic *and* heartfelt, 'The true artist helps the world by revealing mystic truths' (1967).

Eschewing stock notions of the artist as the heroic action painter facing off against vast expanses of the unsullied canvas, Nauman spent days configuring and reconfiguring a pile of flour on the floor into sculpture, recording each variation by means of the neutral gaze of a fixed lens. Often, he devised a series of meticulously choreographed performative tasks for a single witness, the implacable camera: bouncing balls from the ceiling, walking in an exaggerated fashion, manipulating a fluorescent tube into a series of artfully studied poses, stamping around the studio ... Later he hired assistants whom he directed to meld physically into the architecture or, alternatively, to levitate, thereby lampooning – albeit ambivalently – routine assertions that mysterious transformations attend the genesis of a mystical masterpiece.

Sometimes perversely banal, sometimes risible, sometimes absurd, this medley of oblique actions astutely pilloried received notions of inspiration and creativity, of the role and image of the artist, and the practice of art-making. On this account alone, Nauman's deeply impersonal praxis approached more closely the activities of a protagonist in a Samuel Beckett play than it did the standard *Life* magazine profile of a great artist driven by passion and instinct, be it Picasso or Pollock. The struggle to conceive a work of art, these typically low-key, low-budget endeavours implied, is more likely to involve hours of tedious repetitive activity or bleak periods of seemingly fruitless inactivity than macho manipulations of recalcitrant material, virtuoso displays of craftsmanship, or transcendent insights. But irrespective of whether externally imposed or, more frequently these days, self-determined, the discipline of limited means in his case stimulates efficiency, concision and flair. That the results, paradoxically, will tend to be disarmingly nonchalant, deceptively rough-edged, is part of the pleasure of resolving a sculptural conundrum or realizing an insight. Nauman continually refines his aesthetic by sceptically and rigorously scrutinizing his own practice, its precepts and premises. In a gesture as wryly self-mocking as it is generous, he plans to release another version of *Mapping the Studio.* This 'all-action' adaptation, whose duration will be about an hour in length, will focus on the highlights of the first: the gliding moths, the glaring mice, the cat's meow, the gliding moths, and more.

Deeply entrenched is the ubiquitous belief that privileged access to artistic inspiration (which perhaps can never actually be witnessed) proves revelatory to the observer. That consuming desire to witness the creative process and, hence, to invade if not the artist's mind then at least its physical surrogate – his studio – has provoked charged ripostes from Nauman, as exemplified in an audio installation from the series *Studio Aids II* (1968); a looped recording intones, 'Get out of my mind, get out of this room.' In a similar vein, he built spare, archetypal chambers than can never be entered but can, sometimes, be accessed via a mechanical prosthesis, the closed-circuit camera, which provides evidence and surveillance in one. Such psychologically charged situations, involving vicarious and voyeuristic witnessing that occasionally verge on spying, continue to manifest themselves in his latest work.

Considered at once a private arena for artistic investigation and a site of public exposure, in which the creator plays host to visitors in formal as well as more informal encounters, the studio has a long history as a topos, metaphorical as well as rhetorical. Originating in the late nineteenth century with commissioned studies of Rodin's various ateliers, a venerable historical lexicon that includes celebrated photographs of Brancusi's as well as Giacometti's studios, retrospectively shapes contemporary understanding of those artists' practices. Such documents may however become works in their own right, as in the case of the Romanian's delicate shots of his works, tools, and bases bathed in limpid stillness. Testimonies to work as creative labour and, more particularly, to the process of making sculpture, they too haunt *Mapping the Studio I*. In a series exceptionally evocative studies, Giacometti's pale plasters loom spectrally from the tenebrous gloom of his cramped quarters; by contrast, Nauman's chaotic milieu bestrewn with barely distinguishable tools, models, and leftovers, seems caught serendipitously or in a state of transition. Far from his forebears' theatrical, almost reverential portrayals of this sanctum, his scrutiny is surrepticious, requiring subterfuge.

Those celebrated black-and-white still images memorialize a time past, now veiled in nostalgia; Nauman's recording unfolds relentlessly in the present. The real time documented in *Mapping the Studio I* is, literally, time past, yet as it plays out obdurately in the present it is experienced by the visitor as lived time. The extended uninflected continuum in Andy Warhol's epic films of everyday events (such as sleeping) and the near-monochromatic compositions of La Monte Young or Philip Glass provided exemplars for Nauman in his youth. Attesting to his fascination with Warhol's films, the young sculptor's comments are a veritable prescription for *Mapping the Studio I*: 'They just go on and on and on, you can watch them or you can not watch them. Maybe one's showing already and you come in and watch for a while and you can leave and come back and eight hours later it's still going on.' 'I liked that idea very much', he concluded, adding, 'It also comes from some of the music I was interested in at that time. The early Phil Glass pieces and La Monte Young, whose idea was that music was something that was there. I liked that very much, that kind of way of structuring time. So part of it is not just an interest in the content, the image, but the way of filling a space and taking up time.'[2] In *Mapping the Studio I*, the viewer's immersion in the lived moment is enhanced by the scale of the projections, which ensures that the objects represented are a little larger than life, as if seen close-up, intimately, and by their alignment close to the gallery floor, which allows illusory space to extend almost seamlessly into depth beyond the actual space of the room. Moreover, since the speakers are located on the perimeter of the room, recorded sound merges almost imperceptibly with local ambient noise. Sound from different projections, from different moments of past time, overlaps, blending and melding indistinguishably with occasional passing events. Eventually, the illusory and actual prove inseparable, almost indistinguishable.

The ear is prey to that which surrounds it; it cannot block out or refocus as readily as the eye. Sound always places the listener inevitably in the middle of a situation. Opening up to 'infinite' hearing can change the soul and not just understanding, John Cage asserted in his idealistic approach to aural experience. Acting as if sound were a purely formal phenomenon, as if it were not social, as if it did not partake in semiotics, he advocated the use of random procedures as structuring and compositional methodologies to expand and enrich consciousness. Via both his writings and his works, Cage proved inspirational to Nauman, as he acknowledges: 'It had to do with the attitude involved in transforming normal activity into a formal presentation.'[3] A quip as comical as it is challenging, the subtitle of his new work reveals him sparring with the older man's legacy. *Fat Chance John Cage* reads as both an affectionate retort and an equivocal tribute,[4] for all unfurls at night, in the darkest reaches of the mind/studio, in a world neither visible to sight nor to rational, investigative study. Invaded by stealthy creatures who run amok, feral and savvy, impervious to the domesticated feline, this murky milieu takes on noirish overtones, presaging events at once unpredictable, ungovernable, uncanny and unknowable – events whose sole witness will be the surveillance camera. Invested with humor that is as black as it is bleak, as absurd as it is droll, *Mapping the Studio I* insinuates an unexpectedly disturbing register in what is proving to be the abiding thematic in Nauman's art.

1 In his notes on *Mapping the Studio I*, Nauman states: 'The presentation should be in a room about twenty-five by fifty feet with a twelve-foot ceiling and necessary entrance and exit. The projected images are about eight feet high by ten feet six inches wide and ordered as they were in the studio, three images on each of the long walls and one image on one short wall. The scale of the projected images is approximately life-size at the floor-wall junction which generally splits to half floor, half wall.' In the event, he modified this model, tailoring it to the actualities of Dia's gallery.

2 Nauman, 'Keeping It Apart: A Conversation with Bruce Nauman', by Chris Dercon, *Parkett*, no. 10 (1986) 55.

3 Ibid., 57.

4 This subtitle was initially conceived as a work by Nauman for an exhibition planned by the Anthony d'Offay Gallery in London in memory of John Cage. When asked for a contribution to this (never-realized) exhibition, Nauman faxed this in reply.

Lynne Cooke, essay for *Bruce Nauman: Mapping the Studio I (Fat Chance John Cage)*, exhibition guide (New York: Dia Center for the Arts, 10 January – 27 July 2002) n.p.

Daniel Birnbaum
Syncope//2005

The Eternal Return is a necessity that must be willed: only he who I am now can will the necessity of my return and all the events that have led to what I am ...
– Pierre Klossowski[1]

I tend to return – eternally – to the Eternal Return. This doctrine has been formulated in the following manner: the number of particles that compose the world is immense but finite, and, as such, only capable of a finite (though also immense) number of permutations. In an infinite stretch of time, the number of possible constellations must be run through, and the universe has to repeat itself. Once again, you will be born from a belly; once again your skeleton will grow; once again the identical page will reach your same hands; once again you will follow the course of all the hours of your life until that of your incredible death. Since everything is bound to return, nothing is unique, not even these lines, stolen from a writer (Borges) who in turn has pilfered the ideas from someone else (Nietzsche), who in the autumn of 1883 declared:

> This slow spider dragging itself towards the light of the moon and that same moonlight, and you and I whispering at the gateway, whispering of eternal things, haven't we already coincided in the past? And won't we happen again on the long road, on this long tremulous road, won't we recur eternally?[2]

A necessity *that must be willed:* everything that happens in the universe has happened before and is destined to happen again, preceded and followed every time by exactly the same events. The finitude of the universe and the infinity of time make this seeming paradox possible. The same arrangements, dreary or otherwise, are bound to recur. Thus Donny, the good-looking but naïve young guy in Stan Douglas' 1998 video installation *Win, Place or Show,* will again and again present his wide-eyed theories about mystical forces that are responsible for human suffering. And Bob, the slightly older and more rough-hewn tenant of the apartment where the action takes place, will forever explain a game involving horse racing in a manner that irks Donny and leads to a fight that Bob seems to win, but which comes to a close with the laconic remark, 'If I wasn't so tired, I'd slug you again.' And Donny will once again reply, 'I know it.' And so it goes, eternally.

Douglas has produced this finite cosmos, and exactly the same dialogue and camera shots will, in fact, recur – but only after some 20,000 hours, in accordance with a computer programme that randomizes the screening of two wall-size video projections, each of which portrays 'the same' action from a different camera angle. After about six minutes, what appears to be a loop starts all over again, but the repetition is not identical. The slight alteration – the combination of skewed shots mutating constantly – gives one the feeling that maybe this time the outcome will be different. It never is: the two guys always end up carrying out their hopeless wrestling match. They're locked inside a machine that offers no escape.

As is always true of Douglas' installations, there's much more here than meets the eye. My first impressions concerned the various incongruities: here are two lower-class men – dock workers, perhaps – quarrelling and wrestling in lodgings that appear, well, weirdly chic. The chair Bob sits in while reading the *Daily Racing Form* is a Bruno Mathsson. In fact, the whole set reminded me of the Scandinavian modernism revival aggressively promoted in those very years by *Wallpaper** magazine. The hostile dialogue and the heavy rain over a gloomy high-rise cityscape glimpsed through the large windows create a curious contrast to this slick setting. And why exactly are these guys living together? Because they can't afford separate apartments? Because they're gay?

Of course, the cool camera work, with extreme angles and close-ups reminiscent of American TV dramas of the 1960s, should have made it obvious that the setting belongs not to the cynical era of *Wallpaper** but to an earlier time, when this furniture still spoke of utopian hopes. In fact, the theme of this repetitious yet strangely riveting double projection is neither thoroughbred racing nor conspiracy theories but rather the failed promises of modernism. As in all of Douglas' work, the setting and ideological context have been meticulously researched and rigorously mapped out. Together with the architect Robert Kleyn, the artist constructed the set according to authentic blueprints from a 1950s plan for the total redevelopment of Vancouver's Strathcona district, a scheme unrealized but intended as a low-rent high-rise solution to the housing problems facing an enormous population of single, male workers. Donny and Bob occupy one of the dehumanizing units in these complexes, and their circular litany of endless desperation gives expression to a predicament reminiscent of Samuel Beckett's novel *The Unnamable*, living 'like a caged beast born of caged beasts born of caged beasts born of caged beasts born in a cage and dead in a cage, born and then dead, born in a cage and then dead in a cage.'[3] The fact that, a few decades later, their modernist prison cell, intended for low-cost mass production, segues smoothly into the pages of high-end design magazines makes the irony that much more diabolical. From the city planner's grisly dream of rationalized life to a nightmare fetishized by the well-off, this *is* a dismal piece.

Modernism – its failures as well as the fleeting moments of hope in which a constellation of freedom appears possible – is an overriding theme in much of Douglas' work. At Documenta IX, in 1992, the artist presented *Hors-champs*, which offered a glimpse into an alternative social order and the liberating forms of self-expression that modernism promised. Scenes from a free-jazz session – featuring four American musicians active in Paris since the 1960s – are projected in black and white on both sides of a thin screen hanging in the middle of an otherwise empty room. The piece, like so many of Douglas's works, registers on many levels, and I remember enjoying it without worrying much about the exact origin of the music, the social context of the performance, or the camera work involved in capturing the event. That the music of choice, a 1965 Albert Ayler composition, seems to cite two ideologically overdetermined anthems, *La Marseillaise* and *The Star-Spangled Banner*, is no accident: Douglas, after all, stages this performance as part of his research into the emancipatory aspirations of the free-jazz movement, which some took as a marker for an alternative society. Rather than nostalgia, Douglas' double-sided rendition of this moment of hope – ultimately unrealized, like most facets of the '68 revolution – brings out the discrepancy between the way these concerts were presented on TV (where the camera work mainly emphasized solo perfomances) and the group dynamics of the interchange. The music is what ties everything together, but the thin screen holds two realities apart – that of something like the 'official' camera, and that which is perhaps more true but *hors-champs,* or out of reach. It takes plenty of walking back and forth in the room to figure out these twin worlds. You can't get both at once.

Much art from other centuries – Baroque allegories or religious motifs from the Renaissance, say – demands a tremendous amount of knowledge to be fully appreciated; why should today's art be any different? Douglas' most complex installations can certainly be appreciated on a straightforward level, but for the viewer who is willing to delve deeper, the pieces take on much more significance. Douglas is no obscurantist: his writings are crystal clear, and so is his work. At times it's just so multilayered that the ideal viewer – one who comprehends all the parameters involved – hardly exists. Is that a problem? Take the video installation *Der Sandmann* (1995), an elaborate meditation on the mechanisms of recollection and temporal awareness, and, I believe, one of the most sophisticated works of contemporary art I've come across in recent years. A poetic, visually perplexing attempt to come to grips with the German situation a few years ago after the fall of the Berlin Wall, the piece can be viewed and enjoyed simply as a dreamlike scenario about the childhood memories of three people from the small, formerly East German city of Potsdam. But really to appreciate the installation requires a familiarity with numerous sources: the German Romantic writer E.T.A. Hoffmann's story 'Der Sandmann'; Freud's essay 'The Uncanny' and its theory of repetition; as well as certain aspects of German city planning, particularly the *Schrebergarten,* or small plots of land that the poor could lease from the city to grow their own vegetables. These gardens were named after nineteenth-century educator Moritz Schreber, whose son Daniel Paul Schreber's *Memoirs of My Nervous Illness* would play a crucial role in the development of Freud's theory of paranoia. All this is relevant to Douglas' installation, even if it's not ultimately what the work is 'about'.

Der Sandmann is a double video projection with each screen showing a 360-degree sweep of a Schreber garden. Staged in the old Ufa studios just outside Potsdam and shot on 16mm film, the sets are re-creations of the gardens: one as they might have appeared twenty years ago, the other a contemporary version, partly transformed into a construction site. The most curious aspect of this double projection is the vertical seam that simultaneously sutures and separates the halves. Initially the line appears to be only an irritating distortion, and even if you concentrate on the seam, it's not easy to understand what it represents or how, technically, it's produced. The gardens occupy their respective spaces to either side of the cleft in such a way that, in Douglas' own words, 'as the camera passes the set, the old garden is wiped away by the new one and, later, the new is wiped away by the old; without resolution, endlessly.' Thus, the seam is a fissure in time, keeping zones of temporality apart and yet letting them touch via an ultra-thin 'split' that marks a kind of syncopation. The two sides are woven together by a story delivered on-screen by Nathanael, the tragic hero of on the other side. If the line itself represents the present – the conspicuous yet evasive Now of perception – then this work seems to make a philosophical point about the temporality of experience. Is the present ever present? In fact, everything seems to start with deferral, difference, and delay – in short, with what Jacques Derrida gave the name *différance.* The presentness of perception is not the firm foundation it has been held to be, but an effect of a play of differences – and not just temporal differences. Hoffmann's story is full of doubles, uncanny repetitions and puzzling correspondences. Given the abundance of optical metaphors in the tale as well as the central theme of the eye and the fear of losing one's sight, it's perfect material for cinematic experiments. But rather than illustrate the story, Douglas puts the central concepts into motion. There are no sliced eyes à la Buñuel or Bataille but a vertical cut that gives rise to a disharmonious cleft through the field of vision. Yet *Der Sandmann* questions more than the traditional hegemony of vision; it also effectively stages a theory of temporal awareness – a *chronology* – that represents a threat to the understanding of the self as a subject fully present to itself. The work seems to propose a form of temporal awareness that comes close to what Freud understood as *Nachträglichkeit,* or deferred action. Events that have never been given as fully present are experienced only after the fact. In 'Freud and the Scene of Writing', Derrida sums it up nicely: 'It is thus the delay which is in the beginning.'[4]

(This is perhaps the appropriate place to return to the doctrine of the Eternal Return, which a moment ago was given a too simplistic – atomistic – rendering. In an infinite stretch of time, the number of possible permutations is exhausted, and the universe begins to repeat itself, I claimed. But perhaps it's not so much the physical things that must return – historical events, life forms ['... once again you will be born from a belly; once again your skeleton will grow ...'] – but that *difference* which is chronos, or time, itself. *Difference as such returns:* the cleft or fissure that is the Now, the syncopation that is 'presence' thought to an end. The Eternal Return is, in fact, not the thought that the universe must come back the same, but rather that *difference is* always coming back. *Difference* must be affirmed again in each case as such. In this way, the thought becomes a principle of 'selection.'[5] Only that which is affirmed returns, and only *he who I am now can will the necessity of my return.* This selective law of time is *a necessity that must be willed,* says Klossowski, chief promoter of Nietzsche's 'vicious circle', and announces, obviously animated by a sense of inestimable lightness: 'At the moment the Eternal Return is revealed to me, I cease to be myself *hic et nunc* and am susceptible to becoming innumerable others, knowing that I shall forget this revelation once I am outside the memory of myself ... And my present consciousness will be established only in the forgetting of my other possible identities.'[6] What this means to Bob and Donny – the cyclical protagonists of *Win, Place or Show* – I don't want to know. Nathanael, our fractured hero of *Der Sandmann*, will no doubt rotate eternally, out of sync with himself, and, hence, he perfectly demonstrates the relentless return of difference. 'Without resolution, endlessly', says Douglas.[7])

'The doubt, that pronounal doubt, doubt of pronouns, doubt of the certainty of an I, is the a priori of my work', Douglas declared in 1994.[8] The genealogy of the subject is always also a *chronology*. If the self doesn't experience itself in immediate self-proximity but instead realizes things about itself only belatedly, as the Freudian theory suggests, then the implications for subjectivity are significant. With its intricate temporal structure, its perplexing chronology, *Der Sandmann* provides a working model for the historical repetitions that recur, as it were, from work to work. Take *Onomatopoeia* (1985–86), in which a passage from Beethoven's 'C Minor Sonata, Opus III' – famously commented on by Theodor W. Adorno and Thomas Mann – is performed by an old player piano, above which are projected images of textile-factory machinery. What is especially intriguing about the Beethoven fragment is its inexplicable resemblance to ragtime music. This accidental connection seems to transplant the *Nachträglichkeit* of psychological temporality to the stage of history: a few notes by a nineteenth-century genius apparently realize their full significance only retroactively, when the industrial mechanization that emerged during the composer's lifetime finally gained a full grip on artistic creativity.

Douglas' historical explorations are always concrete in their scrutiny of technological changes, and he always seems to be in search of situations in which a particular development could have veered off in an alternate direction, where layers of significance are present but not yet activated. The inquiries into constellations of technology, ideology and art are never pursued in the interest of achieving some overwhelming, all-encompassing final synthesis. On the contrary, most of Douglas' work displays a tragic fracture, a tension that may appear superable in rare hopeful moments but can never be fully redeemed. In *Nu.tka.* (1996), another elaborate installation marked by a tormenting cleft, the soundtrack is kept out of sync and the shot out of focus until sublime clarity finally arrives in the guise of madness. The distorted projections show the gorgeous coastline of Vancouver Island while two eighteenth-century captains, colonialists who claim the land for England and Spain, respectively, deliver a set of delirious narrations revealing their increasing derangement. In *Le Detroit* (2000), a ghost story about a house that 'holds darkness within', two versions of the same 16mm black and white film (one standard, the other inverse and in negative), are projected from opposite sides onto a translucent screen. On either side the corresponding version dominates and is distinctly visible but the translucence creates visual effects: both sides appear a bit washed out and grey. The imagery radiates a ghostlike colourless light; it is, one could say, spectral. The two film loops are also a few frames out of sync, producing a kind of temporal halo of a few fractions of a second so that every movement is surrounded by a spectral echo or premonition of things to come. This increases the ghostlike quality.

The interest in spectral thought or 'spectrology' (a term used by Douglas in his 2002 essay 'Suspiria'),[9] recurs in many works, including the 2005 installation *Inconsolable Memories,* a free remake of Tomas Gutierrez Alea's *Memorias del subdesarrollo* (Memories of underdevelopment) produced in Cuba 1968. In both works, the protagonist is a person who stays behind in Havana during a time when everybody important seems to have left the country. Alea's film is set in 1961–62, a time of Cuban mass emigration; Douglas' protagonist on the other hand is adrift in the same city two decades later during the Mariel Boat Lift when some 100,000 Cubans emigrated. He is arrested for having received a package from abroad. Escaping prison after four years, he tries to find his way back to his old self and into his previous world, but he has turned into a ghost surrounded by individuals that mirror others in an uncanny fashion. Havana itself has turned into a city of doubles. Indeed, the entire work seems to be a study in spectrology: not only does the protagonist mirror the main character in Alea's film (both are named Sergio), but he is also a double of his own earlier self.

Unity is never a given. Works such as *Der Sandmann* and *Le Detroit* both convey a sense of a self that gains (what one might call) self-identity only in rare instances. It would seem that Douglas' work explores the position of the experiencing subject in relation to various technologies and systems of representation, but with the awareness that the construction of subjectivity is an open-ended process. The self emerges not as a closed unit but as a zone of friction where antagonistic forces clash. And it's not always a question of tragic tension and agonizing non-identity: sometimes what emerges is a joyous form of defiance, a determination not to obey. Douglas' early works made for broadcast on Canadian television are more direct than the elaborate installations, but no less mystifying. *In Answering Machine* (1988), a short piece belonging to the series 'Television Spots' (1987–88), a woman is sitting at a table smoking a cigarette when the phone rings. She doesn't answer. In the series 'Monodramas' (1991), the viewer is treated to scenes in which something goes astray. In each tiny narrative, some small error – a school bus driving on the wrong side of the road or a person suddenly vanishing without explanation – produces a situation out of the ordinary. One has the sense that the story has just begun and that the question marks will disappear momentarily. But they never do; no explanation arrives. At the core of Douglas' work one finds the problem of the self that is no longer identical to itself, a self that has no natural link to its own voice. It is no surprise that the artist frequently acknowledges the influence of Samuel Beckett, quintessential interrogator of the coherent self and liberator of the voice. The fundamental doubt of pronouns yields awkward and perplexing situations. If the self remains unnameable, then how can we be certain when we name others? In *I'm Not Gary* (1991) two men approach one another on the sidewalk. 'Hi Gary,' says one of them, and since there's no response, he adds, 'How you doing?' They're standing very close; there can't really be a misunderstanding. Then the reply comes: 'I'm not Gary.'

1 [footnote 2 in source] Pierre Klossowski, *Nietzsche and the Vicious Circle* (1969); trans. D.W. Smith (London: Athlone Press, 1997) 57.

2 [3] From Nietzsche's *Thus Spake Zarathustra* (1891), quoted in Jorge Luis Borges, *Selected Non-Fictions*, (New York: Penguin, 2000) 117 ff.

3 [4] Samuel Beckett, *The Unnameable* (1953), in *Three Novels* (New York: Grove Press, 1965) 386 ff.

4 [5] Jacques Derrida, *Writing and Difference* (1967); trans. Alan Bass (Chicago: University of Chicago Press, 1978) 203.

5 [6] Gilles Deleuze, *Nietzsche & Philosophy* (1962); trans. H. Tomlinson (London: Athlone Press, 1983) 68–71.

6 [7] Klossowski, op. cit., 58.

7 [8] Quoted in Scott Watson, et al., *Stan Douglas* (London and New York: Phaidon Press, 1998) 127.

8 [9] See ibid., 9, for a discussion about the problems of the first and third persons.

9 [10] Stan Douglas, 'Suspiria', in *Documenta 11* (Ostfildern-Ruit: Hatje Cantz, 2002) 557.

Daniel Birnbaum, 'Syncope', *Chronology* (New York: Lukas + Sternberg, 2005); revised edition (Berlin: Sternberg Press, 2007) 47–65.

Katharina Vossenkuhl

A Memorable Walk with Consequences. Francis Alÿs: *The Last Clown* (2001)//2008

The Last Clown (2001), like so many other works by Francis Alÿs, tells an everyday tale. Its images of urban life are described by critic David Torres in his aptly titled essay 'What goes on in the street'.[1] The film is composed of a sequence of watercolour sketches by Alÿs. A man, seen from behind, dressed in a suit and fine leather shoes, wanders seemingly aimlessly up a slightly sloping path, his arms folded behind his back. He has dark hair and glasses. His head and upper torso lean forward pensively; only occasionally does he unfold his arms. The landscape is indicated only by the path and by the shaded areas of pale grey, presumably a meadow, that flank it. In this version of *The Last Clown*, unlike many of his other works, Alÿs does not work with carefully orchestrated colours, but with subtly differentiated shades of black and white. Upbeat jazz music accompanies the man as he walks, his gait underscored by swinging trumpet notes.

Suddenly, a dog comes towards him, wagging its tail in a friendly way, only to pass by him. At that very moment, the man stumbles and falls. It is not clear whether the man and the dog have collided or whether the man has tripped over the dog's tail. The jazz is briefly replaced by the sound of laughter, only to start up again as soon as the man gets up and continues on his way. Is it the laughter of spectators? As film collector Rick Prelinger puts it, 'If you are a typical spectator, what you're really doing is waiting for the accident to happen.'[2] What is also unclear is whether the music stops because the laughter starts, or whether the laughter has broken out because the music has stopped. Chance and uncertainty thus become part of the narrative.

The dog continues on its way, oblivious to the man's fall; only the man glances around furtively and seems confused. The man turns towards the viewer two more times, and each time there is the sound of laughter. We can discern the facial traits of the art critic Cuauhtémoc Medina, a friend of Francis Alÿs. Alÿs' short films, paintings and sketches tell very witty and yet melancholy stories. Without taking a moral stance, he subtly encourages the viewer to look more closely at things and events. Many of Alÿs' works are based on personal experiences, situations or stories from Mexico City, where he has made his home. His video *The Last Clown* is also based on a real-life occurrence. The artist was walking through London's Hyde Park with his friend Cuauhtémoc Medina, chatting about art, when Medina suddenly and inexplicably stumbled and fell. This prompted Alÿs to create a number of drawings and paintings which ultimately formed the basis for this video. The suddenly recognizable face of

Medina in profile creates a link to the actual incident. The slightly shaky images lend the video the characteristics of an early comic or an old black-and-white film – an impression further underlined by the hand-painted sequence of frames and the slightly jerky movements of man and dog. The metallic sounds of the jazz music together with the flickering images recall the films of Charlie Chaplin, making the title *The Last Clown* all the more fitting. Just as Chaplin or a circus clown stumbles from one hilarious accident to the next, so too in this film is humor just one of several possible ways of making a point about something more profound. The video loop turns the man's fall into endlessly repeated slapstick, making the actual event experienced by Alÿs and Medina into a universally valid statement: is it a reference to street life and poverty? This is one of the questions that Alÿs addresses in his works, mainly in relation to the problems in his Mexican homeland. Alÿs tells the story of his friend simply, in ways that correspond to his simple, unframed pictures with their rusty nails still visible on the frame, and the canvas protruding at the sides, or the drawings that he often simply pins to the wall.

Who is the Last Clown? Is it the artist himself, or is it the art critic? Since the artist Alÿs is referring here to a walk during which he and his friend, the art critic Medina, discussed art, the viewer can relate to the task and the significance of artists, art and art criticism. The question here is: who is the clown really, what trips him up, why does he stumble and who is laughing, or being laughed at? David G. Torres comes up with the following answer: 'The artist is the last clown, the ultimate monkey who is called upon to stage an exhibition, to do a few clownish acts so that we can laugh.'[3]

1 David G. Torres, 'What Goes on in the Street', in *Francis Alÿs. The Last Clown* (Barcelona: Fundació La Caixa, 2000) 9 ff.

2 Quoted in ibid.

3 David G. Torres, in ibid., 10.

Katharina Vossenkuhl, 'A Memorable Walk with Consequences. On *The Last Clown*', trans. Ishbel Flett, in *Francis Alÿs* (Munich: Sammlung Goetz, 2008) 102–4.

Tacita Dean
Collections//2000

When I was about eight years old, I went for a walk up the lane behind our family house in Kent. I was probably imagining, as I often did, that I was in a documentary, in dialogue with an invisible camera, talking about horticulture or some other such worldly subject, when I came to a lay-by beside the road. Looking down in amongst a clump of grass, I found my first four-leaf clover. Further visits to the same lay-by harvested a full eight four-leaf clovers. So I wrote to *The Guinness Book of Records*, only to receive some while later a letter with the printed signature of one of the McWhirter twins. It told me that the largest quantity of four-leaf clovers had, in fact, been found by someone in Ohio, and that the record was in the thousands. Indeed, it continued, such mutation in nature was not at all unusual.

Undeterred by the official response to my discovery, I found I had a 'facility'. Whether it was a good eye for a clover or 'good luck', I would find four-leaf clovers wherever I looked and where others couldn't. I would see one crossing a lawn or walking along a road. I would notice it, stop, pick it with care, check for others, because where there is one there is often another, then press it in my notebook. At some future point, I realized I had a collection.

Now, the problem with a collection is realizing you've started one. Recently, I have begun, quite unintentionally, to collect old postcards *thematically*. It started with finding an attractive postcard of a frozen water fountain. On finding the second frozen water fountain, I had begun a collection, although I could delay acknowledging it as such by choosing to call it a diptych, or a triptych, or a quartet. And so it is with postcards marked with crosses, by a hotel window or a table in a restaurant or a mountain climbed, or postcards showing seagulls or thermal spas or four-leaf clovers. All my interests in microcosm: portable, collectible, reproducible.

I know people whose lives are dominated by their collections, ceaselessly searching in flea markets, auction houses and specialist book shops, never resolving their quest. Whether you are collecting versions of popular songs, postcards of lighthouses or votive sculptures of Our Lady of Montserrat, your collection will never let you be. You've started so you must continue, and with most collections, there is no end. Whether it is postcards of lighthouses or four-leaf clovers, there can never be the definitive collection. For what is more inert than a finished collection?

What happened to me and my clover collection was that it became an investigation into my relationship to luck. I had always courted Chance, and the ease with which I found four-leaf clovers made me too sure of this special relationship. When I first showed my collection in 1995, for the first time in my collector's life, I became paralysed by an inability to find any more four-leaf clovers. It was as if I had turned the accidental action of finding a clover into something altogether too self-conscious. I had played an uncomfortable game with Fortune and She had shunned me for my ostentation. I suddenly searched too hard and could no longer find.

My clover collection is not a dead collection, although its constituent parts are dead. No, because I had to surrender it and let it go, and stop my obsessive searching of grassy verges and uncut paddocks, I have at last now managed to re-find something of my ability to chance discover and to find by not looking. And I can now add, from time to time, a new clover to my collection.

Tacita Dean, 'Collections', in *Tacita Dean* (Barcelona: Museu d'Art Contemporani de Barcelona, 2000) 76–7. The collection of clovers was published in the *Book of Leaves* (Artist's book, Bourges, 1995).

Tacita Dean
Send More Cups//2008

The *lumière* [in Fischli & Weiss: *son et lumière*] you understand immediately as you watch the spiralling red and green torchlight make patterns on the wall, but it is the *son* that surprises you: the rhythmic scratching of the plastic cup on the slightly inclined turntable, lolling, as it does, back and forth, back and forth, making sounds indescribably specific to when a plastic cup moves upon a surface. The turntable is grubby and worn where the cup has shifted, and masking tape around the edge forms a lip to prevent it rolling off. It looks homemade, *hausgemacht*, like a work of art should look sometimes but rarely does: thought up and made on the spot. Utterly simple and utterly compelling. One could have pre-imagined the light but not the sound. It is the sound that must have provided the title. Once heard, it needed equal billing: sound and light; *son et lumière*.

Only *son et lumière* normally has greater pretensions: a light show projected on the watered frontage of a castle or chateau with music amplified through temporary speakers to rows of collapsible seats put out in anticipation. It is the spectacle to crown a summer, the height of refined outdoor entertainment, but which quickly can become spectacular boredom or the boredom that can often accompany the spectacular. But this confluence of cultural pretensions and cultural detritus is where Fischli/Weiss find their work. Nothing delights them more than deflating the majestic or elevating the quotidian, playing with our social signifiers, realigning them, redescribing them. Their material is our rubbish, our platitudes and our banalities, which they transmute like alchemists.

I have written about this work before. Then it was in the context of the green ray or *le rayon vert*, a phenomenon not easily seen, when the last ray of the setting sun flashes green briefly before disappearing beneath the horizon. It inspired Jules Verne to write his novel *Le rayon vert* which then inspired Eric Rohmer to make his film with the same title which in turn inspired Fischli/Weiss to sometimes switch their flashlight to green only and make a version of their work called *Son et lumière – Le rayon vert* 1990.

This morning I found in my files an envelope on which I had scribbled notes from a telephone conversation I had had with David [Weiss] two years ago. The notes read like a poem to the moment when they had the idea for *Son et lumière*. You immediately see them ambling down a road in Brazil and spotting the rotating cake stand in a shop window. And then later, in the narrative of this idea, watching people on a beach making light drawings against the night sky, and then finding that particular cross-hatched design on a plastic cup ...

S. America
turntable
we bought something turning
windows
shops
cake turntables
machine line drawings
look like computer drawings
beach Rio de Janeiro
in the dark make drawings
in the dark
geometric drawing
building same spirit
cheap thrills
by chance plastic cup drawings on it

Send more cups

Tacita Dean, 'IX. Send More Cups', in *Fischli/Weiss. Flowers & Questions: A Retrospective*, ed. Bice Curiger (Zürich: Kunsthaus Zürich, 2008) 109–11.

Keith Tyson
Interview with Audio Arts//2004

Helen Sumpter Can we discuss the *Geno/Pheno* series of painted diptychs.

Keith Tyson The left-hand panel is a generator and the right-hand panel is a result. That simple premiss allows me to discuss all kinds of questions that I find interesting, such as how does something come into being, what are the starting conditions of something, and also, the idea of descriptive and prescriptive texts that surround a work. The generators can be very simple, such as an equation, and that produces a certain result on the right-hand side, as an abstract pattern; or they could be quite complicated, to do with making lists of potential titles of works, and breeding those together to form one out of a billion possible results. Traditionally, an artist would say this is a 'masterwork' but this could have been many other things and still been equally as valid. I'm trying to show some of the potential, and serendipity, in the process, and allow the viewer to see those avenues as much as the actual result; to deal with what's there and also with what isn't there.

Sumpter Some of them are more difficult to work out. Is that an element that interests you: the viewer finding it quite hard to see what the connections are, or how they relate?

Tyson Yes, I'm less interested in the game of 'What does this mean?' because ultimately there's a nonsense in the work – you won't be able to gain anything by understanding the origin, 'and therefore he painted this painting'. My children ask, 'Why are we going to school?' 'Because you need to learn how to use language', 'Why?' 'Because we all use it and ...' If you keep asking why, eventually you get down to ontological issues: what's the meaning of life? So the left-hand panel gives you very little more information. It's a system, and what you work out, as you see in the exhibition, is that the exhibition 'isn't', and then by that detachment, you work out what it is.

Sumpter There's one other work exhibited here, *Primordial Soup Paintings*. Can you talk about how that works?

Tyson I put it in the show because, again, it was about a kind of generative methodology. It starts off with a big 'primordial soup'; I've done the imagery without any concern for composition or aesthetic value, or significance. It's just about putting 'stuff' out there, without any kind of idea. Then I make two random selections from that, which will form the background for two further paintings, and they, in turn, become the background for two further paintings, and so on, until you end up with fifteen paintings. I call them 'homoeopathic dilutions', because the end paintings are not present in the original source, and yet somehow there's an echo preserved in that process. I'm asking questions about the inevitability of these paintings' existence. One thing that really fascinates me is the idea of the specificity of things. The universe is vast, but it's actually incredibly specific. If you look at the vast potential of what it might have been, and if you want to eradicate the idea of a decision, then you have to say that everything that could exist does exist, in a kind of specificity bubble of infinite potential. I used to be terrified by that idea but now I find it quite liberating. So I'm trying to offer some of that expansiveness back to the viewer, instead of illustrating my own idiosyncratic ego. When I see the work as a whole, I feel that the exhibition reflects more accurately the state of nature than if I tried to illustrate the state of nature. I actually try to use the methodology, the serendipity, the things that I see out there that are generative forces, and bring them all together to embrace that complexity.

Sumpter You also have an exhibition concurrently in Zurich that focuses on another thread that runs through all your work, concerning gambling and chance. And these you call 'History Paintings'.

Tyson Traditionally, history painting is usually a scene of conflict between a victor and a loser, and it's painted from one position or the other. My 'history paintings' are very minimal works. I guess you could say that they're just red or black stripes that form 49 stripes in a row. So they're like big modernist abstract paintings but the system used to generate them is the spin of a roulette wheel. If it's red, it's a red stripe, if it's black, it's black, if it's zero, it's green. You're left with these minimal works, yet they're titled *St Petersburg 1905*; *Baden Baden 1942*; *Paris 1796* ... These are all places that have famous casinos. They're also places where huge political and social upheaval occurred. So these paintings invite viewers to look for their own humanity in them but what they receive back is the cold mathematics, the law of chance – 'outrageous fortune'. In roulette, if red comes up it's a great victory and if you happen to be on black, it's a loss. It's trying to kind of get rid of that subjective idea of history and show an objective 'fact'. Also, it's extraordinary that where there are casinos in the world they're very often surrounded by extreme poverty. So I wanted to marry those things together. It's not a mimetic representation of history, it's a sort of affirmation of humanity. It's not a simple conceptual artwork about chance. You can't have a reductionist approach to understanding why things come into being. That's what I'm trying to reflect. I find it a quite depressing show, but that's a counterpoint to this, to what seems a very 'carnivalesque' show. It's just two sides of the same coin really.

Sumpter I've read that you have gambled quite a lot, do you still?

Tyson It's rather like an academic studying pornography or something, and pretending that it's purely about the greater view of it, but I was a gambling addict. I'm still fascinated by that 'arrow of time' effect: before the event you don't know what's it's going to be, and afterwards of course the result's there. That seems to me like an essential part of the experience of life, our absent knowledge of what's to come. [...]

Keith Tyson and Helen Sumpter, extract from transcript of interview for *Audio Arts Magazine*, vol. 23, no. 3 (2004).

Sarah Valdez
Substance Abuse: The Films of Jennifer West//2008

For more than ten years, Los Angeles-based artist Jennifer West kept the same canister of 16mm film in her refrigerator. When she decided to process the venerable celluloid, she chose not to do so with chemicals. Instead, she invited friends to provide her with substances she could use, but gave them no specific requests or direction. Artist Jim Shaw – known for his mingling of the quotidian and the discomfiting in his work – offered up his own urine. Nameless others came up with an assortment of other substances: aphrodisiacs, hallucinogenic absinthe, wine, coffee and detox tea.

Marinated Film (2005), the unpredictable result of these soakings, marked the beginning of an increasingly sophisticated oeuvre that has since had West variously sprinkling, dripping, dragging, burying and cooking film, not to mention having people run it over with motorcycles. The film starts out looking like an animated crinkly piece of blue-green cellophane blowing in the wind. Then it morphs into pink snow and hotly hued 1980s-style paint splatters before being taken over by flashes of yellow, flickering electric blue, and red-purple static.

In 2005 West also produced a series of 'Psychosomatic Films', again made without a camera. For these somewhat monotonous, all less-than-one-minute projections (West transfers her footage to DVD for gallery installations), she experimented with soaking 16mm film leader in virile-sounding performance-enhancing beverages like Amp, Full Throttle, Rockstar, Adrenaline Rush, No Fear and Essential Superpowers. Surprise colours and patterns emerged, similar in their abstract randomness. *Psychosomatic Film #1*, for one, starts out with what one might mistake for a swarm of little black bugs on the red planet Mars; *#5* has purplish hues and discrete forms outlined with fuzzy edges. Each piece winds up energetically charged in a way that brings to mind the drawings of California-based conceptualist Tom Marioni, who has declared drinking beer with friends the highest form of art and, like West, engages in physically expressive processes reminiscent of Happenings to make his abstract work.

'I know now how certain things will affect the film', says West, who has become increasingly controlling about the substances she uses, and cites Tony Conrad, Ed Ruscha and Carolee Schneemann as heroes. Mint, as it turns out, has the capability to rot away a layer of celluloid, as do other acidic mediums, like tomatoes. Furthermore, West – who now works with a traditional colour chart in her studio – has discovered that pigments tend to appear their complementary opposite when directly applied to film: purple comes out yellow, for instance, and orange turns into blue. 'As the project goes on, I'm coming at it more as a mark-maker and painter', she explains. All the same, West uses some materials she knows will have no optical effect, but keeps them in her titles for drama's sake.

Indeed, the visceral impact of reading the lists of media she uses accounts for much of her project's psychic power. (How many artists can claim to have made literal use of a cocktail called Adios Motherfucker or a body spray called Purple Haze in their work?) For her *Skinnydipping Carbon Beach Malibu Film – In Front of David Geffen's House* (2008), West did use a 16mm camera – shooting herself with three friends on the media mogul's grudgingly public-access beachfront property 'lit by the full moon and searchlights' – then sprayed the footage with fried pickle juice, painted on it with celery stalks she'd dipped in Bloody Marys, smeared it with ash from the Malibu fires, and submerged it in the ocean. And while one may or may not have interest in catching glimpses of West and her pals naked on the beach, the appealing footage begot by the cocktail of chemicals has its own draw: a dance of electric blue, neon yellow and hazy green against a deep black background (sort of a hippyish version of Jeremy Blake's mod, abstract digital animations, which he also punctuated with figurative footage).

West recently switched to working with extra wide 70mm film, which she feared wouldn't work on account of revealing too much detail, thus destroying the seductive abstract qualities of the films. Yet due to that switch she's created the appealing *Rainbow Party on 70mm Film* (2007) and *A 70mm Film Wearing Thick Heavy Black Liquid Eyeliner That Gets Smeared* (2008). Despite the somewhat peevish fact that the former was based on the urban myth that twelve- and thirteen-year-old girls wear different lipsticks to try to give boys 'rainbow'-effect blow jobs (West and friends kissed the film repeatedly) and the latter was subjected to Jell-O vodka shots, rubbed with glitter and painted with black eyeliner, the level of detail afforded by the large film makes the nuances of West's media all the more visually palpable. In fact, the work practically begs a soundtrack and, in so doing, heightens the purely visual experience.

Sarah Valdez, 'Substance Abuse; The Films of Jennifer West', *artonpaper* (May–June 2008) 28–9.

Walead Beshty
Statement//2009

[...] There is a set of chance operations and material conditions that define how some of my work is made – in particular with the photograms[1] and glass boxes[2] – and in the case of the glass boxes, it is the means of transportation, FedEx, that acts as the generative mechanism of the work. [...] I'm not particularly concerned with the denaturalization or decontextualization of a pre-existing organizational structure in its static form. I'm more concerned with how the material traffic of an image – the contingencies produced by this traffic – whether the work is on photographic paper or exists in a digital file, or as an object in transit, might generate other possibilities for aesthetic production. This is distinct from being simply a reflection of the dominant structures that define, sometimes arbitrarily, and often with self-validating authority, the meaning and organization of images. A defining impulse in my work is an attempt to avoid tacitly reifying these prescribed models for meaning, neither embracing their spectacular, abstract or alienating aspects, nor dealing with them negatively, i.e. proposing them as false models and attempting to undermine them. In the end, for me, doing so would be one and the same reifying gesture. Negation is, in my understanding, a perverse form of preservation.

In the photograms, the paper is folded into a free-standing geometric form, each side gets a colour, and the colours are dependent on the spectrum of emitted and reflective light. I'm blind in the dark room, where I am managing this huge piece of paper, an operation involving the tensions between my body, the material of the paper and the light source. I would not use the word 'chance' but would liken the operation, instead, to a game: it's really an aleatory process. There is a set of rules that dictates the parameters for a range of outcomes, and there are no hierarchies for these outcomes, all of which are indicative of the particular rules at work. My procedure might be an 'appropriated' model, modified from the avant-gardes or conceptual art, which allowed one to be freed up from certain aesthetic conventions. But my emphasis is on the active application of this logic to the contemporary context as a way of moving past certain conventions, of finding another way of dealing with potentially repressive structures that isn't based on the false options of negation or affirmation.

More recently, I have been preoccupied with the idea of how to deal with the material component of the digital image, in that digital images are essentially comprised of text. There is a similarly aleatory process I use with digital images, by dealing with the information that composes the image as a text file, and using automatic functions in word-processing programmes to reform the text. In my earlier work the materiality was stable, but things have changed with digital media. When I've shown this work, it has essentially functioned like wallpaper, a pattern, a space-filling object: it can be reproduced as many times as one might want for a particular context. This gets away from the photogram, a unique object. Which is not to say that the uniqueness or specificity of the object was a problem, just a fact. The reflexivity of my work has never been 'about photography' or 'about the digital', but a response to the specific conditions related to their use. I'm not particularly invested in, nor do I really care about, photography in a general sense. It's a medium that is relatively ubiquitous, readily accessible, and that I have some facility with, so it makes sense for me to use it.

I believe there's a kind of 'aesthetic unconscious' of a medium, one formed through its applications, cultural associations and technological development. I have heard people claim my work looks like something called 'modernist' photography. But when pressed, they seem to be referring to something amorphous, indistinct. I think of my work, and that of others, in relation to the specific contexts of their production and reception, not in loose formal or historical categories. [...]

1 [For example, *Fold (45 degree directional light source), December 22nd, 2006, Valencia, CA* (2007)]

2 [For example, *Fedex® Kraft Box ©2005 FEDEX 330504 REV 10/05 CC, Fedex International 2-Day, Los Angeles-Brussels (Tracking No. 8652 8205 7953)* (2008)]

Walead Beshty, statement from round table discussion with Erika Vogt, Elad Lassry, Carter Mull and Aram Moshayedi: 'Pictures Generation: After Materiality and Style', *Art in America* (April 2009) 135–6.

Walead Beshty
Interview with Nicolas Bourriaud//2009

Nicolas Bourriaud Two questions. Firstly, how does travelling (and displacement) function in your work? Would you say that you are inscribing forms in space, rather than on paper or canvas? Secondly, in history, 'Modern' moments have always been linked to uprooting, nomadism, exodus. Do you think postmodernism is therefore coming to an end?

Walead Beshty In the airport, the aeroplane, in customs and security queues, abstraction is forced to reconcile itself with materiality; there the relation between the abstract rule of Law and the movement of bodies is realized with banally vulgar immediacy. I'm not speaking in the classic sense of abstraction or materialism within art (especially not in the sense that the term 'abstract' is misused to mean 'non-figurative', or that materialism has come to be synonymous with a claim for ontological purity), but in how abstractions are manifest in compromised form within the quotidian, how they govern our experience of the 'real', or, more exactly, how they become concrete, and how this becoming produces moments of friction and error. In transit, concepts as amorphous as subjecthood (as constituted in the right to privacy, of personal property, free speech, etc.) are identifiable simply by their being momentarily subject to revision. In these marginal connective tissues, tacit hierarchies become spatial, physical: one's belongings are inspected, one's body relegated to queues, numbers, compartments, 'class'. Normally, the fragility of the state's guarantees manifest itself only in moments of direct conflict and massive collapse (such as the recent credit crisis, or the revelations regarding the conditions at the American military prisons at Guantanamo Bay or Abu Ghraib), but in the case of air travel, the fragile malleability of social order is always close at hand, delineated by temporary post and rope stanchions, bracketed by pavilions and kiosks in linoleum-topped chipboard, in colour-coded wall-to-wall carpeting, and the eye of the x-ray machine. It is a commonplace that the reason one is more likely to cry while watching a movie on an aeroplane is the implicit trauma of air travel, i.e. the fear of death, of crashing, which leaves us emotionally vulnerable. But the trauma of air travel is quite literally one's confrontation with one's tenuous grasp on autonomy, its little humiliations emphasizing the conditional nature of selfhood: an alchemical transformation that allows inalienable rights to become suddenly alienable, subject to revocation.

In this constellation of forces, the x-ray has pride of place, marking the edge between the 'real' world, and the siteless limbo of air travel. Its accidental discovery in the late 1800s fits seamlessly into modernity's fascination with, and belief in, the power of technological transparency: the desire to domesticate time (cinema), to preserve and capture the surface of the fleeting (photography), to see inside (x-ray). For me, these apparatuses are made concrete in moments of error in the translation between the abstract and the material, when there is a friction between organizational systems, as when enlightenment principles rub up against the rule of law they were the foundation for (as when one is searched without probable cause in the airport), or optical devices affect what they are meant to only inspect (like when vacation photos are marred by passing through baggage xrays), or the transport of an object results in its transformation (as when an object is damaged by shipping).

Abstractions have reached the level of facticity. Financial markets, national sovereignty, the corporation as individual under the law, international airspace, property rights: all are interwoven, ephemeral constellations that delineate the rights of the citizen subject, the conditions of the social contract, and the character of lived 'reality'. The Bush Administration understood this fully, bending this abstract foundation to its whim. As a senior White House aide told a reporter for the *New York Times*: 'We're an empire now and when we act, we create our own reality. And while you're studying that reality – judiciously as you will – we'll act again, creating other new realities, which you can study too ...' (One is left with an image of former President George W. Bush as a character akin to Neo from *The Matrix*, able to reform the solid world – to which the unenlightened are subject – to his messianic whim.) Old notions of critique seem rather quaint in light of this formulation. The modernist transformation from the tangible to the intangible, from the object to the image, the haptic to the visual, is only half of the contemporary equation. With the passing of the last century and a half, these abstractions have been naturalized, entrenched and built upon to such a degree that they have the quality of concreteness and stability. It makes no sense to claim that either is more 'real' or 'fictional' than the other. These have always been false oppositions; the actual circumstance is far less discrete. After all, the solidity of objects is as much an abstraction of the social systems that produced them as the social systems are abstractions of these objects: the cumulative effect of both is a kind of capitalist realism. Classic critiques of power, some of which fall under the umbrella of the 'postmodern', rely on a 'reality principle', an idea that the real and fiction can be separated, that the revelation of power can threaten (not simply reify) dominance, that there is even something behind the curtain to be revealed, but these categorical delimiters are untenable. Monolithic expressions of power are simply an accumulation of compromise and negotiation, they all contain gaps; we, too are collaborators, even if we choose to relinquish this role. These momentary openings, the pockets between, their transitory spaces, ignored seams and forgotten vistas, promise a site from which the either/or of utopian and apocalyptic thinking, or the political/formalist opposition can be dismantled, and production can be understood as embedded and at stake in all things, not at the level of grand abstraction, but as a bare fact, evidenced in every moment of life. I think part of the problem is the search for 'endings', the desire to cleave the past from the present, to hope for liberatory rupture. Abandoning this search might be the way to an affirmative proposition of critique, rather than a negative one. This is the choice between presence and absence, between ascetic refusal and active negotiation. Perhaps, as the documentary filmmaker Hito Steyerl put it, 'the closer to reality we get, the less intelligible it becomes', but still this 'reality' is what it seems like it is most important to confront, one that is camouflaged in plain view, the unintelligible that is everywhere around us. [...]

Walead Beshty and Nicolas Bourriaud, extract from interview in *Altermodern* (London: Tate Publishing, 2009) 54.

Vito Acconci founded the New York-based architecture practice Acconci Studio in 1988. Formerly he was internationally known as a conceptual artist since the 1960s. Retrospectives include Museum of Contemporary Art, Chicago (1980); Museu d'Art Contemporani de Barcelona (2004).

William Anastasi is an American artist based in New York since the early 1960s when his work foreshadowed developments in conceptualism and Minimalism. Retrospectives include Nikolaj Contemporary Art Center, Copenhagen (2001) and The Drawing Center, New York (2007).

Michael Archer is Reader in Art and Course Leader in Undergraduate Studies in Art Practice at Goldsmiths College, London. A frequent contributor to international art journals for several decades, he is the author of *Art since 1960* (2002).

Paul Auster is a New York-based novelist, poet, translator and writer. His writings on art have included a text in the catalogue *Edward Hopper and the American Imagination* (1997) and his collaboration with Sophie Calle, *Double Game & Gotham Handbook* (2000).

Jacquelynn Baas is Director Emeritus of the University of California Berkeley Art Museum and Pacific Film Archive, and Programme Director of the arts consortium *Awake: Art, Buddhism and the Dimensions of Consciousness.*

John Baldessari is an American conceptual artist based in California. Retrospectives include The New Museum of Contemporary Art, New York (1981), Museo Nacional Centro de Arte Reina Sofía, Madrid (1989) and Tate Modern, London (2009, touring).

Georges Bataille (1897–1962) was a French writer and thinker and 'dissident' associate of surrealism. His works include *Inner Experience* (1943/1954; trans. 1988), *On Nietzsche* (1945; trans. 1992) and *The Accursed Share* (1949; trans. 1991).

Walead Beshty is a British-born artist and curator based in Los Angeles. Solo exhibitions include Armand Hammer Museum of Art, Los Angeles (2006) and Hirshhorn Museum and Sculpture Garden, Washington, DC (2009).

Daniel Birnbaum has since 2001 been Rector of the Städelschule and curator of Portikus, Frankfurt-am-Main, and was Curator of the 2009 Venice Biennale. He is a regular contributor to *Artforum, frieze* and *Parkett.* His books include *Chronology* (2007).

Claire Bishop is Associate Professor of Art History, The Graduate Center, City University of New York. Her books include *Installation Art: A Critical History* (2005) and the edited anthology *Participation* (Documents of Contemporary Art) (2006).

George Brecht (1926–2008) was an American artist and composer, based in Europe from 1965 onwards, who was one of the central figures in the international Fluxus movement. Retrospectives include Ludwig Museum, Cologne, and MACBA, Barcelona (2005–6).

Guy Brett is a critic and curator based in London. His exhibitions include *Force Fields: Phases of the Kinetic* (MACBA, Barcelona; Hayward Gallery, London (2000) and the Cildo Meireles retrospective at Tate Modern (2008). His books include *Carnival of Perception: Selected Writings on Art* (2004).

Benjamin H.D. Buchloh is the Andrew W. Mellon Professor of Modern Art, Harvard University, a co-editor of *October* and a contributor to *Artforum*. His books include a first volume of collected writings, *Neo-Avantgarde and Culture Industry: Essays on European and American Art from 1955 to 1975* (2001).

Sophie Calle is a French artist based in Paris who has made work since the late 1970s. Significant solo exhibitions include 'à suivre', ARC Musée d'art moderne de la Ville de Paris (1990), Centre Georges Pompidou, Paris (1999; 2005) and Whitechapel Gallery, London (2009).

Stanley Cavell is Walter M. Cabot Professor Emeritus of Aesthetics and the General Theory of Value at Harvard University. His books include *The World Viewed: Reflections on the Ontology of Film* (1971) and *In Quest of the Ordinary: Lines of Scepticism and Romanticism* (1988).

John Cage (1912–92) was an American experimental composer, artist and writer, and a leading figure in the post-1945 American avant-garde and international Fluxus movement. His books include *Silence: Lectures and Writings* (1961/1973).

Lynne Cooke is Chief Curator at the Museo Nacional Centro de Arte Reina Sofía, Madrid, and Curator at Large for the Dia Art Foundation, New York, where she was Curator at the Dia Center for the Arts from 1991–2008. She is the author of numerous major monographs and essays for art journals.

Tacita Dean is a British artist based in Berlin. Solo exhibitions include Witte de With Center for Contemporary Art, Rotterdam (1997), Institute of Contemporary Art, Philadelphia (1998), ARC Musée d'art moderne de la Ville de Paris (2003), Solomon R. Guggenheim Museum, New York (2007) and Dia: Beacon, Riggio Galleries, Beacon, New York (2008).

Gilles Deleuze (1925–95) was a French philosopher influential for his work on historical philosophers such as Nietzsche, Leibniz and Spinoza, his co-authored studies with Félix Guattari on contemporary philosophical and psycho-social conditions, and his studies of the cinematic image.

Anna Dezeuze is a Postdoctoral Research Fellow at the University of Manchester and a contributor to *Art Monthly* and *Papers of Surrealism*. Her current research includes preparation of two co-edited volumes and the book *The 'Almost Nothing': Dematerialization and the Politics of Precariousness.*

Brian Eno is a British experimental composer and musician. His innovatory ambient music recordings drawing on chance procedures include *Another Green World* (1975), *Discreet Music* (1975), *Ambient 1/Music for Airports* (1978), followed by *Ambient 2, 3* and *4*; and *Apollo* (1983).

Cerith Wyn Evans is a Welsh-born artist based in London, who was initially an experimental filmmaker. Solo exhibitions include Museum of Fine Arts, Boston (2004), Frankfurter Kunstverein (2004), Musée d'art moderne de la Ville de Paris (2006) and Tramway, Glasgow (2009).

Fei Dawei is a Chinese curator and scholar who was the founding Director of the Ullens Foundation (2003–7) and first Artistic Director of the Ullens Center for Contemporary Art in Beijing (2007–8).

Russell Ferguson is Chair of the Department of Art, University of California at Los Angeles. Formerly Associate Curator at The Museum of Contemporary Art, Los Angeles, he has written, edited and curated extensively in the field of contemporary art since the late 1980s.

Peter Fischli and David Weiss are Zurich-born artists who have collaborated since 1979. Major solo shows include Centre Georges Pompidou, Paris (1992), Walker Art Center, Minneapolis (1996, touring) and retrospective, Tate Modern, London (2006–8, touring).

David Frankel is a contributing editor of *Artforum*, where he served as an editor (1981–95) and is senior editor in the Department of Publications at The Museum of Modern Art, New York.

Branden W. Joseph is Frank Gallipoli Professor of Modern and Contemporary Art at Columbia University. His books include *Random Order: Robert Rauschenberg and the Neo-Avant-Garde* (2003) and *Beyond the Dream Syndicate: Tony Conrad and the Arts after Cage* (2008).

Allan Kaprow (1927–2006) was an American artist whose influential ideas from the late 1950s onwards are collected in *Essays on the Blurring of Art and Life* (1993). Retrospectives include Haus der Kunst, Munich (2006) and The Geffen Contemporary at MOCA, Los Angeles (2008).

Klara Kemp-Welch is the Leverhulme Early Career Fellow at The Courtauld Institute of Art, London, for 2009–12. She has published reviews, articles in journals and catalogue essays on East European artists including Tadeusz Kantor, Jerzy Beres, Endre Tót, and Sanja Ivekovic.

Siegfried Kracauer (1889–1966) was a German-Jewish cultural critic, sociologist and film theorist. He left Frankfurt for Paris in 1933 and in 1941 emigrated to New York. His works include *Theory of Film: The Redemption of Physical Reality* (1960) and *The Mass Ornament: Weimar Essays* (1995).

Jacques Lacan (1901–81) was a French post-Freudian psychoanalyst whose seminars and writings were influential on the Surrealists in the 1930s and on the emergence of poststructuralism in the 1960s. Key translated collections of his writings include *The Language of the Self: The Function of Language in Psychoanalysis* (1968) and *The Four Fundamental Concepts of Psychoanalysis* (1977).

Sarat Maharaj is Professor of Visual Art and Knowledge Systems, Lund University and Malmö Art Academy, Sweden. He was formerly Professor of History and Theory of Art at Goldsmiths College, London (1980–2005) and was a co-curator of Documenta 11 (2002).

Cildo Meireles is a Brazilian artist based in Rio de Janeiro who was an early exponent of installation in the late 1960s. Solo exhibitions include the New Museum of Contemporary Art, New York (1999; retrospective, touring to Rio de Janeiro and São Paulo) and Tate Modern, London (2008).

John Miller is an American artist and writer on art who has contributed to numerous catalogues, publications and art journals including *October, Artforum, Parkett, Tate Etc.* His books include *When Down is Up: Selected Writings* (2001).

Robert Morris is an American artist based in New York whose interrogations of established aesthetic positions from 1960 to the late 1970s were central to the emergence of conceptual art and Minimalism. Retrospectives include Centre Georges Pompidou, Paris (1995).

Alexandra Munroe has since 2006 been Senior Curator of Asian Art at the Solomon R. Guggenheim Museum and was formerly Director at the Japan Society, New York, where her exhibitions included *Japanese Art After 1945: Scream Against the Sky* (1994) and *Yes Yoko Ono* (2000).

Bruce Nauman is an American artist based in New Mexico whose works have been influential since the late 1960s. Touring retrospectives include Los Angeles County Museum of Art (1972), Walker Art Center, Minneapolis (1994) and Centre Georges Pompidou, Paris (1998).

Gabriel Orozco is a Mexican-born artist who lives and works in New York, Paris and Mexico City. Retrospectives include The Museum of Contemporary Art, Los Angeles (2000) and Museo del Palacio de Bellas Artes, Mexico City (2006).

Cornelia Parker is a British artist based in London. Recent solo exhibitions include Wurtembergischer Kunstverein, Stuttgart (2005) and Ikon Gallery, Birmingham (2007). Her video work *Chomskian Abstract* (2007) was shown at the Whitechapel Gallery in 2008.

Gabriel Pérez Barreiro is the New York-based Director of the Colección Patricia Phelps de Cisneros. His publications include *The Geometry of Hope: Latin American Abstract Art from the Patricia Phelps de Cisneros Collection* (2007) and *New York Graphic Workshop: 1964-1970* (2009).

Robert Rauschenberg (1925–2008) was an American artist who lived and worked in New York and Florida. From the early 1950s onwards he influenced the eventual emergence of Pop and conceptualism. Retrospectives include Solomon R. Guggenheim Museum, New York (1979).

Jasia Reichardt is a writer on art and exhibition organizer based in London. She was Assistant Director of the ICA, London (1963–71) and Director of the Whitechapel Gallery (1974–76). She has written extensively on art, science and technology and was a director of the ARTEC biennale (1989–98).

Gerhard Richter is among the most influential German artists of the post-1960 period, who has been described as a conceptual painter. Retrospectives include The Museum of Modern Art, New York (2004). His work is extensively documented at http://www.gerhard-richter.com

Julia Robinson is Assistant Professor of Art History at New York University. She has contributed essays in exhibition catalogues of John Cage, George Brecht and Claes Oldenburg, and articles in art journals including *October, Art Journal, Grey Room* and *Performance Research.*

Luc Sante is a Belgian born writer and critic who emigrated to the United States in the early 1960s. He teaches writing and the history of photography at Bard College, Annandale on Hudson. His books include *Evidence* (1992), *Walker Evans* (1999) and *Folk Photography* (2009).

Brad Spence is an American artist and curator based in Los Angeles and a contributor to international art journals. In 1999 he curated a landmark Bas Jan Ader retrospective at the University of California at Irvine. His solo exhibitions include University Art Museum, Long Beach (2003).

Ann Temkin is Chief Curator of Painting and Sculpture at The Museum of Modern Art, New York. Among her publications are monographs on Barnett Newman, Alice Neel, Joseph Beuys and Raymond Pettibon, and *Colour Chart: Reinventing Colour, 1950 to Today* (2004).

Marcia Tucker (1940–2006) was Curator of Painting and Sculpture at the Whitney Museum of American Art, New York (1969–77), Founding Director of the New Museum of Contemporary Art, New York (1977–99), and series editor of *Documentary Sources in Contemporary Art.*

Keith Tyson is a British artist based in London. Solo exhibitions include Kunsthalle Zurich (2002), South London Gallery (2005), Louisiana Museum, Denmark (2006), De Pont Museum, The Netherlands (2007). His website is at www.keithtyson.com

Sarah Valdez is associate editor at *ARTnews.* She has also regularly contributed articles and reviews to other international art journals such as *Art in America* and *Artforum*, and an essay in the publication *Curve: The Female Nude Now* (2003).

Katharina Vossenkuhl is a curator, editor and writer on contemporary art and Managing Director at the Sammlung Goetz in Munich. Her writings include essays on Francis Alÿs, Matthew Barney and Mike Kelley.

La Monte Young is an American experimental composer and musician whose work was foundational in the Fluxus movement and in the emergence of Minimalist composition. His website is at http://melafoundation.org

Bibliography

This section comprises selected further reading and does not repeat the bibliographic references for writings included in the anthology. For these please see the citations at the end of each text.

Armstrong, Elizabeth, and Rothfuss, Joan, eds, *In the Spirit of Fluxus* (Minneapolis: Walker Art Center, 1993)

Arp, Jean/Hans, 'Looking' (Meudon, May 1958), in James Thrall Soby, ed., *Arp* (New York: The Museum of Modern Art, 1958)

Banes, Sally, *Democracy's Body: Judson Dance Theater, 1962–1964* (Epping: UMI Research Press, 1980)

Benn Michaels, Walter, 'Action and Accident: Photography and Writing', *The Gold Standard and the Logic of Naturalism: American Literature at the Turn of the Century* (Berkeley and Los Angeles: University of California Press, 1987)

Bogle, Andrew, *Chance and Change: A Century of the Avant-Garde* (Auckland, New Zealand: Auckland City Art Gallery, 1985)

Borchardt-Hume, Achim, Introduction, *Stan Douglas: Journey into Fear* (London: Serpentine Gallery/Cologne: Verlag der Buchhandlung Walther König, 2002)

Bowie, Malcolm, *Un Coup de dés n'abolira le hasard: Mallarmé and the Art of Being Difficult* (Cambridge: Cambridge University Press, 1978)

Brassaï (Gyula Halász), *Marcel Proust sous l'emprise de la photographie* (*c.* 1924–84); first published posthumously (Paris: Éditions Gallimard, 1997); trans Richard Howard, *Proust in the Power of Photography* (Chicago: University of Chiccago Press, 2001)

Breton, André, *L'Amour fou* (Paris: Éditions Gallimard, 1937); trans. Mary Ann Caws, *Mad Love* (Lincoln: University of Nebraska Press, 1987)

Breton, André, *What is Surrealism? Selected Writings*, ed. Franklin Rosemont (New York: Monad Press/London: Pluto Press, 1978)

Broodthaers: Writings, Interviews, Photographs, ed. Benjamin H.D. Buchloh (Cambridge, Massachusetts: The MIT Press, 1988)

Cabanne, Pierre, *Dialogues with Marcel Duchamp*, trans. Ron Padgett (New York: Da Capo Press, 1987)

Campany, David, *Photography and Cinema* (London: Reaktion Books, 2008)

Dalí, Salvador, *Oui: The Paranoid Critical Revolution: Writings 1927–1933*, ed. Robert Descharnes (Boston: Exact Change, 1998)

Demos, T.J., 'Zurich Dada: The Aesthetics of Exile', in Leah Dickerman and Matthew Witkovsky, eds, *The Dada Seminar* (Washington, D.C.: National Gallery of Art, 2005)

Duchamp, Marcel, *The Bride Stripped Bare by Her Bachelors, Even* ('Green Box', 1934); typographic version by Richard Hamilton, trans. George Heard Hamilton (New York: George Wittenborn, Inc., 1960); reprinted edition (Stuttgart, London, Reykjavik: Edition Hansjorg Mayer, 1976)

Ernst, Max, *Beyond Painting* (New York: Wittenborn, Schultz, Inc., 1948)

Elliot, Patrick, et al., *Boyle Family* (Edinburgh: National Galleries of Scotland, 2003)

Fer, Briony, 'The Laws of Chance', *On Abstract Art* (New Haven and London: Yale University Press, 1997)

Focillon, Henri, *La vie des formes* (Paris: Presses Universitaires de France, 1934); trans. Charles B. Hogan and George Kubler, *The Life of Forms in Art* (New York: Wittenborn, Schultz, 1948); reprinted edition (New York, Zone Books, 1989)

Foster, Hal, *Compulsive Beauty* (Cambridge, Massachusetts: The MIT Press, 1993)

Foster, Stephen, C., ed., *Dada/Dimensions* (Ann Arbor, Michigan: UMI Research Press, 1985)

Freud, Sigmund, *The Psychopathogy of Everyday Life* (1901); *The Standard Edition of the Complete Psychological Works of Sigmund Freud*, vol. VI (London: Hogarth Press/ Institute of Psychoanalysis, 1960)

Gamboni, Dario, 'Fabrication of Accidents: Factura and Chance in Nineteenth-Century Art', *Res*, no. 36 (Autumn 1999)

– *Potential Images: Ambiguity and Indeterminacy in Modern Art* (London: Reaktion Books, 2001)

Hapgood, Susan, *Neo-Dada: Redefining Art, 1958–1962* (New York: American Federation of Arts, 1994)

Henderson, Linda Dalrymple, *Duchamp in Context: Science and Technology in the Large Glass and Related Works* (Princeton, New Jersey: Princeton University Press, 1998)

Iversen, Margaret, *Beyond Pleasure: Freud, Lacan, Barthes* (University Park: The Pennsylvania State University Press, 2007)

Janson, Horst W., 'Chance Images', in Philip P. Wiener, ed., *Dictionary of the History of Ideas: Studies of Selected Pivotal Ideas* (New York: Scribner's, 1973)

Joseph, Branden W., *Random Order: Robert Rauschenberg and the Neo-Avant-Garde* (Cambridge, Massachusetts: The MIT Press)

Kaprow, Allan, *Essays on the Blurring of Art and Life*, ed. Jeff Kelley (Berkeley and Los Angeles: University of California Press, 1993)

Kelsey, Robin, 'Photography, Chance and The Pencil of Nature', in *The Meaning of Photography*, ed. Kelsey and Blake Stimson (New Haven and London: Yale University Press, 2008)

Kotz, Liz, 'Post-Cagean Aesthetics and the "Event" Score', *October*, no. 95 (Winter 2001)

– *Words to be Looked At: Language in 1960s Art* (Cambridge, Massachusetts: The MIT Press, 2007)

Krauss, Rosalind E., *The Optical Unconscious* (Cambridge, Massachusetts: The MIT Press, 1993)

Lachman, Charles, '"The Image Made by Chance", in China and the West: Ink Wang Meets Jackson Pollock's Mother', *The Art Bulletin*, vol. 74, no. 3 (1992)

Lautréamont, Le Comte de (Isidore Ducasse), *Maldoror* (Paris, 1868); trans. Paul Knight (Harmondsworth: Penguin Books, 1978)

Laxton, Susan, 'The Guarantor of Chance: Surrealism's Ludic Practices', *Papers of Surrealism*, no. 1 (Winter 2003) www.surrealismcentre.ac.uk/papersofsurrealism

Malone, Meredith, ed., *Chance Aesthetics* (St Louis: Mildred Lane Kemper Museum/Washington University in St Louis, 2009)

Motherwell, Robert, ed., *The Dada Painters and Poets: An Anthology* (New York: George Wittenborn, Inc., 1951); reprinted edition (Cambridge, Massachusetts: The Belknap Press of Harvard University Press, 1989)

Parkinson, Gavin, *Surrealism, Art and Modern Science: Relativity, Quantum Mechanics, Epistemology* (New Haven and London: Yale University Press, 2008)

Pincus-Witten, Robert, *Against Order: Chance and Art* (Philadelphia: Institute of Contemporary Art, 1970)

Richter, Hans, *Dada: Art and Anti-Art* (London: Thames and Hudson, 1965)

Ruscha, Ed, *Leave Any Information at the Signal: Writings, Interviews, Bits, Pages* (Cambridge, Massachusetts: The MIT Press, 2002)

Schimmel, Paul, and Stiles, Kristine, eds, *Out of Actions: Between Performance and the Object 1949–1979* (Los Angeles: The Museum of Contemporary Art, 1998)

Spoerri, Daniel, et al, *Topographie Anécdotée du Hasard*, pamphlet (Paris, 1961); first re-anecdoted edition, *An Anecdoted Topography of Chance* (New York: Something Else Press, 1966); final re-anecdoted edition (London: Atlas Press, 1995)

Strindberg, August, 'New Arts! Or, The Role of Chance in Artistic Production', *La Revue des revues* (Paris, 15 November 1894); trans. Shaun Whiteside, in Olle Granath, *August Strindberg: Painter, Photographer, Writer* (London: Tate Publishing, 2005)

Sylvester, David, *Interviews with Francis Bacon 1962–1979* (London: Thames and Hudson, 1980)

Tompkins, Calvin, *The Bride and the Bachelors: Five Masters of the Avant-Garde* (New York: Viking Press, 1962); revised edition (New York and Harmondsworth, Middlesex: Penguin Books, 1968)

Watts, Alan, *The Way of Zen* (New York: Pantheon Books, 1957)

Index

ACKNOWLEDGEMENTS

Editor's acknowledgements

This anthology was supported by a grant from the Arts and Humanities Research Council, which funded a three-year interdisciplinary project: *Aesthetics after Photography*. I am grateful to the other members of the research team: Diarmuid Costello, Wolfgang Brückle and especially Dawn Phillips, for their incisive comments on the draft. Audiences at the Universities of Essex and Oxford, The Ruskin College of Art and the Fotomuseum in Winterthur, Switzerland, made helpful suggestions. I am very grateful to Series Editor and Director of the Whitechapel Gallery, Iwona Blazwick; Achim Borchhardt-Hume, Chief Curator at the Whitechapel Gallery; Hannah Vaughan, Project Editor; and most of all to Commissioning Editor, Ian Farr.

Publisher's acknowledgements

Whitechapel Gallery is grateful to all those who gave their generous permission to reproduce the listed material. Every effort has been made to secure all permissions and we apologize for any inadvertent errors or ommissions. If notified, we will endeavour to correct these at the earliest opportunity.

We would like to express our thanks to all who contributed to the making of this volume, especially: Vito Acconci, Michael Archer, Paul Auster, Gabriel Pérez Barreiro, Walead Beshty, Daniel Birnbaum, Claire Bishop, Nicolas Bourriaud, Benjamin Buchloh, Sophie Calle, Stanley Cavell, Caroline Dayton, Tacita Dean, Anna Dezeuze, Thomas McEvilley, Russell Ferguson, Susan Hapgood, Branden Joseph, Klara Kemp-Welch, Jorge Macchi, Sarat Maharaj, Hans Ulrich Obrist, Gabriel Orozco, Cornelia Parker, Gerhard Richter, Julia Robinson, Luc Sante, Charlotte Settle, Brad Spence, Helen Sumpter, Lisa Tickner, Keith Tyson, Katherina Vossenkuhl and La Monte Young. We also gratefully acknowledge the cooperation of: American Federation of Arts; The Americas Society; *Art History*; *Art on Paper*; *Artforum*; *Audio Arts Magazine*; Charta; *College Art*; Columbia University Press; Dia Center for the Arts; Ediciones Polígrafa; Éditions Gallimard; *frieze*; Harry N. Abrams; Japan Society, New York; MoMA; McPherson & Company; Museo Nacional Centro de Arte Reina Sofía; The New Museum, New York; Other Minds; Oxford University Press; Printed Matter; Smithsonian Institute; Solomon R. Guggenheim Museum, New York; *Studio International*; Thames & Hudson; University of California Press; University of Wisconsin Press; VAGA; W.W. Norton; Walker Art Center; Wesleyan University Press.

Whitechapel Gallery is supported by
Arts Council England

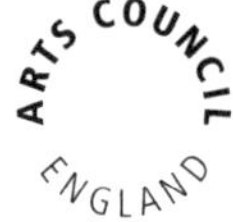